Give Me the Hills

OVERLEAF: The Matterhorn at dawn.

GIVE ME
THE HILLS

Miriam Underhill

THE CHATHAM PRESS, INC.
RIVERSIDE, CONNECTICUT
in association with the
APPALACHIAN MOUNTAIN CLUB

DISTRIBUTED BY THE VIKING PRESS, INC.

All photographs, excluding those in which she appears or which are otherwise credited, were taken by Mrs. Underhill herself. The sources of two
photos (those facing pages 82 and 161) are unknown.

Foreword

We were driving across the prairies of eastern Montana one sunny day in early autumn. I had recently passed my fiftieth birthday, the first one to seem to me of any particular significance. But these first fifty years, I mused, had made up an outstandingly satisfactory life! And not the least of its interests through all but the very earliest years had been the climbing I had done, so much of which was now fading away into the hazy past and would soon be forgotten by everyone, including me. As if it had never existed.

I turned to my husband. 'I'm going to write a book,' I said.

'Good idea,' he replied idly. It did not occur to him then, either that I would actually set out on this project or, touching him more closely, that it would involve him in such a great amount of work. For he has looked over every word (except these few), occasionally muttering under his breath, 'Literary primitive'. I can see him now, my manuscript in one hand, the other holding his head, exclaiming in mock despair, 'We've got to get some English grammar into this thing *somewhere.*'

To him, then, I owe my first and greatest thanks.

*   *   *

I wish to express my gratitude, too, to the editors of the following publications where parts of this book have appeared in more or less similar form, for allowing me to republish the material here: *Alpine Journal, Alpinisme, American Alpine Journal, Appalachia, British Ski Year Book, Canadian Alpine Journal, Ladies' Alpine Club Year Book, National Geographic Magazine, Rivista Mensile.*

CONCORD, MASSACHUSETTS
April 28, 1956

Publisher's Note

Give Me the Hills was originally published in England in 1956, by Methuen & Co., Ltd. of London, although no American edition has ever appeared. Mrs. Underhill's climbing career was by no means concluded in 1956, however, and it has seemed to many who know her that the book should not only be enlarged to include more of her wonderful photographs and more recent episodes, but should certainly be made available to an American audience as well. With the cooperation of Miriam and Robert Underhill this has now fortunately been made possible, through an association with the Appalachian Mountain Club of Boston.

For the first thirtèen chapters the original British text has been reproduced, with grateful acknowledgement to Methuen & Co. To these there has now been added a final chapter which originally appeared in a slightly different form in the December 1967 issue of the magazine, *Appalachia*, published by the Appalachian Mountain Club. The number of illustrations has been more than doubled and the book as a whole has been produced in a larger format than before, giving greater scope to the photographs.

RIVERSIDE, CONNECTICUT
February 25, 1971

Contents

Give Me the Hills

I
Beginnings

‘One thing is sure—she doesn't want dolls for her birthday. I got one downtown and she turned away in disgust. Aunt Ellen came last night. She says she is going to buy her a greased pole or a tree to climb or something of that order.' This, the first written record of my inclination towards climbing, occurs in a letter from my mother to her mother, back in the last century (by a few months). The letter goes on to record that I weighed, with clothes, twenty pounds.

My early childhood's most memorable experience was a trip, the summer of my sixth birthday, into a remote wilderness region of northern New Hampshire. Hellgate Camp at Deerlick Falls on the Little Dead Diamond River was a fishing camp ten miles from Wentworth Location, the nearest inhabited place. It took all day to get in there, riding on a buckboard (a wagon with long resilient planks joining its axles) pulled by two big strong horses. Men had hewn out a narrow track through the forest, but had done nothing to smooth the surface underfoot. How we jounced along, over boulders and ledges, through deep holes of clinging mud! The camp, one log cabin and a few tents, stood in a little clearing beside the river. The mountains around, the northern foothills of the White Mountains, were merely hills. It was the forest that entranced me and the feeling of primitive remoteness.

Although I was a little young to undertake any extensive exploration on my own, still there were certain places where I was allowed to go by myself, to the brambles on the river bank to pick raspberries, to a great boulder in the dark, cool woods,

13

towering above my head and all covered over with mosses and ferns, to another moss-and-lichen-covered boulder small enough for me to climb on, where I went many times. How I loved the fragrance of the northern balsam firs, the sight of the deer at dusk stepping delicately into the clearing to browse, the sound of the falls as I lay in bed at night! And most particularly the knowledge that for miles and miles in every direction, there was nothing but unbroken forest. I got there my first taste of the wild, uncrowded places of the earth and even at six years old, I liked it. For years afterwards I cherished these impressions in my thoughts.

For thirty-seven years, to be exact, for in 1941 I went in there again with my husband. On foot this time, we walked across the wild North Country forests from the Connecticut Lakes on the northwest. As we approached I knew from the clear memory-pictures in my mind just exactly how everything was going to look and it was a disillusioning moment when I found at first glance that things weren't quite right, particularly those two buildings. But these few details were soon explained. The building of 1904 had long since mouldered away and the 'new' ones were soon to go too, if I am any judge. To account for the fact that the falls did not loom up above me in such an overpowering way—that they were, in fact, very small falls—I had only to reflect that in these thirty-seven years I myself had grown a good bit bigger! But the fragrance was the same, a deer stepped into the clearing at dusk, and the next morning as we walked out I'm sure I recognized, still covered with its lichens and mosses, the smaller boulder where I used to climb. The old feeling of happiness had come back. Wild and beautiful places have brought a great deal of joy into my life. In those thirty-seven years I had been to other regions more remote, more spectacular. But this had been the beginning, the first experience, and so held a special place in my heart.

In 1914 my mother (Mrs. Robert Lincoln O'Brien) took her two children, my brother Lincoln and me, to Europe. Looking

14

back now, one might say that for a woman who had never before been outside her own country, 1914 was perhaps not the wisest year to choose. But it looked all right in the spring when we started. Early in July we were in Chamonix, the most glorious mountain region that we had yet seen. Mother and I walked the 5,000 feet up to the Brévent—there was no *téléphérique* in those days—and since this was considered too long a climb for the seven-year-old Lincoln, he stayed below with the concierge and had a most enjoyable time driving to the station to meet all the trains, perched up on the box of the hotel bus, behind the two dashing horses. The high point of the climb, for me, was the ascent of the Chimney, that little rocky gully where it was just barely necessary to use our hands. From the summit of the Brévent, spread out in front of us across the Chamonix valley, rose the enormous mass of Mont Blanc and the jagged, rocky spires of the Chamonix Aiguilles. I found it most impressive and it never occurred to me that I should stand on many of those summits in time to come.

When war actually broke out we were in Switzerland, staying with Professor and Madame Piguet and their daughters Madeleine and Gabrielle at their mountain chalet at Mayens de Leytron, a three-hours' climb above Riddes in the Rhône Valley. We had walked up, while a horse pulled our baggage on a primitive cart with great solid wheels. It was a beautiful spot near the village of Ovronnaz, where we spent our time mostly walking over the idyllic Swiss mountainsides, with their waterfalls and alpine flowers and grazing cows—just the sort of country, I felt sure, that Heidi must have lived in.

All this time, through the last days of July, Mother was writing letters home about picnics and mountain walks but with never any mention of the possibility of war. It is astonishing how slowly news penetrated up to our secluded chalet. When we finally heard that there actually was war, it was an immense surprise, but we were not extraordinarily alarmed. Only two German girls, who were spending the summer with the Piguets to learn French, burst into uncontrollable tears. Their fathers were army officers and they had more of a feeling for the seriousness of the situation than anybody else. Professor Piguet had to leave at once. Along with every other able-bodied Swiss man, he was mobilized. We children found it very exciting and romantic to see him start off with rucksack, climbing rope, ice-axe and heavy nailed boots, the army equipment that he was required to keep in readiness at all times.

Then the mountainside was thrown into confusion. All the work of the harvest had to be done and nobody was left but women, old men, children and idiots (quite a lot of these last). We children at the Piguets' turned to and helped. I don't remember just what we did; I have an impression it had something to do with vegetables, but perhaps so much of my energy went into vegetables in the Second World War that I am confusing the two. Mother felt that the simplest thing to do was just to stay on at the Piguets' for a few days. Meantime my father in his newspaper office in Boston, having much more information about the gravity of the situation, was frantic with anxiety. He sent us cables, as Mother did him, few of which got through at all, and those often incomprehensible. I remember the *facteur* from the post office slowly plodding up the hill bringing us one of Father's cables, which read, '*Essayez table de commerce.*' Was that the board of trade? And if so, what should we try it for? We did nothing. Later we found out that Father had sent, 'Try Commercial Cable.'

A bit later, since there were still no trains for civilians running across France, we thought we might as well have a quick look at Zermatt. On the little train from Visp, when we rounded that last corner and the Matterhorn came into view, it took my breath away that first time as it has so often since.

We set out one day to walk up to the Gornergrat accompanied by an English maiden lady of some forty or fifty years and a lone English gentleman from our hotel, who were waiting for transportation home, as we were. As the path wound across the open alpine meadows and pastures towards Rotenboden, the last station before the summit, with more and more flowers, and more and more great peaks coming into view at every step, my mother said that since her children were tired she proposed

16

to take the cog railroad from there up to the top. The Englishwoman was appalled, with a you-can't-do-this-to-me expression.
She was quite firm about not wanting to take the train herself,
but clearly she did not want Mother to do so either. Finally,
blushing with embarrassment, she took Mother aside and
explained the trouble: never before in her life had she walked
alone with a gentleman; it was the sort of thing a gently-reared
Englishwoman did not do!

From the Gornergrat, right opposite rose Monte Rosa with
its enormous glaciers winding miles long down the valley. At
that time, in common with most Americans, I had probably
never seen any skis or even heard of the sport of skiing. I
wonder what I should have thought if someone had told me
that I was going to slide, standing up on boards, the 10,000 feet
from the ridge of Monte Rosa right down those glaciers into
Zermatt? And the Matterhorn over there to the right, the
Dent Blanche, Obergabelhorn, Rothorn, Weisshorn—I was to
be on the summits of them all.

Near the end of August we got word from the American
consul in Geneva that a special train for Americans would leave
for Paris and we were to take with us 'food and water for
48 hours'. What a trip that was across France! Ordinarily
requiring eight hours, this time it took twenty-eight. Many
times we were left on a sidetrack while troop trains went by,
and once, in the night, a brightly lighted hospital train, coming
back from the front, with attendants hurrying around. As we
got nearer Paris, we met great crowds of refugees pouring out
of the city, and we seemed to be alone in wanting to go in.
It was the time of the First Battle of the Marne, and we
reached Paris the day the Germans were the nearest they ever
got to it—in that war—and people were afraid it would be only
hours before they entered the city. We saw the Paris taxicabs
jammed with soldiers, taking the troops to the battle lines only
forty miles away. The Regina Hotel where we had stayed in
the spring let us have a room for the night—the first night
bombs were ever dropped on Paris—although they were dis-
organized by the mobilization and were not serving any meals.

We saw only two men employees, with whom Mother exchanged some moving words about *la Patrie*. They turned out to be Austrians. For meals, Mother cooked eggs for us in our bedroom on her little alcohol stove.

In 1920 we were back in Switzerland again. All of us six years older, it showed up most in Lincoln. Thirteen is a much better age for mountain walks than seven. It would be gratifying to report that we started in at once on a serious climbing career, but far from it. Our biggest achievement was the Grand Muveran, which we climbed from the Piguets'. With Professor Piguet, Madeleine, a cousin and an uncle, we walked one afternoon up to the Cabane Rambert, one of the Swiss Alpine Club huts. The Piguet family proposed to climb the mountain guideless, but I expect that Professor Piguet, reasonably enough, felt that he had all he wanted to do to look after his own party without taking on the three of us as well. In any case, when we reached the hut, Professor Piguet took aside the *guardien*, Jules Alexandre Crettenand, and asked him if he would act as guide for Mother, Lincoln and me. The next morning, as it turned out, we all got to the top of the mountain with ease. It is not a difficult climb and it takes not much more than two hours from the hut. But how we all loved it! And what a thrill to be roped up (my first time on a rope) to cross a snowfield which seemed very large to me at that time; it was still quite hard in the morning chill. Then we climbed rocks mixed with snow. Quite frequently the Piguet uncle, out of breath, would announce, 'Hush, I think I hear a marmot. Everybody stand still for a moment.' But who am I to ridicule the uncle and his marmots? I do the same thing myself now, only I am more likely to put it, 'Bob, do you mind stopping for a moment? Here's a flower I'd like to look at.' What would ageing mountaineers do without the alpine flora and fauna? When we returned from the climb Mother sent a money order for two dollars to Crettenand. Whether that was the whole fee for his guiding services I do not know.

Back at Zermatt again, we engaged a guide to take us up the Riffelhorn and one day I succeeded in picking up an attractive

American boy with whom I climbed the Ober Rothorn above Findelen, 11,215 feet, but cow pastures nearly to the top. Still we did no serious climbing, and again in 1921 it was the same story. That year my best accomplishments were the Unter-gabelhorn and the Zermatt Breithorn, that classic trip for beginners, an impressive-looking mountain but, by the ordinary route which we took, nothing but a somewhat tedious snow walk. I cannot understand why I was so slow in getting started. For one thing, my mother held a firm conviction that high-altitude climbing 'strained the hearts' of young people. Lincoln, admittedly, was still young, but I wasn't. Even in 1924, the next time we were in Zermatt, we still managed for the most part only simple things like the Pointe de Zinal. On the balcony outside the Schönbühl Hut George Finch, who had been on the 1922 Mt Everest Expedition, pointed out his spectacular route of the year before on the north face of the Dent d'Hérens and advised me not to waste time on trivial climbs like the Pointe de Zinal but to take on some real stuff. 'You could do the Matterhorn,' said he. This was a purely casual remark, but although he had no way of knowing it, I believe now that it was true. Subsequently we did do that nice little rock climb on the Riffelhorn, the Matterhorn Couloir, and two days later I traversed the Wellenkuppe and Obergabelhorn, perhaps the first of my real climbs.

In 1925 we stayed in North America and travelled, with climbs here and there, out through Canada to the Pacific Coast and back through the United States. Besides sampling the climbs in the Canadian Rockies and some of the more obvious peaks in the United States, such as Rainier, Hood, Long's Peak, etc., on this trip, I suffered my first mountaineering 'accident'. On Mt Edith near Banff a loose rock, falling from above, hit my fourth finger, cutting it and breaking the bone. Exactly the same thing happened to the same finger on the other hand a few years later, just under the summit cairn on the Meije in France. In each case I applied a *pansement d'allumettes* as the Chamonix porter Georges Cachat, whom I was leading over the traverse of the Meije, called my splints of matches. That disposes of two-thirds of the mountaineering accidents that I have undergone and from neither of them did I lose a day's climbing, although I did find, when I reached the Zsigmondy Crack on the Meije, that my splint was so overlarge and awkward that that hand was of little use; I had to give up the lead to Georges, to his great joy. The third accident was also trivial. None of these, of course, would be in any way worthy of mention were it not to offer some evidence against the popular concept of the 'danger' of mountaineering. There are few sports one could practise for so many years with so little physical wear and tear. And as for the enormous physical benefits—leaving aside for the moment any consideration of benefits of other sorts—it is not for nothing that members of the Alpine Club enjoy an expectation of life four and a half years greater than the average healthy male!*

* W. W. Naismith, 'Climbing and Longevity', *Alpine Journal*, XXXIV, p. 266.

II
New England Rocks and Snow

For years I had been climbing summer and winter, spring and autumn, whenever the opportunity came up, in the White Mountains of New Hampshire, densely forested hills rising some 4,000 feet or more above their valleys. I think it probable that I have climbed Mt Washington, the highest (6,288 feet), every month in the year. My mother had taken me as a child on many of the climbs and later, with family or friends, I had become familiar with most of them. In 1915, on a visit to Isabel Arnold, one of my classmates at school, I had gone with her, her father and sister Sally up Mt Washington through Tuckerman Ravine, one of the series of large glacial cirques gouged out of the eastern wall of the Presidential Range. Poor Dr Arnold! It was a strenuous climb for a hot day, particularly up the 1,000 feet or so of the headwall of the cirque. I'll never forget the sight of him ceaselessly mopping his brow with a big white handkerchief and—theological school professor that he was—muttering heartfelt imprecations in a variety of erudite foreign tongues, living and dead. In 1915 Isabel and I were big girls and although we wore, with our middy blouses, the big, full bloomers of the period, we considered it more seemly to wear a skirt outside. Sally, being younger, could go with only bloomers. But that was about the beginning and end of the skirt period for me. Trousers for climbing and skiing were just coming into fashion about the time that I needed them.

In the early 1920's a group of us around Boston, mostly members of the Appalachian Mountain Club who had learned the sport in Europe, started rock-climbing. A mounted police-

man, placidly riding his beat through the Blue Hills Reservation just south of Boston, spurred his horse to a frantic gallop
when he caught sight of my brother Lincoln on the end of a
rope over the sheer face of Rattlesnake Cliff. 'Are you com-
mitting suicide?' he shouted up, breathlessly. That was in the
early days; later the policemen never gave a second glance. We
tried out the Quincy granite quarries where the faces were firm
and precipitous but the rock, freshly cut, had often not
weathered into a sufficiency of hand- and footholds. Some
glacial boulderfields north of Boston gave us a few good, but
short, routes. 'The glacier must have been back again last
winter,' said little Nicky Helburn, 'and brought that new
boulder that wasn't there before.' Nicky has since developed,
as might have been foreseen, into a professor of geology. But
for good longer climbs we got up into Maine, to the walls of the
cirques of Katahdin, or to the cliffs of New Hampshire, where
we could find as much as 800 feet of continuous rock-climbing.
I cannot help thinking that we skimmed the cream, in working
out these routes for the first time..

The winter climate of the White Mountains, in spite of their
low elevation, is one of great extremes of cold and wind. I
believe it is a general rule that those regions that lie near the
western edge of a continent (Washington, Oregon, California;
England, France, Switzerland) enjoy a milder climate with a
narrower range of temperature due to the moderating effects of
water—oceans—on the prevailing west winds, than the regions
some thousands of miles to the east. In any case the weather
station on Mt Washington has clocked the highest wind
velocity, over 230 miles an hour, ever recorded, and the general
severity of its winter climate compares with Spitzbergen in the
Arctic or Adelie Land, 'Home of the Blizzard', in the Antarctic.*

This rigorous climate brings to the White Mountains in winter
real alpine conditions of snow and ice and it seemed reasonable
to us to give our Swiss crampons, rope and ice-axes a little work-
out at that season. Most of the serious winter climbing in those

---

* Charles F. Brooks, 'The Worst Weather in the World', *Appalachia*, XXII, pp.
194 ff.

days was done on snowshoes as far as timberline, crampons above. These snowshoes are not the Alaskan type, narrow and long, sometimes six feet long, with a turned-up tip, but a bearpaw (oval) or beavertail (oval with a short projection in back), slightly larger than a French *raquette*. The binding around the boot, unlike that on a *raquette*, is fastened to the snowshoe only at the sides of the toe, so that the heel can rise up in a normal walking fashion at each step, and the toe of the boot can project downwards through a matching hole in the snowshoe webbing. A good binding does not allow the snowshoe to twist sideways relative to the boot. Although the webbing is made of heavy gut, well shellacked, it still requires a soft-soled shoe like an Indian moccasin if it is to last for many days. Those of us who like to wear nailed boots or ski boots on our snowshoes must lace on with thong a leather patch under the boots. The front of the snowshoe is flat—not turned up—so that on steep slopes one can kick steps by driving the snowshoe in horizontally. Finally, for ice, the snowshoe has its own crampons, so-called 'snowshoe creepers', a plate with short spikes affixed under the snowshoe below the ball of the wearer's foot. In using snowshoes it is not necessary, as one might suppose, to keep your legs spread apart the full width of the two snowshoes. Instead, at each step you merely lift the snowshoe and draw it forward over its mate, clearing only your own leg.

Although snowshoes are efficient tools for winter mountain travel, there is little pleasure involved in their use as such, as there is with skis. Still, twenty-five or thirty years ago there were no proper ski trails in the White Mountains as there are now, through the dense forest, and the narrow, twisting, summer climbing trails were hardly feasible for descent on skis, particularly at that stage in the development of our ski technique.

The day after Christmas in 1925 Lincoln, Tom Rawles, Rupert Maclaurin and I went up to the Glen House at the foot of Mt Washington equipped, at least I was, with both skis and snowshoes. The eight-mile Carriage Road on Mt Washington—or rather the four miles of it below timberline—and an occasional old lumber road on other peaks were about the best ski trails we had in those days, but after a day or two of running them we decided on a more ambitious trip: we would go up through Huntington Ravine, the steepest of the glacial cirques on Mt Washington, and down the Carriage Road. Tom and I, conservatives, went on snowshoes; Lincoln and Rupert, who were at a more dashing age anyway—still in their teens—chose skis. But the first result of this separation was that we had to break two sets of tracks. The ski tracks did not help the snowshoers a great deal, and vice versa. And the snow was very, very deep and heavy, quite exceptionally so for so early in the winter. I don't mind admitting that we had a tough time, with only four of us, to break trail. Although we left the Appalachian Mountain Club's Pinkham Notch Camp (2,000 feet in elevation and the highest point on the valley road) at eight in the morning, it was well along in the afternoon before we got up into the floor of the Ravine, less than three miles away and hardly two thousand feet higher up. Now in winter when the temperature is well below zero (Fahrenheit) it is more prudent to get back home by dark, or at a reasonable approximation thereto, and to do that we should have had to turn back, and at once. But the two skiers reasoned that it would really be quicker for them to go on, that once they were up the headwall they could ski down the Carriage Road in the twinkling of an eye. Although I was a little uneasy about it all, I was powerless to sway them, and in any case I could sympathise with their desire to avoid skiing down the steep and narrow trail that we had come up. In a later year I once skied down the Huntington Ravine brook. Although the brook bed between its forest borders was admittedly wider than a trail, perhaps ten to twelve feet, the turbulent stream, cascading down over huge boulders, afforded a most uneven ski trail. Still, it was good sport working our way down and avoiding the occasional patches of open water swirling blackly over the brink of some waterfall.

But on this, our first winter trip up into Huntington Ravine, no one thought of using the brook as a ski trail. And it really did seem as though, once the skiers reached the Carriage Road, they would have a much more practicable as well as agreeable route to the bottom of the mountain. What everybody passed over pretty lightly and casually is that the Huntington Headwall, the precipitous, thousand-foot-high rock wall of this great glacial cirque, was at that moment sheathed in ice, and it wasn't going to be easy, even with ice-axes and crampons, for anybody to get up it in a hurry, particularly with a pair of skis on his arm. In any case the snowshoers would have to turn back. Even if we got up the headwall, one cannot snowshoe down the Carriage Road in the twinkling of any eye.

As the others started on, Tom and I went back. It was a trifle shorter for us to cross by the Raymond Path to the Carriage Road, which we counted on doing while we could still see the blazes on the trees well enough to find the trail; for the two miles from there down to the Glen House we could follow the wider road all right even in the dusk. But that meant more trail breaking. We forced the pace here all right enough, putting forth our last ounces of strength while lifting, it seemed, tons of snow on our snowshoes at every step. When we got to the road we were disturbed to find no ski tracks there, since if the other two had gone according to their schedule they should have been down before we were. And when we reached the Glen House, ate our dinner, and the evening wore on without any skiers showing up, we began to get seriously alarmed. The crux of the matter was getting up that headwall. It was steep and icy and a person could fall there as easily as not.

At nine o'clock we set out on the rescue party. In those days there weren't many people around the mountains in winter. It was eight miles from the Glen House to the next inhabited house and the road was open only for horse-drawn sleds. Even the Pinkham Notch Camp, now so busy and bustling, was in those days locked up tight and deserted under its snow blanket all through the winter months. The largest rescue party we could muster consisted of Fred Pike, farmer at the Glen House, Tom and me. I don't know that Fred even had snowshoes and Tom in any case had had trouble that day with his bindings. He and Fred thought that if we went up the trail from Pinkham

Notch that we had broken out so thoroughly earlier in the day, we could travel all right without snowshoes. This was a most grievous error. Strolling along on my own snowshoes (which I had tied on to my rucksack when we set out, just in case), I really felt sorry for Tom and Fred as they sank into the snow with every step deeper and deeper the higher we got up the mountain. In truth, they struggled courageously but the time finally came when we all had to admit that they could not possibly get up into the ravine. There was no question of my stopping too; someone had to find out if those boys up there needed help. I left Tom and Fred to wait for me—and why they did not freeze while doing so I shall never know—and raced along alone for an hour or more longer, up through the forest and into the ravine. I reached the bottom of the headwall above timberline at almost exactly midnight.

Strangely enough, it turned into one of the most glorious experiences of my life. Of the first importance, there were no mangled bodies lying at the base of the rocks, and that afforded me, I may say, a measurable amount of relief. The full moon was shining brilliantly and I could make out the line of tracks the two boys had left in the snow and ice, up the headwall and over the top. So they had got up all right. (As a matter of fact, they had reached the top—probably the first winter ascent— at just about midnight too, and we had missed seeing each other by minutes.) So then as my apprehension flowed away, I felt an airy joyousness in the beauty and splendour of the scene. I was in a magical world of diamonds. In the gorgeous moonlight every snow-frosted rock, every sugared twig, every ice-sheet on the majestic walls above, every frost feather, sparkled and glittered. The air was cold with that exhilarating dry cold that excites and stimulates, and that contrasted so pleasantly with the glow of warmth my vigorous exercise had given me. And the silence! Not a breath of wind stirred. Not a bird, not a creature. Every little wild animal was tucked away deep in his hole. As I stood there motionless for a few minutes the sense of solitude was perfect and complete. To be alone, at midnight in the dead of winter, in a scene like this! I felt

Huntington Ravine in winter. RIGHT:
The Odell Gully and the Pinnacle;
BELOW: The Central Gully and the
Headwall. OVERLEAF: The Obergabelhorn, above Zermatt. The first
important mountain I climbed, by
the ridge on the left.

myself a privileged intruder in a world not meant for human beings.

Had I been a disembodied spirit I might have stayed there happily through eternity. As it was, I lingered perhaps a bit longer than I should have done before turning down. But I had not become totally dissociated from the usual concerns of life. As I flew along back down the trail my first care, even before speed, was for placing each foot with precision, and in the background of my mind there had been lingering a pleasant awareness of my warm clothing, my sturdy snowshoes, and even the vigour of my muscles, each one of those things important to me that night as never before.

It turned out that the boys had not got to the top of the headwall before dark. They had been obliged to wait on the rocks about halfway up, good and cold, too, I gather, several hours for the moon to rise above the high Carter Range to the east and give them light enough to see their way on. Those four nice boards they had with them might have made a little fire to take the chill off, and I understand they were tempted, but they managed to keep in mind how agreeable skiing down the other side was to be. However, this skiing down, for Lincoln anyway, was not the joy he had anticipated, what with his being so chilled and stiff from the cold. We were all back at the Glen House about 2 a.m.

But that trip gave me the biggest boost towards becoming a real mountaineer that I had as yet had. From it I learned that the sensation of fatigue may be very misleading; that one has enormous unsuspected reserves of strength and endurance. What had happened? Tom and I had got back to the inn at night, after a long and exhausting day in the mountains, breaking trail through that exceptionally heavy snow, done in, unable, we should have said, to take another step. After a short rest we had started out again and on this second trip the incentive to keep going—and fast—had been so strong that I had not noticed any fatigue at all! After this eye-opening experience I adopted the belief that for practical purposes there was no limit to physical endurance. This may have been intellectually untenable, but for the years of my youth it seemed to do well enough as a working hypothesis. I have been, in my lifetime, extremely tired more than once. I have been too tired to eat, too tired to sleep. But I don't remember any occasion when I couldn't have walked another mile if my life had depended on it.

In a day or two the Washburn family arrived at the Glen House. Dean and Mrs Washburn were friends of our parents and they asked us if we would take their two young sons, Bradford and Sherwood, with us on the trip we proposed for New Year's Day, up Mt Washington through Tuckerman Ravine. They would pay us as if we were Swiss guides. This part of the proposal we declined on the ground that it would seriously compromise our amateur status, but we agreed to take the boys if they would send Fred Pike along too, to come back with them if need be. We felt that the chances were good that the kiddies would be able to make it all right, but, after all, it was the first time we'd ever seen them and they were on the young side. We had a splendid climb and all reached the summit without incident—so different from our frustrated attempt to climb the mountain through Huntington's. The boys came along like veterans with never a moment's hesitation, but their guardian, Fred Pike, climbing in his long winter overcoat, had some heavy going and needed a bit of assistance in getting up the ice steps we cut on the headwall of Tuckerman's. Later Bradford Washburn, after a few years of apprenticeship in the Alps, has become the foremost explorer of the great Alaskan ranges, particularly of Mt McKinley, and one of America's most outstanding mountaineers.

In February Margaret Helburn, daughter of an old friend of my mother's, and her husband Willard invited me to go with the Bemis Crew, a select group of tough and experienced mountaineers. Initiated in 1923, this group gathered every February for a week of climbing, finding in the winter White Mountains the technical problems of the Alps. In 1926 the Bemis Crew met at the Glen House as it does regularly every alternate year. If you want to go to the Glen House in February in the present age of powerful rotary snowploughs, you just drive up there in four or five hours from Boston. But in those days we took the night train to Portland, Maine, thence another train to Gorham, New Hampshire, where the Glen House sleigh met us for the eight-mile drive up the notch.

We had a week of vigorous climbing on the Carter-Moriah Range as well as on the Presidentials and I must have passed some sort of test because Margaret and Willard told me about a small party going in to Katahdin, the highest mountain in Maine, on March 6, and invited me to come along. Katahdin was deeper in the wilderness in those days, before the construction of recent roads, and was not ordinarily accessible in winter. But in 1926 the Great Northern Paper Company were lumbering near Grindstone, twenty-seven miles from Katahdin as the bird flies, and had opened up tote roads running up towards the mountain; we would snowshoe the rest of the way. We were to spend a week at the warden's cabin at Chimney Pond in the Great Basin, that big cirque on the east side of the mountain. Leroy Dudley, the warden, was going in with us and had arranged for getting the bulk of the food supplies in there ahead of time, before the snow came the autumn before. Naturally I was delighted, and much complimented, to be included on this rugged trip. In the North Station, in the Boston and Maine sleeping car, Margaret introduced the other members of the party. One of them was Robert L. M. Underhill, Harvard philosophy instructor and a keen mountaineer. That name will come up again.

We reached Grindstone a little before six in the morning and were invited to a Gargantuan breakfast at the Great Northern Paper Company's camp. Lumber-camp meals are of course legendary and this was one of the best. Great thick steaks and other meats with fried potatoes, tinned fruits in variety, pies of apple, mincemeat and pumpkin, frosted cakes, cookies and doughnuts all went down well. Then a big sled drawn by a pair of powerful horses carried us all to Burns' Tie Camp, some thirteen miles away on Mud Brook. Mrs Burns had another stupendous meal ready for us at 11.30, which we handled all

29

right. Then we had to get down to work and proceed under our own power. Arthur Comey and Robert Underhill travelled on skis, the other eight of us on snowshoes. After some six hours we reached the remains of the old Depot Camp, used in previous lumbering operations. There was one small shack still upright, but just barely, with a stove and wooden bunks. It was 6.30 and dark, and the Helburns, Bob and I decided to spend the night here. We were carrying our sleeping-bags in our packs. We had some of the perishable food supplies with us, but I don't believe we needed much to eat. The theory was that Margaret and I were to sleep undisturbed while Willard and Bob, dividing up the night between them, would in turn be awake and on duty stuffing the stove with boards from the buildings that had fallen down. Even so, and I have been accused of the most preposterous ingratitude in saying this, we passed a very cold night.

The others, Avis Newhall, the only other woman, and five men, made of sterner stuff, kept on to the goal in below-zero temperature, arriving at eleven and much fatigued. The sleeping accommodations at the warden's cabin were divided into two 'rooms' by a partition some six feet high. On one side were two beds, eventually occupied by the Helburns and Avis and me, but that first night by Avis and Roy Dudley. The others slept in bunks on the other side of the partition, but in no great privacy at that.

'Don't, Roy, don't! No, no! You mustn't do that!' Screams from Avis roused everybody from sleep.

'What's Roy doing, Avis?' the alarmed leader of the party finally asked.

'He's trying to put a grand piano under my bed,' Avis replied in great indignation.

They say that laughter from the other side of the partition finally woke Avis up from her nightmare. The embarrassed Roy was glad enough to sleep on the other side of the partition from then on.

The next morning in a snowstorm we four made our way in to the cabin and found it down a hole in the snow some ten feet deep. We had a pleasant slide to get to the door, but no view other than blank whiteness out the windows. When the boys dug the snow away from a spot on the lake and chopped through the ice, they found the water alive with small wriggling red creatures, curling first one way and then the other.

'If they were smaller we'd eat them and call them germs,' remarked Arthur, 'and if they were larger, we'd eat them and call them shrimps, so why not eat them anyway?'

For the following week we led a primitive life. Arthur was the only one who made any gesture towards bathing, and his was to go outdoors now and then and roll naked in the snow. While I never actually saw this from close up, I have a picture of him doing it, with great clouds of snow flying in all directions. It must have been refreshing.

Roy, who cared little for mountain climbing in March, stayed at the cabin, chopping for wood and water, and preparing meals. The food supplies had been chosen by Margaret and he thought little or nothing of her choice.

'Pancakes, now,' declared Roy, 'is the only food for breakfast. These new-fangled things you brought, oatmeal, bacon and eggs, digest right away on you and don't do you no good. But pancakes, they lay on your stomach and nourish you all day long.'

We had some excellent climbs that week. We reached the high tableland of Katahdin and its summit by various routes, by the Basin Slide and also up the Chimney, a big rocky gully that leads to the outlying summit of Pamola. The huge chockstones of this Chimney were buried deep in snow and it was a steep climb getting around them out on the wall. From Pamola we made our way to Katahdin itself along the rocks and ice of the Knife-Edge (real alpine going here), crouching low in our tracks to cut the force of the violent wind and glad enough for our sturdy parkas and the woollen scarves over our faces. We also had a good ice climb up the Elbow Gully in the North Basin. Arthur and Bob took skis up the mountain for the first ski ascent. Two hundred feet below the summit, where the surface became unrelieved hard ice, Bob changed to

31

crampons. But not Arthur. Although it was neither easy nor, perhaps, any too safe, he planted his skis right on the summit cairn.

On the way out, we snowshoers spent the night at another old lumber camp.

'I'll learn you to be a game warden,' Leroy offered, as he went poking around, turning over the boards of the bunks until finally, sure enough, he found marks where beaver pelts had been stretched out to dry.

The skiers stayed at the Basin Pond Cabin one night longer and then came through in one day. Arthur, in fact, disdaining to ride in the sled from the Tie Camp, skied the twenty-seven miles to Grindstone.

From all these people on the Bemis Crew and the Katahdin trips, experienced mountaineers that they were, I learned more about climbing in the Alps and about the plans that should be made ahead of time. Engaging the right guides was of first importance, they said. I had often had good guides, but more by luck than anything else. The Helburns, particularly, gave me invaluable help of all sorts towards a mountaineering career. In 1927 I spent the summer climbing in the Alps with Margaret, and it was on our return from that trip that I experienced my one and only fall, as far as I can remember, while leading a climb.

Willard had met us in Montreal and as we drove down through the White Mountains we stopped off long enough to make an attempt on the unclimbed Central Gully of Huntington Ravine. Although a small stream ran down this gully, it bothered us not at all in the early part where we could climb up the rocks beside or, occasionally, in back of it. About halfway up, however, there was a step in the gully where the stream gushed out through a narrow V-notch in a nice little waterfall. As we stood under the overhang and looked the situation over, the side walls seemed unalluring and we decided that our route obviously led up and out directly through the water. I was leading and I found it easy enough to climb up in back of the waterfall, reach out and grasp what seemed to me excellent handholds a few inches above the brink. Up to this moment, only my hands and arms were in the water. But as I swung out into the current, preparatory to pulling myself up over, I found that I had completely underestimated the force of that water and I was amused at the ease with which the waterfall swept me away as lightly as if I had been a feather. As I went down past Willard, entirely comfortable, cushioned all around as I was by a powerful curtain of water, I was astonished when I looked out by the expression of anguish on his face, and I realized that perhaps he was thinking of the time a few years earlier when his guide, Alfred Couttet, had fallen down past him to his death on the Dru. I felt sorry to be reminding Willard of this, particularly since I was enjoying such a novel and entertaining experience.

What does one think about while falling? In my case, nothing much. I don't suppose I had time to do much logical thinking. Certainly the events of my past life did not pass in review before my mind. My thick shell of water gave me an impression of impenetrability, a sensation of complete security, complete protection. I was wrapped up in something so much stronger than I; nothing could get at me here! I experienced not the slightest alarm. Nor, as it turned out, did I need to. Willard's rope pulled me out of the stream only slightly below him, completely unharmed, and as for being wet, it was a lovely warm September day. I unfastened my knickerbockers at the knee to let the water run out and we finished the climb by making a detour around our waterfall so wide that we could not consider that we had climbed the central gully after all.

III

The Dolomites

In the summer of 1926 I set out for Europe at the end of May with very definite plans in mind. Rock-climbing was what I wanted. I would start in the Dolomites and later go on to Chamonix and its granite aiguilles. Dolomite rock is a magnesian limestone, about as firm and hard as rock can come, so that the striking peaks and walls can be, and often are, almost vertical. The texture of the rock, when you get up into touch with it, is like a solidified sponge with all sorts of little roughnesses, little holes and peaks, that make fine fingerholds.

Antonio Dimai, who had been the most outstanding Dolomite guide for some twenty years around the turn of the century, was to be my guide. His two sons, Angelo and Giuseppe, although young at the time, were already brilliant climbers and he proposed taking one or the other of them along too, a reasonable suggestion considering my inexperience. In difficult rock-climbing the two guides would work together as first and second men, while I came along at the end. (And twenty years later, whenever my husband and I took along an inexperienced climber on an ascent in the Rockies, we too liked to run a double-header with the two of us up front, and our 'tourist' at the end.) Although the whole Dimai family was quite extraordinary, Angelo Dimai was the most beautiful rock-climber I have ever seen, so graceful that when he climbed he seemed to float up the rocks with no effort. And his footwork was so delicate that never did he kick down so much as a pebble. For several years I watched him with the closest attention, trying

RIGHT: Angelo Dimai in 1926, and BELOW: in a typical performance crossing from one Dolomite tower to another in the Misurina group. *Photos courtesy of Ghedina Studio, Cortina.*

Antonio Dimai
in 1926.

The Pomagagnon Group from Cortina. Punta Croce is the second, or central peak (Punta Fiames is the first) in the lefthand set of three.

to analyse his style with a view, of course, to copying it, and if I am not a prettier rock-climber than I am, it is not for lack of trying under a perfect example.

Punta Croce, one of the peaks in the Pomagagnon group, was my first climb, and nobody will ever convince me that it is not the hardest climb in the world! It was my first experience with that extreme Dolomite exposure—that climbing out in the open with nothing below but a big drop. Some years later my thirteen-year-old son, Brian, was to observe on the Cima Piccola, 'I like difficult rock-climbing and I like exposure. But I don't like them both together.' That's the way I, too, felt on my first Dolomite climb. Punta Croce was one of those Dolomite south walls, quite short as they run, but a good deal longer than any rock-climb that I had done before. And a good deal steeper. The exposure all seemed so startling that I even lost my sense of the perpendicular and at one point wondered why Giuseppe, who was leading, went up a certain thirty or forty feet so slowly, although it looked as though he was finding it quite easy. But when he reached his stance and pulled the rucksacks up on the rope they swung out away from the wall, showing that the whole pitch had really been overhanging. And then my shoes, on this first day, were not holding well. They were new, the local *scarpe da gatto* (cat shoes) whose soles were made of many layers of woollen cloth stitched together. When these got worn a bit and frayed out they really held very well indeed on the Dolomite rock and better than rubber when the rock was wet. But mine had just been made and were not yet in the best condition. Today everyone wears rubber, but not then. *Scarpe da gatto*, manchon felt or even rope soles were the style and when I took to wearing, as I soon did, my ordinary sneakers from home, people shook their heads.

From the top of Punta Croce we could look across to Punta Fiames and its magnificent southeast ridge, the famous 'Spigolo', sharp as a knife-edge and straight up in the air.

'Angelo has climbed that,' remarked Antonio, 'but I never shall. It is too dangerous.'

I shuddered dizzily at the very thought of climbing such a

place. How *could* anyone? And yet, that same season, both Antonio and I did go up the Spigolo and I, for one, enjoyed hugely every step of the way. It is remarkable how fast one can get used to exposure, and even acquire quite a taste for it. To my mind, it spiced up the climbs enormously and without adding any element of danger—not for me, at least, for in that first year I never climbed without being held on a good strong rope.

And this Dolomite climbing hardly needed any spicing up at all, being about the best fun I'd met in life! In common with many women, I felt that these Dolomites were made just to suit me with their small but excellent toe- and finger-holds, and pitches where a delicate sense of balance was the key, rather than brute force. While it helps of course to have tough muscles, the prizefighter would not necessarily make a fine Dolomite climber. But the ballet dancer might.

II. COL ROSÀ

After a few days Col Rosà appeared on the programme. While 'col' in French—and English—means pass or notch, in Italian it means peak. Col Rosà, in those days of *arrampicata libera*, of free climbing without artificial aids, was one of the more difficult climbs.

'Not all Cortina guides can lead it because it is very perilous for the first one who goes up,' Antonio, who had made the first ascent, informed me. 'The King of the Belgians says Col Rosà is harder than the Grépon at Chamonix.' (It is certainly more delicate and subtle, though shorter and less fatiguing.) That day Antonio wanted to go to market, and was going to send Angelo in his place. This was the first climb I ever did with Angelo, the first of many fine ones.

Although the weather was uncertain in the morning, we set out anyway. At the beginning of the rocks, it started to rain a bit, gently.

'If it rains, it will be quite impossible to go up,' announced Angelo, very firmly, but there was something curiously unconvincing in the tone of his voice. Just what did he mean? I

36

agreed, of course, that if he thought best we would turn back. The danger would be his. At the same time I intimated that if it were merely a matter of getting wet, I should not mind. There had been a lot of rain that June, and a lot of dull days at the hotel.

'It might stop,' suggested Angelo cheerfully. 'And it's not raining very hard.'

Meanwhile our preparations for doing the climb were going on as usual, changing our boots to *scarpe da gatto*, roping up, and it was clear to both of us that we both wanted to go on. It was only when we reached the summit that Angelo told me, with a slight chuckle, that his father's definite instructions had been: don't do the climb if it rains.

A slow drizzle, however, will get rocks as wet, mud as slippery and hands as cold as a torrent will, and as the minutes went on that day, the slow drizzle turned into a torrent, anyway. One bad-looking place was a wall of smooth, wet rock not much more than twelve feet high but slightly overhanging, topped by grass and a loosely-anchored pine tree. There was a crack going up the middle, too narrow for a foot and too wide for a finger-hold.

'Shall I draw?' Angelo called down.

'No, thanks,' I answered, but not from any real conviction that I should be able to get up unaided.

However, I finally managed by treating the crack as a 'corner' (which it certainly wasn't). Standing a bit off to one side, I pulled with the fingers of both hands on the nearer wall of the crack, while pushing against the farther wall with my feet. For this I had to bend my ankles about at right angles. But it worked all right.

The traverse that I had been warned was quite terrible did not seem so bad, even though wet and slimy with mud. Halfway across I saw some beautiful large clumps of *Primula auricula* about six feet below me, but on second thoughts decided not to get any, even though I had promised some of the other guests at the hotel I would bring them some. This lovely little deep-yellow flower had a reputation for being rare and growing only in the highest and most inaccessible places. Still, to a mountain climber it seemed to be everywhere, and more than once I had to dig it out of a handhold I needed.

The rain came down in earnest. I couldn't wear my hat because it interfered with my view of where I was supposed to be going, which always seemed to be directly above my head, and I had to be content with a dripping wet handkerchief tied over my new wave. Near the top came an interminable chimney, nothing 'perilous', but hard work, especially since it was so wet and it came at the end of the climb. As I reached up to grasp the handholds mud and water poured up my sleeves, the hand-kerchief came off my head, and my wet clothes, a nice light-grey woollen climbing suit that I had just had made in Paris, caught and tore on every projection.

The porter was waiting on the summit with our boots. Nowadays climbers wear their vibram-soled boots both up and down, but in 1926 it was standard practice to have a porter bring your nailed boots to the summit by the easy route, so that you might have them to walk home in instead of the too-light *scarpe da gatto*. This was a pleasant little luxury that I missed in wilder mountain regions.

The war had not been over very long in 1926 and there were signs of it everywhere in the mountains. Occasionally, still, some melting snowbank would uncover a soldier's body—that spring on Tofana climbers had discovered the body of a soldier from a Bavarian regiment. The gentler north side of Col Rosà had been fought over bitterly for three years and was covered with dugouts, fortifications, and networks of trenches. And over everything hung the horrid smell of mouldering rags and rubble.

On the summit we enjoyed an hour of warm sun, the only sun of the day. But when we started our descent, rain came down in torrents again as we ran down the easy side, leaping trenches and crawling through entanglements of barbed wire, adding, I am sorry to admit, a few more tears and a great deal more mud to my sorry clothes.

During the First World War Cortina, which was Austrian,

was taken by the Italians in May, 1915. They evacuated it in November, 1917, to return for good in November, 1918. Although the people had always talked Italian, the sympathies of most of them were Austrian and still were in 1926, I suspect. The engaging story of the Cortina guide who changed sides with the town, and spent the whole war on Tofana, the mountain behind his own house, fighting in whatever army was at the moment occupying it, visiting his family at night quite frequently to bring them a loaf of bread or two, is unfortunately not true!

The Dimai boys had been too young to be in the war but when the Italians were about to evacuate the town in 1917 they rounded up all the young lads approaching military age, sixteen to seventeen years old or so, and drove them off like a herd of cattle to Italy, where they spent the rest of the war. Angelo was one of these and he told me the boys all considered it an immense lark, and were happy and excited at the thought of a trip to the south. It must have been quite a scene in the village square, with all the mothers in despair, weeping—how Angelo laughed when he said *le madri piangevano*—and the boys cheering and singing in glee. Although the Italian soldiers tried to keep their charges quiet, they could not make much progress at it. The boys were well treated, not only by the soldiers, but also when they reached Italy—Angelo was apprenticed to a cabinet-maker—and at the end of the war they came home. Giuseppe, a young child, was left at home with his mother. In the Second World War things worked out tragically for Giuseppe. He had diabetes, and whether there was a lack, during the war years, of the proper food and drugs, I do not know, but in 1946 he died of his disease, leaving a charming young wife, Paola.

On our way home from Col Rosà we stopped at the Dimai house where two sisters, Maria and Alma, gave us some delicious milk and lent us an umbrella for the walk to my hotel. Even though the upper route through the fields was a bit longer, it seemed better to go that way rather than through the village, considering my appearance.

A friend of mine, I'll call her Clementine, had arrived at Cortina to join me in some climbs.

'I met Antonio in the village this morning,' she said. 'He certainly was surprised to hear that you and Angelo had started out. But then he thought it over and said that when you saw the weather wasn't good of course you would have changed your plans and climbed something easier. As we stood there a moment it was easy to see that two thoughts were struggling for possession of his mind: first, that it was unthinkable that any son of his had disobeyed him so flagrantly as to do Col Rosà in that rain and, second, that he might perhaps have done just that!'

The next time I met Giuseppe I gathered, from little grins and half-hints that he dropped, that Angelo had certainly heard from his father about this.

And my nice grey suit. When I took a look at it the next morning I decided that a walk to the tailor shop in the village was imperative. I was checking over in my dictionary to be sure I knew the Italian words for mend, clean and press.

'Don't bother,' suggested Clementine. 'Just show the suit to the tailor and words will not be necessary.'

III. CLIMBS WITH CLEMENTINE

For Clementine's first trip we chose the Cinque Torri, that classic starting-ground for Dolomite beginners, which I had not visited before because the snow had been too deep to get there. The climbing on this group of small towers, although none of them is more than 400 feet high, is nonetheless most spectacular. When Clementine, like me, first came to grips with Dolomite rock-climbing she did not find it too obvious, either. Antonio excitedly and volubly shouted at her, pouring out a whole mass of suggestions and instructions. Giuseppe and I were convulsed with laughter as Clementine looked at us in mock dejection.

'Half of what he says I can't understand,' she complained, 'and the other half I can't do.'

I'm afraid I allowed Clementine scant time to get in training

40

but in the next few days took her right along on climbs that I wanted to do myself, those great deep chimneys, the Pompanin Camin on the Croda da Lago and Camino Barbaria on the Becco di Mezzodì. At the top of the last one, squirming out from under the huge chockstone, Clementine apparently found the outlook immediately in front of her a bit bleak.

'Tira! Tira! [Pull! Pull!]', she called out vehemently. I was appalled.

'Oh, Clementine!' I protested, embarrassed. 'I'm sure you didn't mean to say that. That's the second person singular, the familiar form. What you should have said is *Tiri.*'

But Clementine made no reply. In any case, she seemed to have gone up with no untoward incidents. Somewhat later, however, when we were comfortably settled over the lunch bags on the summit, she spoke to me with great and solemn emphasis:

'The next time I am hanging between life and death, Miriam, do not talk to me of verb forms.'

Clementine should have known about those verb forms, and no doubt did, since we had had some Italian lessons together in Boston from a young Italian student, Michele Cantarella, whom we took rock-climbing on weekends. (His experience with us apparently got him off to such a good start in teaching that he has subsequently become a professor.) I always liked to pick up what bits of languages I could as I travelled about. In 1924 in Rome my father refused the services of an interpreter, in an interview with Mussolini, on the ground that his daughter spoke Italian and would do the job. This was a considerable overstatement. But, although we promised beforehand that we would not publish the contents of this interview, I think it would be all right to say that the subjects discussed were of sufficient simplicity so that my Italian was adequate. I had to translate only one way, anyhow. Mussolini understood our English, but talked in Italian himself. This is not the only contact with the 'great' that our family has had. In 1932 my husband rode up in the elevator in a Frankfort hotel with Hitler. Hitler was just about to come to power and although

41

he needed a few big, tough bodyguards, not so many as he had later, and there was room in the elevator for Bob too. Hitler, however, had nothing to say to Robert.

IV. PUNTA FIAMES, BY THE SPIGOLO

On July 1, I went up the Spigolo of Punta Fiames. This was a difficult and delicate climb which only a few people had done by 1926. And it was, quite seriously, considerably more difficult in those days before the general use of pitons. Pitons are those metal spikes, some six inches long, that you hammer into crevices in the rocks. They have a loop or ring at the end through which you snap a carabiner, which is much like a large and strong safety-pin. Through this carabiner in turn you thread the rope and the whole arrangement adds considerably to the safety of the climb, as well as making it distinctly easier. Pitons were just beginning to come into use at that time. In those early days, certain climbers looked down on them as just one more artificial aid that was not quite sporting. But styles change, and in order to do more and more difficult climbs, people must of necessity make more and more use of artificial aids. Some climbers have made otherwise impossible ascents by drilling a line of holes in the rocks and putting in expansion or contraction bolts, up which they climbed. Although I belong to the generation which feels that may be going a little far, I don't like to take a dogmatic position on the question. It is too easy to date yourself by the things you disapprove of. Everybody uses 'artificial aids'; it is only a question of degree. Consider the following list, all artificial: clothing, boots, nails in boots, ice-axes, crampons, climbing rope, roping-down rope, pitons for security, pitons as direct climbing aids, expansion bolts, rope-ladders, oxygen, benzedrine 'pep' pills, etc. Where will you draw the line? Or why draw one? (Yes, one must draw one after all. For it wouldn't do to land by helicopter above all the difficulties and 'climb' a peak by strolling up the final few easy feet!) I don't think I regret, though, that I did my rock-climbing in those simpler days when it was still done pretty much with one's own arms and legs, fingers and toes.

Two Dolomite chimneys.

Punta Fiames of Pomagagnon. The Spigolo route is shown as number 2. *Photo courtesy of Ghedina Studio, Cortina.*

Torre Grande of Cinque Torri. Via Miriam is the route marked on the photo. *Photo courtesy of Ghedina Studio, Cortina.*

It seems to me it was just as much fun that way, even though there were places we couldn't get up at all, and the rucksacks must be heavy with so much hardware (ironmongery) now in these days, when it is hard to tell where rock-climbing ends and engineering begins.

When we climbed the Spigolo in 1926 there was not one single piton anywhere on the route. The Spigolo route diverges from the regular one about halfway up and traverses over to the 'cutting edge' of the ridge, which it hits only about 500 feet below the summit. Those 500 feet took us three and a half hours. The climb was nearly vertical all the way and occasionally overhanging, with good stopping places quite infrequent. The holds were small and the whole climb was a study in balance and delicacy, fields in which Angelo was a master. The hardest pitch was a smooth wall of the most startling exposure and something over seventy feet high. This was the place that Angelo had told me about where he proposed to take off his climbing rope and go up with just a small fishline tied to his waist, just strong enough to pull up the climbing rope when he reached the first stopping place. Climbing ropes were heavier in those pre-nylon days and seventy feet tied to his waist and dragging him back would have made it much more difficult to maintain his balance on the minute holds. Although I remonstrated that I did not like to have him do that, Antonio pointed out quietly that it was safer that way. And of course it was.

As we watched Angelo moving up the wall we realized that we needn't have worried. And then when it came to my turn, what glorious fun it was!

Several years later Angelo and I made the first descent of the Spigolo and I was astonished to see a few pitons here and there embedded in the rock.

'I put most of those in myself,' said Angelo, 'when I took King Albert of the Belgians up this climb. It wouldn't do, you know, to have any accident happen to the King. . . . Of course, when it's only you,' he added quickly, with the customary twinkle in his eye, 'it wouldn't matter.'

43

V. VIA MIRIAM (MIRIAM ROUTE)

In early July of the following year I arrived in Cortina again. There were some half-dozen of us there, and it was a gay occasion when our guide friends came to welcome us. Quickly Antonio, excited and barely concealing it, led me aside and in a conspiratory whisper warned me, 'Don't go to the Cinque Torri tomorrow!' Although there was no time then for an explanation, I caught the contagion of his mysterious enthusiasm and steered the group into planning a training climb for the next day up Punta Fiames.

The exciting news turned out to be that Angelo had a new climb for me on the Torre Grande, the first route that any climber had succeeded in working out up its precipitous south wall, the hardest route so far made anywhere on that tower, and one of the most difficult in the whole Dolomite region. He, Giuseppe and Arturo Gaspari had accomplished this feat the week before. I was to make the first tourist ascent and— Angelo had his father tell me this—he would like to call it the Via Miriam. Naturally I accepted this honour with pride and pleasure and I still find it entertaining, more than a quarter-century later, to overhear in Cortina young Italian climbers, strangers to me, discussing 'the Miriam'. For it is one of the good climbs even today.

Although the three boys had meant to keep this climb a secret, word had got out, and some Italian alpinists had telegraphed Angelo to ask if they might be the first tourists he took up this new route. Angelo had replied that the route was destined for the Signorina Miriam. Then some of the other Cortina guides had asked to be taken up. Harder to refuse, this request was, and about all Angelo could do was put them off from day to day. Obviously we must make the climb as soon as possible. So we did, as the very next climb after Punta Fiames, and it was a brusque surprise for my arm muscles, not yet much hardened up after a winter's lack of practice. On July 7, 1927, Margaret Helburn and I with Angelo Dimai, Antonio Dimai and Angelo Dibona did the new Via Miriam. We found here no chance for warming up, no easy pitches to start with. On the contrary, after a pleasant stroll up through flower-decked meadows, the difficulties began the moment we first laid our hands on the rock. For this side of the Torre Grande rises almost perpendicular. Angelo made the claim that in the first eighty metres (260 feet) of rise in this route of his, there is one metre (three feet, three and one-third inches) deviation from the vertical. ('Which way?' a facetious friend once asked me.) But such fun it was, not only steep and exposed, but delicate, and strenuous as well.

Angelo led, backed up by Dibona, with me next, then Antonio and Margaret; so at least it was at the start, for the order changed from time to time. The first passage of 100 feet, a face climb with small holds and two overhangs to surmount, set the keynote. By the time I reached Dibona, who had a good belay just below a small cave, I was wondering if perhaps it had been the wisest course to undertake so hard a climb as this for the second one of the season. But I got some rest lying in the cave and waiting while Angelo went on up and the other two came to us. The next pitch went better; a little crack, not so terribly hard, led up for perhaps twenty-five feet. Here a ponderous overhanging band of rock above, running across the whole south face, definitively blocked our advance upward. So we traversed to the left, towards the southwest face, along a narrow, slightly ascending ledge, a traverse that was technically easy—no hands needed—but stimulating in its exposure.

Some fifty feet along this traverse Angelo diverged from the ledge to ascend diagonally to the left a difficult small crack filled with loose stones, by which he arrived up under a massive out-thrust of red rock. For the next thirteen feet his progress depended on his hands alone, with no support whatever for his feet, as he traversed immediately under this red rock, along a delicate little crack that provided only minute fingerholds. Today this is the regular route for all the members of the party, but when we made the climb Angelo sent the rest of us traversing still farther along the ledge, sensational here, to rejoin him by climbing straight up for some thirty feet, a route that was later abandoned because of the looseness of the rock. On this ascent I struggled hard to surmount two small overhangs while Angelo held the rope firmly, practically on the borderline between 'holding' and 'pulling'. Not over it, I hope, for I felt strongly that I should do this climb—*my* climb!—on my own. And I believe in the end I did, all of it, although at times I had to work hard and on one or two pitches take a second try. Later in the season I should have found the climb more within my strength.

After I reached Angelo, another good rest fell to my lot and indeed I was to need it, for the rest of the climb, to condense the details a bit, seemed to grow more and more strenuous the higher we got. I remember particularly the great black wall, with no stopping place really worthy of the name for the whole length of the rope. I kept moving mainly because I had to, even though the handholds diminished in size and, instead of supporting the fingers properly from on top, turned into the kind that have to be pinched from the sides. When even these gave out completely, I came to two pitons, one of which bent down under my weight. The other did afford me a moment's pause, long enough to wonder what Angelo had been standing on when he had driven it into its crack in the first place.

Near the top came what was in those days perhaps the most difficult and certainly one of the most dangerous passages of the climb, a short but vertical little crack filled with earth and grass. Don't touch it, shouted down Angelo, nothing there would hold. Just put your feet on each side of the crack, out on the wall. It seemed to be Angelo's opinion that even though the holds on this wall were admittedly so small that they would support a person's weight only for an instant in passing, if I maintained a continuous and calm rhythm, momentum would carry me up! Perhaps this crack has been cleaned out now; I hope so. It led towards an easy chimney that joined the ordinary route, and in ten minutes we were on the summit. We had needed three hours and a half to climb this 400 feet.

The climb was repeated several times that same summer.

And in July, 1928, I received a postcard from Clementine reporting on the Cortina climbs she had done, several of them easy '(facile), the Spigolo (difficile ma non troppo) and the Via Miriam (*molto* difficile—1 "tiri" and 2 "tene benes")!'

VI. CIMA UNA

Lightheartedly, Angelo and I romped over many other good climbs in subsequent years and I think almost all of them were as new to him as they were to me. For I made a rule that he and I would climb no peaks where he had been before. I liked to see Angelo baffled, I explained to Antonio, when he gently questioned this curious notion of mine and pointed out to me reasonably that many people take a guide because he *does* know the way. Perhaps a more accurate reason would have been that I found it not only entertaining but of course immensely instructive to watch Angelo choose a route. And Angelo as well, always game for anything, found this rule quite to his liking. For a guide is usually occupied in leading tourists up the same climbs, over and over. Although Angelo protests that no aspect of guiding ever became tedious, he did, after a few years, get himself a business job (and today he is director of the Cooperativa and one of the leading business men of Cortina). I noticed, however, that he always managed to take a few days off whenever he wanted to climb. But that apparently wasn't with everybody. For several years only two signatures alternated in his guide's book: Albert, Roi des Belges, and Miriam O'Brien! (I need scarcely mention that this is the only manner in which these two were ever associated.)

The north wall of the Cima Una in the charming little Val Fiscalina had been climbed by only two Cortina guides, Antonio Dimai and Angelo Dibona. A long climb it was, some 2,600 feet of rock, of which about one-half took place in a great deep chimney. On the single occasion when it had been done the year before, the party, one tourist with two guides, had taken two days for the climb, sleeping out on the rocks. Back in 1898 Antonio had put twelve hours on the first ascent of this route. Angelo, affectionately teasing his father, told him that although twelve hours might be good time for *him*, we—*alpinisti come noi*—would go up much more rapidly. Antonio was doubtful, but it turned out that Angelo was right! (Seven hours we put.)

On our way, when we stopped in Sesto to get one of the two good guides there to act as porter for our expedition, the mayor told us that neither of them would think of doing the climb. Quickly Angelo explained that we did not want him to go on the climb itself, but merely to carry our boots to the summit by the easy route. I remember how appalled the mayor was to learn that we two intended to go alone! Angelo must be a rash young man indeed. To show how things change: today the guide-book rates that climb as only third degree* with passages of fourth.† (The Via Miriam, I am happy to notice, is still fifth degree.) Since our day, however, improvements may have been made in the route. And then, too, in the guide-book description I find here and there the word *chiodo* (piton), which may explain something of why it is now considered easier than it used to be. There was no piton along the route when we went up. The raising over the years of standards of difficulty is due in large measure to the use of improved equipment, and particularly of pitons.

Even we found much of it quite easy. And of the four difficult places that Antonio had warned us about, we considered the first one hard but possible, the second we never found at all, and the fourth I do not remember. But the third, oh! that third used up an hour of our time and caused me more than a little uneasiness. The chimney was here quite wide and deep. We had climbed up inside, at the very back where the walls were close together, until we came to some enormous blocks of rock wedged in the chimney, closing it off completely. To get around these we had to traverse out along one wall underneath this great roof. There was nothing whatever to support the feet, and for the hands only a few unsatisfactory holds and those wet

---

* Rock-climbs are classified in 'degrees', from 'first degree', where it is just necessary to use your hands, to 'sixth degree', the limit of human possibility. Sixth degree requires artificial aids.

† Antonio Berti, *Dolomiti Orientali*, 1950, p. 563.

and slimy. Not even Angelo launched out on this in his usual debonair manner, but first looked about until he found a small wedged stone around which he could run his rope for a belay. As he made his way across the traverse he kept warning me of the smoothness, the slipperiness and the general inadequacy of the handholds.

When it came my turn to start and I glanced at my rope, which stretched out horizontally for some fifteen or twenty feet before it could turn the corner around the blocks and go up to Angelo above, most dismal ideas were running through my mind. If I fall off here, I thought, I shall swing out in an impressive pendulum, and when all is calm again there I'll be, hanging in the air with nothing in reach of either my hands or feet. How shall I get up from there? I'm sure Angelo could not pull me from above with the rope first running over that overhang. And so on and so on. But with every step I progressed the length of the horizontal stretch of rope diminished until I finally reached the outer edge of the chimney still in contact with the rocks, somewhat to my surprise. The rest of the climb, as I remember it, was uneventful and we were back in Cortina that afternoon.

VII. ANTELAO, SOUTH FACE

I enjoyed climbing rapidly. And, going with Angelo, it was as well I did. At one time or another I have been with guides (none of those mentioned here!) who climbed in an unlively, heavy-gaited manner, putting a bit too much time into overcoming the problems, not only physically, but intellectually as well. This takes a lot of zest out of the adventure. But never with Angelo. Quick as lightning he was, and deft and sure as well. Walking to the *attacco* in the cool morning air, we occasionally surmounted some two thousand feet of elevation an hour. I remember a time or two when we raced up or down easy rocks in two parallel lines; that the rope between us rarely snagged was due to its rapid and skilful manipulation on Angelo's part.

Whenever we could, Angelo and I preferred to do our climbs

straight out from Cortina. We would either start early in the morning on Angelo's *motocicletta*, which could roar up the steepest path or, if we went by car, we hardly noticed an extra bit of climb up to the *attacco*. We did the south face of Antelao, starting that same morning from Cortina. The usual custom on this climb, which involved an ascent from the valley of approximately 8,000 feet* was to spend the night in a bivouac cave at the foot of the big cliffs of the face and complete the climb the following day, for all of which the guide-book counted about fourteen hours in total time.

Besides doing the entire climb in one day, and cutting three or four hours off the time, we made a new route for well over a thousand feet of the ascent. Many a new route, I may as well admit, is made because the climbers cannot find the usual one; ours was no exception. Angelo says that his father had not explained with sufficient clearness where the route went. ('But I remember,' writes Clori, Angelo's wife, 'that his father used to say Angelo mistook the way because he had not been sufficiently attentive to the explanations.') In any case, Angelo's new route was a splendid one, which I enjoyed immensely. Angelo himself, when he later repeated it, found it most interesting, in particular a long traverse of fourth degree superior. At the time, he had not recognized the beauty of the route for, as mist now and then obscured the face, he was too intent on his search for a way, any sort of way, to get up.

Those three to four thousand feet of rock-climbing were hard on my *scarpe da gatto*; the layers of woollen cloth that formed their soles began to fray out to an extent that alarmed me. I might soon have no soles at all. In the little bag that I habitually carry in my rucksack, however, among the safety-pins, band-aids, compass, waterproof matchbox, etc., I found needle and cotton as well. (The woman's handbag, whether for town or mountain, is notorious for including a bit of everything.) It took me an extra half-hour to sew up those soles well enough so that they lasted to the summit.

* Cancia, 936 metres. Antelao, 3,263 metres, with an intermediate descent of 100 metres.

Down we went by an easier route to San Vito, where Giuseppe met us with the motor-cycle and drove me to Cancia where I had left the car. We were all back in Cortina in good time for dinner.

VIII. CAMPANILE BASSO DI BRENTA, VIA FEHRMANN

The Via Fehrmann on the Campanile Basso di Brenta would be a good one, Angelo suggested, when I asked him to recommend an agreeable climb.

'The Campanile Basso . . . is a fantastic obelisk of rock, extraordinarily bold and without doubt the most elegant, the most classic and the most difficult of the Alps . . . [it] rises for fully a thousand feet with absolute verticality . . . [The only break in its symmetry is] a comfortable ledge'—called, for obvious reasons, the Stradone Provinciale (State Highway)— 'on the north side, which ends in an almost horizontal shoulder, the only healthy (*igienico*) place on this extraordinarily smooth phantasm of rock,' I read to Angelo from the guide-book.*

He stared at me in amazement. 'But the book was published in 1926—four years ago. Of course you know that all climbs are much easier now!'

While perhaps not any too easy, the climb was a splendid one, and we were enjoying it hugely when, all of a sudden, great black clouds swirled up from nowhere to envelop us, and down poured rain and hailstones as thunder rolled and lightning flashed. True, the weather had been a bit cloudy beforehand, but we never expected anything like this. Quickly we glanced around for some sort of shelter, or at least a secure position for waiting out the storm. Nothing, absolutely nothing but sheer walls met our eyes in any direction. We were perhaps two-thirds of the way up and there simply wasn't shelter on that face of 'absolute verticality.' We just stayed where we were. What else indeed could we do? I perched sideways on a narrow little ledge, five or six inches wide, with my feet dangling over several hundred feet of space. Angelo stood beside me, with his toes on two little toeholds in the rock. We waited there for more than one hour.

* Pino Prati, *Dolomiti di Brenta*, 1926, p. 149.

Soaked by the rain, chilled by the wind, and later covered with snow, we should have been warmer had we been able to move about, but practically the only motion we could make was that of shivering (and that warms you, too). One bolt of lightning hit Angelo, so he reported, directly on the jack-knife which was in his pocket. I had supposed that I was the one the lightning hit, but was willing to admit that it might have struck both of us at once. Later, when we joined two other parties who had been climbing at different points on the peak, we found that each separate person had thought himself the direct target of that lightning flash. I have heard the questionable tale that when lightning hits a person it sometimes stimulates his muscles in such a way that he leaps forward. Had that happened to any one of us on the Campanile Basso it would have been too bad!

Just as suddenly as the storm had come, it left, and the beautiful warm sun was shining down on us again. For an instant we were pleased, until we glanced up and saw the great wall above us sheathed with snow and ice and realized that our situation had for the moment deteriorated. For all this began to melt quickly and showers of water and wet snow poured down on us, with slabs of ice as well. We both knew that this melting stuff could also bring down with it showers of loose rocks. It would be pleasant to get off the wall fast! Angelo started on up, scratching with his fingers to dig away the snow and ice and uncover whatever he could find that we could use as holds. Up the slippery rocks he went, with only an occasional pause to warm his aching hands. How thankful I was that no one less expert than he was with me! Angelo intimates to me now, indeed, that the only reason we succeeded in getting off that wall—[alive]—was because that was the period of his top form; that the last part of the wall [difficult enough even in good condition] became extraordinarily difficult and dangerous as well, done with the cold and the snow.

The famous Bavarian guide, Emil Solleder (who lost his life the following summer on the Meije), was looking down at us from the edge of the Stradone Provincale on the regular route

The Companile Basso di Brenta, Brenta Dolomites. The Via Fehrmann goes up the wall (in shadow) directly under the highest point.

ABOVE: Angelo and I approach the tent occupied by the German woman on the shoulder of the Campanile Basso. (Later such tents, known as "bivouac sacks," came into more general use.) *Photo by Emil Solleder.*

Our three parties, crowded into the tent, share a cheerful meal.

and shouting encouragement. He told us he had erected a tent there, on that one 'hygienic' spot on the great tower, and urged us to join him and his tourist, a German woman, inside it. When we arrived the 'tent' turned out to be a thin cloth supported entirely by the German woman's head. But we crawled inside with her, as did two Italian boys, Francesco and Tony, and their guide, who came down from the summit. Even though the tent did not quite cover the seven of us, still the companionship warmed and cheered us, and so did the shared food, for we all brought out everything edible we had in our rucksacks and passed it around. As a result, everyone consumed some curious mixtures.

Although we had accomplished the Via Fehrmann we had not yet climbed the peak, which rose directly above us and not far away. But since there was still a great deal of snow and ice on the rocks, and Angelo and I seemed to have lost our taste for climbing under these conditions, we simply went down the regular route with the others.

IV

Chamonix

After my first season in the Dolomites in 1926 I went over to Chamonix to climb with Alfred Couttet, one of the outstanding rock-climbers, whom Willard Helburn had picked out as guide for me. Chamonix! That fabulous region of firm granite that offers not only rock-climbing technically difficult to an extraordinary degree, but also mountaineering on a larger scale. The snowfields and glaciers in the higher mountains, as well as the mere size of the peaks, make a scene of striking beauty, particularly in those enchanted hours around dawn. There is something about even the start of the high-mountain climb—setting out early in the cool starry night, stumbling up the path or the moraine by the uncertain flicker of the candle lantern, trudging long hours up scree slope, snowfield and easy rock before reaching the main problems of the day, the final precipitous walls—that sets the mood of a more momentous expedition.

After a few of the standard climbs, Alfred proposed our trying a small pinnacle that had not yet been done, the Aiguille de Roc. This was my first experience with a new route, and although I contributed nothing of judgment or skill to the enterprise, merely following along as an observant passenger, still, even I felt a more stirring emotion just from being a part of this pioneer undertaking than I had felt on climbs where many others had succeeded before. The most satisfying experience in all mountaineering, that of leading a first ascent without professional help, was in the future, but this did very well as a foretaste.

The pinnacle of the Aiguille de Roc, a most striking pinnacle indeed, stands out on the eastern (Mer de Glace) face of the wall between the Grépon and the Bec d'Oiseau. On August 7, 1926, we—my brother Lincoln, Couttet, a second guide and I— approached it from the Montenvers (the Refuge de la Tour Rouge was not built until 1930) by way of the Mer de Glace, the Trélaporte Glacier and the Tour Rouge. This first attempt turned out to be only a reconnaissance, and indeed, since we had been having a long period of bad weather, it would have been extraordinary to find conditions suitable for making the actual ascent. As we stopped for lunch and the swirling mists occasionally lifted long enough to give us a view ahead of the forbidding-looking wall of the Aiguille de Roc, the second guide, although continuing to devour his food with much gusto, began clutching his stomach and moaning with discomfort. *Mal au ventre*, he said; he was in great distress and would not be able to climb farther. Being in those days more naïve than perhaps I am now, I believed this tale and suggested solicitously that in that case it might be wiser to eat lightly. At this suggestion, which caused the other guide some discomfiture, Alfred laughed and I understood that I had not been very astute. We acquiesced in the guide's subterfuge, of course—what else could we do?— and left him with scant show of sympathy at the luncheon place while we three went on.

But even we didn't go far. The large quantities of ice that filled the cracks and chimneys, and the snow frozen on those massive slabs, made it quite obvious that these were no conditions for climbing on such terrain. As for getting a view of a possible future route, for that the mists gave us little opportunity, but what they did allow convinced us that it would be a better idea to look around on the other side.

To the other side, then, we went six days later: Alfred, Vital Garny (of more intrepid character than the first guide) as porter, and I. From the Col des Nantillons we climbed up to Brèche 3385, a small notch between the Grépon and the Bec d'Oiseau, and looked through it towards the Aiguille de Roc. From here our peak stood not so very far away, but in order to reach it we should have to descend the couloir running down from the brèche, on the east wall, for nearly 400 feet to where this couloir joined another coming down from the notch between the Aiguille de Roc and the wall of the Grépon.

Since Alfred, on his many descents from the Grépon, had had opportunities of glancing down this couloir before, he knew that with the icy conditions that still obtained its descent would be more easily accomplished *en rappel* [by roping down], especially at the top where it overhung slightly, and for this purpose we had carried along an 80-metre (260-foot) rope. One end of this Alfred tied at the top of the couloir so that we might use its full length. Since our climbing rope, however, permitted only 65-foot intervals between the members of our party, we had to cut several platforms in the ice to wait in while the others were on the way. And from the foot of our long fixed rope we roped down farther a couple of times in the usual fashion. All this took a great deal of time.

From the junction of the two couloirs we had an excellent view of the Bec d'Oiseau face of the Aiguille de Roc. The lower part in particular looked most inhospitable. Search as carefully as we might for some line of cracks or chimneys that we could try to follow up, we could discover nothing of the sort. We then turned to the left and ascended the other couloir, somewhat shorter than the one we had come down, to the notch at the base of the final spire of the Aiguille de Roc, that part of it which was entirely detached from the Grépon wall. The ice in this couloir was hard, but once the steps were cut they were firm and permanent.

The notch provided an excellent vantage point from which, for the long time before it became my turn to start, I could watch some spectacular climbing on Alfred's part. Hard ice, with snow frozen to it, covered every break on this precipitous wall of the Aiguille de Roc. But up these treacherous holds Alfred climbed a moderate distance to a small platform. From here he carried on an elaborate rope-throwing manoeuvre in order to lasso a projecting spike of rock some twenty feet above and slightly to the left. He then climbed up the rope

56

The summit of the Aiguille de Roc.

The couloir at the base of the Aiguille de Roc.

Alfred working his lasso.

diagonally, reaching a narrow ledge from which he hoped to traverse a slab to the left. But to no avail. As he roped down again, the rock spike that supported him was moving, suggesting that what held it in place was ice. (And on our third attempt by this same route, two weeks later, this rock spike did indeed pull out.)

Alfred then dropped down slightly from the farther end of his platform to a lower ascending ledge, narrow, outward-sloping, and of course covered with a large accumulation of snow and ice, while the wall above was somewhat overhanging. By much ice-axe work—he sent the axe back and forth to Vital at the notch by a sort of aerial tramway rigged up with a spare rope—and by the use of a couple of pitons, he did succeed in making his way up across this ledge for a certain distance. But conditions were too bad for our explorations to be pushed far. We did not accomplish much, but we carried out a few fruitless investigations, more than I reported fully in contemporary accounts.

A great man for mystery, Alfred was. So much must be kept a secret, either to endow the climb with more romance for me, or because there were others who would like to make this first ascent. Furthermore, Alfred was a little ahead of his day in the use of artificial aids such as pitons. In those earlier days at Chamonix, where they were just coming in, pitons were not yet quite accepted. (They came into use first in the Eastern Alps, in Austria and Italy.) Armand Charlet says in his description of the first ascent of the Isolée in 1925,* 'At that time pitons were not yet used, either as an aid to climbing or for assurance. Carabiners were absolutely unknown.' By 1926, however, Couttet was using pitons, and using them skilfully. But at the time he wished it kept a secret! I think it can also be revealed that he practised, too, the more ingenious method of getting a rope over a distant target by first throwing a small cord to which he had attached a lead. Other guides, said Alfred, threw the climbing rope itself, which wouldn't go nearly so far.

Late that afternoon, after an arduous climb back up the

* Charlet, *Vocation Alpine*, p. 175.

couloir (I particularly remember pulling myself up that 260-foot fixed rope!), we reached Brèche 3385 again and I was glad enough to relax and eat in the warm sun. Three guideless climbers appeared, making their way up from the Col des Nantillons. To Alfred they were objects of derision. Everything about them, and guideless climbing in general, it seemed, was at once laughable and deplorable. But as Alfred emphasized the extreme folly and peril of guideless climbing, I knew what his motive was. While I had already done modest bits here and there, I planned soon to do more and on a bigger scale.

The three men who now arrived were members of the Groupe de Haute Montagne, the crack French climbing club (this I found out only afterwards, naturally), coming up to bivouac at Brèche 3385 preparatory to making an attempt on the Aiguille de Roc by the route we had just followed. They bowed to us briefly but did not waste time in conversation; obviously I was an incompetent girl coming down very belatedly indeed from the Grépon. Alfred, for his part, wished to have nothing whatever to do with them, and even when they peered down the couloir and excitedly began speculating on whether it could be possible that they detected steps in the snow down there, he explained nothing, and hurried me away. But not too long afterwards these same men were among my friends.

After two weeks of warm sunshine in Zermatt I came back to Chamonix and found conditions very much improved. The same three of us reached the notch between the Aiguille de Roc and the Grépon a good hour earlier than on our first attempt. The rocks were looser now, but dry, and we progressed somewhat farther—perhaps, roughly, halfway between the notch and the summit. We were stopped finally by a large overhang composed of blocks of rock which were most unstable in appearance. The thought of touching them from underneath was not an attractive one, and there seemed to be no other way up the peak from this side. So ended attempt number three. Back we went to Brèche 3385, but since we hadn't thought it necessary this time, with the couloir much drier, to leave the long rope fixed in place, we had to turn the overhanging part at the top

58

Alfred on the Aiguille de Roc on our third attempt.

Alfred on our final ascent, BELOW: in the chimney, and LEFT: on the slabs.

by a delicate bit of climbing along the face of the Bec d'Oiseau.

In 1927 we returned to our original route on the east face by way of the Tour Rouge. Our porter was Georges Cachat, with whom I subsequently did many climbs, including the first traverse of the Aiguilles du Diable. I also took Georges with me on climbs I wished to lead, the Meije, Rimpfischhorn, Grépon, and others. This was a step in the right direction, although, of course, not guideless climbing, for Georges was too good, and even though young and technically only a porter, he would have been entirely capable at any time of taking over the lead had it seemed desirable.

On the morning of August 6, 1927, as I dressed, bearing in mind that we might well spend the night out, I took along extra woollies, mittens and gloves. We left the Montenvers at 2.20 a.m., a few minutes later than the other parties and without using a light until we were well beyond the railway station, for no one must know where we were going! Soon we made out a lantern ahead of us and experienced a moment's trepidation: was that party going to 'our' climb? When, however, they took the upper path instead of dropping down to the glacier, Alfred concluded that they must be guideless climbers, in trouble right at the start. He implied that this, although regrettable, was to be expected!

By 5.45 we had reached the platform beyond the Trélaporte Glacier where we had lunched on our first reconnaissance. Here, with a good deal of satisfaction, we found and ate a tin of apricots that we had hidden in a crack almost exactly a year earlier. Although they must have frozen and thawed many times in those months, they still tasted delicious.

After about fifteen minutes we went on, Alfred leading, Georges second, and I at the end. We passed behind the Tour Rouge, the limit of our last year's trip, and traversed horizontally towards the south for a considerable distance to reach and cross the couloir that comes down on this side from the notch between the Aiguille de Roc and the wall of the Grépon. The two couloirs running down on its two sides from this same notch define the Aiguille de Roc; one, where we were now, running

59

down to the east along the north side of the peak; and the other, which we had ascended on our second and third attempts, running down to the southeast along the southwest side of the peak. Each couloir is bounded on the Aiguille de Roc side by a well-marked ridge; up along these ridges and on the great slabby face, roughly triangular, between them, we succeeded in making the ascent of the peak.

By this Mer de Glace face we knew that the climb would be a long one, and Alfred was not at all sure we should be able to get back to the Montenvers that night. We were therefore looking for a ledge suitable for a possible bivouac on the descent where we could now leave extra clothes, much of the food, and Alfred's heavy boots. Georges and I climbed throughout in nailed boots but Alfred, as leader, preferred to wear his rope-soled scarpetti. After crossing this north-side couloir we reached a region of easy rocks and several large terraces where we found a most satisfactory bivouac emplacement.

At 7.50 we left this platform and traversed somewhat farther to the south, reaching the crest of the east ridge immediately below its first important gendarme. Here we discovered, just behind the ridge and hitherto invisible, a long chimney, which turned out to be the key to the climb as it enabled us to make a substantial amount of elevation without marked difficulty.

When the chimney ended at a little notch on the ridge, above a higher gendarme, the serious difficulties began. The rock was firm and solid, but steep, and the climbing most delicate. Aiming always towards two small red gendarmes high up on the farther (southeast) ridge, we worked a devious route diagonally up towards them, across the great face, mainly over slabs, but making use of whatever small chimneys or cracks we found. 'Traverse with the hands,' Alfred instructed time after time. The climbing was first-class, exposed and entertaining to a high degree, with those firm holds characteristic of Chamonix granite. For the rough rock at Chamonix is filled with little crystals and sharp-edged particles that make for good adhesion but, incidentally, toughen and harden the fingertips to such an extent that in the autumn after a climbing season if I considered buying a dress in Paris (much less expensive in those days!), I would have to feel the material with my wrist or the back of my hand. And I know a violinist who goes to the Montenvers and looks with longing at the peaks, but cannot climb for he must keep his fingertips sensitive.

We finally reached the farther ridge somewhat above a series of small gendarmes and proceeded up along it to the foot of the summit block. Most startlingly, this immense block was split completely through. The crack between the two sections, which we should have to climb for eighty feet, rose vertically above us —a narrow crack, far too narrow for the neat and easy back-and-foot chimney technique. The opening, in fact, was barely wide enough for a person to enter, and the two walls offered very few holds and those far apart.

Even before I came in sight of this crack, Alfred was halfway up it, and both Alfred and Georges were much higher and quite out of sight before they were ready for me to start. Georges, in the meantime, had left his pack, with an end of the extra rope tied to it, planning to haul it up when he and Alfred reached a suitable position. Certainly this was no crack to climb with a rucksack on one's back! When they tried hauling, however, and found that the rucksack caught below all the overhangs and jammed in the crack as well, they shouted to me to untie it and leave it at the bottom. I heard them well enough, but what a time I had to make them understand me in return! I was shouting that they had not lowered the rucksack as much as they thought they had; that it was still wedged in the crack some fifteen to twenty feet above my head, jamming my rope behind it; that I would untie it as soon as I came within reach; but that I preferred not to tackle the beginning of this crack where Alfred, so he told me later, had used a *courte-échelle* [climbed up on Georges' shoulders] until they took up my rope, coils of which were still lying loose on the rock ledge at my feet. They finally got the idea that I wanted a rope pulled, but then they pulled the wrong rope! Hardly an important incident, any of this, but I give it as an example of the little mix-ups that complicate the joys of climbing.

The crack I found most difficult and exhausting. By friction I wriggled up, with a little tug from Georges now and then to hurry things along, for the weather was turning bad. And on my part perhaps all these nine hours were beginning to tell!

At the top of the crack the right wall of rock ended in a small horizontal platform; the left rose above us some twenty feet more, a sharp-pointed granite pinnacle with no way that I could see of getting up it. But Alfred had discovered a rounded mushroom of rock over to the left near the farther edge of this spire, above us and some ten feet off. After climbing six to seven feet up beyond the platform he succeeded in throwing his rope over this mushroom. By swinging over in pendulum fashion, climbing up the rope to its point of support, and finally standing erect on the mushroom itself, Alfred was able to gain the farther edge of the summit block and to make the few remaining feet to the summit itself. At 11.20 I, too, was on top, a most airy perch indeed.

We did not stay long. The space was far from adequate and —a much more disturbing circumstance—the weather looked most threatening. If the dry weather would only hold until we were down across the slabs on the face to the top of the long chimney, we could manage the rest even if the rocks were wet. We hurried as I have rarely hurried. To save time we roped down frequently, as fast as three people could, but even so we did not reach our goal before the storm broke at about 1 p.m. A violent thunderstorm it was, with lightning, rain, hail and snow, and it caught us in a most unpropitious position on the great slabs of the face, considerably above the chimney, when we were just about to start the seventh of our twelve rope-offs.

Up to this time I had acted the well-looked-after tourist, with a good guide and a good porter, my only function on the climb being my personal enjoyment. When the storm came I had to drop that role completely and go to work as a member of the team. With the rocks wet and later taking on a glaze of ice under a cold wind, and with the ropes wet, icy, and consequently hard to manage, we had a serious struggle to carry out our descent. Georges pushed down ahead to hunt out the route in the face of the storm. Alfred, still in his thin, wet climbing shoes two and a half hours after the rain started, came down these icy slabs as last man. My job, in the middle, was to handle the ropes, to keep them from getting mixed up, and to belay Georges. Him I might have succeeded in holding had it been required, for when he tackled a ticklish passage I took his rope around my body with my feet braced against the line of an eventual pull. I had held people below me before now. But with Alfred it was another matter. I could take in his rope as he came down, keep it from getting tangled in the *corde de rappel*, and arrange it in a coil so that it would run out again smoothly when it was my turn to move down again. But occasionally when Alfred was faced with the problem of descending a gully filled with snow and ice in his slippery shoes, he would warn me to be ready to haul in his rope quickly in case he slipped. Fortunately he never slipped, and a notable achievement that was, but it was in my mind that I shouldn't care to do what he was doing with only a person like me to hold the rope! Although it is possible to hold a man who falls from above if you know how (the chief rule is: don't try to stop the fall abruptly, but let the rope run a bit and brake it gradually), the thing is by no means easy to do. I should have tried my hardest, but should I have had the strength? Georges was, of course, the man to belay Alfred, but Alfred wanted Georges to keep on constantly and rapidly with his job ahead. We had no time for any precautions that could possibly be dispensed with.

For hours I handled those twisting, kinking ropes, cold, wet and icy, and in general I kept them in order pretty well. For Alfred did not omit comment on any lapse! My gloves, such a comfort for the first few minutes, soon became sodden masses of slippery leather and I had to discard them. Although my hands grew more and more uncomfortable from all this handling of the rough wet ropes, and became more or less numb from the cold, perhaps the really vigorous work I was doing was good for their circulation. And every time I put my hands in water —a mixture of rain, snow and hailstones as it was—it warmed them up.

At one time the centre of the storm passed very close, the thunder and lightning being simultaneous. I felt a strong blow along my right arm which momentarily knocked my hands off the rocks. All my fingers were tingling. I wondered if my hair was standing on end, but no doubt it was held down by the water dripping off it. 'Chauffage électrique!' shouted down Alfred. For spirits were high during this foul descent. For the first few hours, at least, all three of us, keyed up by the emergency, were exchanging the gayest of banter. Privately, however, '*Forsan et haec olim meminisse juvabit*' kept running through my mind, and I wondered if that could really be true. (If so, the day has not yet arrived.)

We finally reached the ledge where we had left our things, but although soaked and shivering I realized that putting on the sweaters would entail untying the climbing rope and taking off my jacket, and decided I would rather use that time in getting along down. From there the climbing was easier, but just as uncomfortable, because of the pouring rain and the cold. I shivered for the last six hours of the trip. More or less mechanically I kept on making the same motions I had been making and felt a certain confidence that habit would carry me through to the end!

Through, perhaps, but not in first-class shape. For there occurred a couple of little incidents that suggested that fatigue was creeping up on me. For the most part we were now climbing silently, but once or twice when I did utter a word it came out not French but English, which was incomprehensible to my companions. Vaguely this disturbed me, for that summer I had been talking a lot of French and thought that the simple remarks one makes while climbing came to me equally easily in either language. Then towards the end of the descent I noticed just below us, not fifty yards away, another party of three men who were climbing along in the same direction as ourselves. This was certainly astonishing, for here we were near no usual route. I asked Alfred where they could have come from. He stopped, surprised, and both he and Georges looked down directly at this other party, below them to the glacier, out across the glacier, to the left and to the right. 'I can't see anybody,' said Alfred. Georges, too, ahead of me, was shaking his head in puzzlement. A wave of intense embarrassment swept over me. If Alfred and Georges could not see these people, close as they were, it must mean that I was seeing things that weren't there. This I could reason out, although I didn't really believe it. I said nothing more, hoping that Alfred and Georges would think merely that I had been mistaken. I didn't at all like the idea that there was something the matter with me, something altogether too much like a touch of insanity! But there the people were, still climbing along, slowly but well. Whenever my attention was not absorbed by my own problems, I watched them. When we get to the glacier, I thought, we'll have to meet, and then all this will be explained. I'll wait. . . . But when we did get to the glacier, not even I could see them any longer.

When we stopped below the Trélaporte Glacier to take off the rope, we found each knot a shrunken and hard-frozen mass of ice on which no amount of prizing with the ice-axes seemed to have any effect. In the end, I remember, Alfred simply cut mine. We finally reached the Montenvers at 8.10 p.m., having spent eighteen hours on the climb. As our enthusiastic friends surrounded us, a curious shift of emphasis took place. They seemed to think that the important achievement of the day had been our getting up, and on that they congratulated us. I had pretty much forgotten that part of it; for the last nine hours the only thing that had counted for me was our getting down!

A week later, with Margaret Helburn and her guide Armand Charlet, we climbed the Grépon by the Mer de Glace face. (Armand and Alfred told us that we were the first women to do this climb, and also the first party to accomplish it in one day, straight out from the Montenvers without a bivouac.) I found it most interesting, of course, to compare the two routes and to find that these two adjacent walls, as might have been expected, presented quite similar problems. On the whole I found the Aiguille de Roc more delicate and, although some 200 feet lower, much more fatiguing, this latter impression being due, no doubt, to our arduous descent in the storm. And certainly, except for the Knubel crack at the top, nothing on the Grépon face seemed to me so difficult as the final eighty-foot crack near the summit of the Aiguille de Roc.

The Grépon by the Mer de Glace face had not, however, been my first chance to watch the incomparable Armand, the foremost guide of France,* at work, for a few days earlier we four, Margaret and I, with Armand and Alfred, had made a new route on the northwest face of the Aiguille du Midi.

One incident of that day rises up in my memory above a general background feeling of hunger. For we made our first stop for food and rest just five hours after leaving the little Hotel des Glaciers, which was then being finished. Before that we had found no stopping place large enough for sitting down and eating a lunch. Five hours is longer than I like to go without food when doing a climb so unrelievedly strenuous. At the particular passage that I remember most vividly, as I climbed laboriously at the end of this five hours up a sort of chimney filled with ice and the most friable and treacherous rocks, I thought I had really come to the end of what I could do. Here, if ever, I should certainly fall off ('peel off', they say nowadays). But wasn't Armand on top holding me? In my mind's eye I could see him, intent, poised to haul in instantly on my rope as I went down. To enjoy this reassuring vision in reality, I glanced up when I came near enough, and what did I see? Armand was opening a tin of pineapple, having casually tossed aside the coils of my rope, which were lying in an untidy heap on the ground. The shock was just what I needed! If Armand thought I could get up untended, the climbing was undoubtedly easier than it had looked to me, and I went on with renewed confidence.

II. AIGUILLES DU DIABLE, FIRST TRAVERSE

The following year, 1928, Robert Underhill and I found ourselves in Chamonix with two or three days to spare before meeting the members of an Appalachian Mountain Club trip to the Dauphiné which we were arranging. Just time for one

* Recently made Officier de la Légion d'Honneur.

outstandingly fine climb. What should it be? Something that we might do guideless, or perhaps those Aiguilles du Diable? Among the most spectacular recent climbs had been the conquest of the Aiguilles du Diable, the Corne du Diable, Pointe Chaubert, Médiane, Pointe Carmen and Isolée, five striking 4,000-metre spires on the southeast ridge of Mont Blanc du Tacul. By now they had all been climbed, and all but the Médiane had been climbed twice, but never more than two of them had been attempted on any one expedition. Armand Charlet had led the first ascents of four of the five. In the *Annuaire* of the G.H.M. for 1926 Charlet had written that 'the complete traverse of the Aiguilles du Diable seems possible under normal conditions.'* Nevertheless, the full summer season of 1927 and parts not only of 1926 but also of 1928 had passed by without any party's attempting this bold project. We would ask Armand to do it with us. The fact that Armand had been searching for two years for clients who had *la classe suffisante pour tenter l'aventure* and had considered favourably *Sous-la-Colline* (Underhill) and Miss O'Brien we did not learn till twenty-two years later when, in 1950, he sent us a copy of his book, *Vocation Alpine*. With Myriam O'Brien, he there says, he had already climbed; of Sous-la-Colline's climbs he knew by hearsay. Furthermore, discussing these two with Josef Knubel, Knubel had answered, 'Ah! charrette, tout à fait bon, c'est sûr, oui, moi qui pense,' which for some reason struck Armand as most reassuring! Still, Armand never allowed a whisper of these thoughts of his to reach us, taking it for granted that the project of doing the Diables would be likely to occur to us. 'Quoi de plus naturel à ce que Sous-la-Colline portât ses vues sur l'arête du Diable!'† And, indeed, it did occur to us.

But what a time we had finding him! By telephone and on foot we searched the town and surroundings of Chamonix before finally running him to earth in the P.D.A. (Patisserie des Alpes, hang-out of G.H.M. members on their off-days in the valley), facing an impressive plateful of cakes in the company of his client, Mr Burford, Scottish schoolmaster, and a handful

* P. 69. † Armand Charlet, *Vocation Alpine*, p. 200.

of Mr Burford's schoolboys. Mr Burford had Armand engaged,
and it is a delicate business getting a guide away from the man
who has engaged him—in fact, it is simply Not Done. So Bob
and I had two problems on our hands, those of persuading Mr
Burford to lend us Armand and of persuading Armand to come.
That we succeeded with Mr Burford was due to the fact that
he is a gracious gentleman and a friend of mine. Even so, he
agreed only that we might borrow Armand for just one day,
August 4. As for Armand, he took small part in these negotia-
tions for his transference, simply sitting back and eating cakes
until it was settled that we would all go together to the Rifugio
Torino on the Col du Géant, whence Mr Burford and the boys
would do the Aiguille du Midi with their porter while Armand,
with Georges Cachat as porter, took Bob and me for a climb
on the Aiguilles du Diable.

Only then did Armand inquire, 'How many of them do you
want to do?' We murmured, apparently with diffidence but in
reality with caution, that we should like to do as many as
possible. Armand thought this over quite a long time and
finally ventured the opinion that it might just be possible to
do the three upper ones. Armand's intention, of course, was to
traverse the whole lot, just as ours was, so although the subject
was not mentioned again, I don't think anybody was surprised
to find, when the time came, that we started at the bottom and
went over all five.

On our way up the Glacier du Géant to the hut a brisk thunder
shower wet us more than we cared for, and dampened our spirits
as well. Arriving at the hut, we gazed in silence at the heavy
black clouds lying low over the Peuterey Ridge. We had
planned to start at 11 p.m., but when we went to bed that night
it looked uncertain whether we should start at all. At eleven
Armand found the weather cloudy and much too warm. But
about midnight when he went outside again, a little north
wind had sprung up. Possibly better weather was on the way.
We had only that one day. So we, too, had to spring up and
start as soon as possible, even though two hours later than we
had planned.

Since no one disputed that this was going to be a long climb, we galloped up the upper west branch of the Glacier du Géant towards the Cirque Maudit, and up the southwest flank of the Diable Ridge. Even though the bergschrund presented some slight difficulty and the rocks that followed, although not too exacting, were also not too reliable, we reached the crest of the ridge between the Corne du Diable and the Pointe Chaubert at 4.30, a fair achievement for slightly over three hours. (The times I give are all my own, as fourth on the rope. Armand, of course, arrived in each case considerably earlier, sometimes by as much as half an hour.) Here began a glorious climb of more than nine hours over these spectacular needles, all the while above 4,000 metres. There is some magic in that figure of 4,000 metres (about 13,120 feet) which in the Alps divides the really big climbs from the lesser ones.

The Corne du Diable (5.10) and the Pointe Chaubert (5.45) went off without incident and very rapidly indeed. The cold was intense and the north wind had increased to a quite uncomfortable velocity. We welcomed it, of course, for it should bring good weather with it, but, casting merely the briefest glance at the beautiful sea of clouds over Italy, we did not pause for leisurely contemplation of our grandiose surroundings.

Our descent of the Pointe Chaubert on its northwest face, towards the Médiane, was the first new part of the climb. I always feel a pleasant little tingle of excitement when the first man—Georges, here—slides down a rope along a sheer wall where no one has been before. When he reaches the end of the rope will he find a perch on the rock? And a supporting spike for the subsequent rope-off? (On other occasions I have myself been the first explorer down an unknown rope-off—lighter to pull up again if it came to that, and the men would still be on top to do the pulling. I find this, of course, even more exciting and pleasurable than watching someone else.) We descended the Pointe Chaubert with two rope-offs of sixty-five feet each and a third shorter one; then a traverse led us to the notch at the base of the Médiane, with a substantial advance over Armand's calculated times. Everything was going famously. Our spirits

69

were sky-high. Armand writes that Myriam O'Brien and Georges Cachat kept up a continuous stream of jokes about everything and nothing; that Sous-la-Colline's expression was one of high contentment, even though he joined little in the badinage of the other two. (The language of this group was French, which Bob speaks but slightly.)

The final tower of the Médiane, rising 260 feet, offers the longest climb of any of the five Aiguilles du Diable. After working up to the base of a high open chimney and ascending this for some fifty feet, we traversed right, very delicately, to the east ridge. Then up by cracks on the faces adjoining this ridge, to traverse back again across the head of the chimney, which involved a sensational *enjambée*, or long stride across nothing. Some easier climbing led to a large terrace out of which rise the three massive, upright blocks that form the summit, with two narrow and tall slits, or windows, between them. On this terrace I found Armand already busily engaged arranging the ropes for the descent which was to start off through the slit on the right. Up the left slit, then, I chimneyed by back-and-knee work until I could get a handhold on the top of the centre block. A *rétablissement* (pulling oneself up by arms alone) on to this centre block and a second *rétablissement* on to the higher left-hand block got me to the summit of the spire (8.15).

The earlier party to make this climb had come down by approximately the same route as that of the ascent but we, wishing to continue up the ridge towards the Pointe Carmen, made a descent of the northwest face, much the most serious new problem of the day. Had we had a rope of 160–200 feet here we should have met with considerably less difficulty, but as it was we had to split our rope-off into two sections. To find stopping places for the four of us on this face, on minute and slippery snow-and-ice-covered holds, to retrieve the rope from its first position and arrange it again for the second rope-off, all the while standing on almost nothing, posed no small problems, particularly since we had the greatest difficulty in communicating with each other above the roar of the howling wind. How well I remember this nightmarish descent, knowing

70

Pointe Médiane in the Aiguilles du Diable. We started our long rope-off down this face through a small hole at the top.

Armand Charlet shown in four successive steps, left to right, during the ascent of the most difficult passage in the Aiguilles du Diable, the first hundred feet on the Isolée.

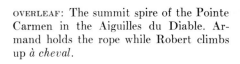

OVERLEAF: The summit spire of the Pointe Carmen in the Aiguilles du Diable. Armand holds the rope while Robert climbs up *à cheval*.

that people were shouting urgent directions that I could not quite hear, shivering with cold as the wind penetrated to my very bones while I waited for those ropes to be untangled! And then, after we were finally down the rope-offs, making my way over the most delicate traverse towards the narrow notch between the Médiane and the Carmen. With some trepidation I edged across this steep north face of ice and loose rock covered with *verglas* (a thin coating or glaze of ice), clasping minimal holds with fingers so cold and stiff they were almost without feeling.

How our spirits rose as we reached the base of the Carmen! Of the two parties who had already climbed the Pointe Carmen, the first had gone up by the north face and the second by the long chimney on the west face. We took a third route, straight up the east ridge, at first by fissures between big, unstable blocks. Above a large platform, more cracks and grooves led to the foot of the east spire, which we turned on the north. We reached the summit (west) spire (9.50) as our predecessors had done by crawling 'on horseback' up the sharp, steep ridge, some thirty-five feet high, pulling with hands clasped low in front of us over the keen edge of rock, and pushing with knees on each side. Your hands hold better if you keep them near enough to get your weight above them. The real holds are few and small along this delectable knife-edge, the situation most exposed and airy. And as we climbed up here the cold, strong wind blew a few flakes of snow along with it.

We roped down the west face of the Pointe Carmen to the Brèche du Diable, and traversed to the Brèche de l'Isolée, the notch at the base of the Isolée, the last of the five needles. We had started to eat another of our brief lunches when a sudden flurry of snow interrupted us. We'd better be getting on with this last peak without delay! Although cold and windy, the weather so far had been passably good. Now we weren't sure how much longer it would hold. Fortunately, this particular snow flurry dwindled away to an occasional flake now and then as Armand started up.

The initial stretch of 100 feet on the Isolée is the most

difficult single pitch on the Aiguilles du Diable and was at that time one of the hardest rock passages in the Mont Blanc massif. Armand is of the opinion that it is less difficult than the Knubel Crack on the Mer de Glace face of the Grépon, but he wonders if the Knubel Crack would be climbed at all if it were at the elevation of the Diables instead of 3,000 feet lower. The difficulty of a passage may often be gauged informally by the number of photographs of the climber that you have time to take. One, usually, is all you can snap of a climber of Armand's proficiency as he floats up like a wisp of breeze-blown cloud. Here I took eleven. But even though Armand was of necessity climbing with less than his accustomed speed, he moved with an extraordinary precision and skill that were most heartening to watch.

To reach the start of the passage Armand descended the couloir on the southeast, an uncomplicated fifty feet, to traverse afterwards on to the wall of the Isolée itself. Then he went straight up the wall, nowhere easy but getting even less so as it grew steeper and the cracks, fissures and small scratches less convenient. Then came a tough little overhang, but not the hardest one. As I watched Armand dealing with these increasing difficulties I began to consider, privately, that the day had already held for me a fair amount of serious rock-climbing and I hoped I still had strength sufficient to handle this long and demanding passage.

Finally Armand came up into position to grapple with the crux, the culmination of the difficulties. For a few yards he had been following roughly a wide-angled line of junction between two slabs, too open to be called a crack. Now this route was definitely closed off by a great overhanging tongue of rock, projecting downwards. Supporting himself under the bottom of the tongue with his right arm, with his left he disengaged his ice-axe from the cord that held it, reached out around the side of the tongue to the left and above, and jammed the adze of the axe into the smooth-sided, open crack between the tongue and the wall, three feet away. A difficult manœuvre, and a clever solution to this problem, it seemed to me when I had a chance to look at the place from near-by; he must have put the axe in side-ways and then twisted it. Armand then relinquished his right-arm hold, swung out from under the overhang, pulled himself up along the axe handle, stood on the head of the axe, and from there reached the ridge to the left, taking his axe with him.

When my turn came to get out from under this tongue of rock, since (according to instructions) I had left my ice-axe at the notch below, I tried to follow Armand's advice to jam my fist in the crack around to the left of the tongue. The fourth finger of this left hand, however, recently broken on the Meije, was still unbendable, being wrapped up in its splints of matches. I could not jam my fist, I could not get up any other way, and poor Georges had to pull me. I suppose this broken finger provides as good an excuse as anything. Whether I might otherwise have got up unaided we shall never know and I, for one, feel content that this was not put to the test!

There are now three pitons and a little fixed rope, Armand tells me, in this pitch alone, which of course diminishes markedly its difficulty. Climbers have driven in pitons, too, as is the custom of the day (and indubitably safer), at other places on these five needles where they are useful for the security of the leader or even for direct aid in climbing. As for this matter of pitons: morally, I see little difference between using a piton and jamming in the ice-axe. In the years I climbed with Armand, however, I never saw him use a piton for anything except roping down.

But even with pitons the traverse of the Aiguilles du Diable still remains today one of the fine long rock-climbs of the Alps. The edition of the Mont Blanc-Tour Ronde volume of the *Guide Vallot* (the climber's guide-book) which was published in 1930, two years after the first traverse of the Diables, remarks: 'Given the high degree and the length of the climbing difficul-ties which one finds here, it does not seem exaggerated to say that this itinerary constitutes probably the most difficult big ridge climb of the Alps. It is reserved for rock-climbers of exceptional power.'* It is not extraordinary that a statement

* *Guide Vallot*, Mont Blanc—Tour Ronde, 1930, p. 123.

so sweeping should be modified with the passage of years and the increase in the general level of difficulty in climbs accomplished. Still, the 1951 edition of the same guide-book describes this traverse as 'without doubt one of the finest climbs in the Mont Blanc group'.*

But to come back to 1928 again, when we were making the first traverse. Once we had turned the great tongue of rock, the climbing again became possible even for me, though not easy; a ridge with small holds, a six-foot chimney closed by a chockstone, and I arrived on a platform beside Armand, who was most impatient to be on his way. The last hundred feet to the summit (11.40) seemed child's play compared with what had gone before. The weather now looked bad and we wondered if we were at last in for a real blizzard. 'Not dangerous now,' remarked Armand thoughtfully, 'but it might become so.' Down we went as fast as we could to the notch, gathered up our things and started on at once. For our day's climbing was not over; we still had one more peak to go, Mont Blanc du Tacul, nearly 14,000 feet high. And I was not so fresh as I had been earlier. All day long we had been forcing the pace much more than we should have done in settled weather, and this extra exertion was beginning to have an effect. My legs dragged a bit.

On the summit of Mont Blanc du Tacul (1.10) we found thick clouds and more snow falling and Armand set off once more at a lope. Down the steep snow slopes towards the Col du Midi we ran, leaping the terrifying great open crevasses on the way. I tried to keep up with those three long-legged men, but I have never distinguished myself in the long jump, and my courage even lags a bit behind my ability, which makes it mediocre indeed. But we could afford no time for hesitation and even when I felt sure that the approaching crevasse gaped open far too wide for me to jump, I ran boldly down towards it, knowing that when the edge crumbled away under my weight Armand, already arrived on the lower side, would give the necessary pull on the rope to hale me to an adequate, if not always elegant, landing. Once, and I blush to admit this, all four of us sat

* *Guide Vallot*, Mont Blanc—Trélatête, 2nd edition, 1951, p. 282.

down—those of us who were not already sitting!—and slid rapidly down the steep snow towards a huge crevasse, with Armand shouting that we must keep going fast. All four slid completely over it, a startling sensation and one perhaps unsuited to the timid, but not bad fun at all. Speed is a requisite for success in this sort of thing. If any of us had put on the brakes, we might all still be in the depths of that crevasse. But even when I really did jump and land upright on my feet, things could still go wrong. Once I landed with such vigour in the soft snow that I sank in to my knees and by the time I had got back my breath found that my feet were solidly frozen in and immovable. Armand chopped with his axe to free me, expostulating that in such a case I must move at once and pointing out the danger I should be in had I been here alone—and without an ice-axe. This possibility seemed to me remote. And so to the Col du Midi, the Requin Hut and the Montenvers (7.30). I have seldom run so hard, and for eighteen and a half hours.

Twenty-three years later, in 1951, on the path down to Zermatt from the Zinal Rothorn I walked along chatting with an Austrian, one of the crack young climbers of the day, and as he told me about the rock-climbs he had done and among them the traverse of the Aiguilles du Diable, he suddenly stopped short and gazed at me in astonishment. I must have said something, I thought to myself, that showed too much familiarity with this climb. Eyeing my grey hair and considering my moderate pace down the path, the boy exclaimed in disbelief, 'Surely you haven't been there!'

III. PRIDE GOETH BEFORE—A NIGHT OUT

'A', 'B' and 'C', from the top-layer cream of French climbers, were discussing their forthcoming expedition, something new and exciting but not too long for the first climb of the season, when, most unexpectedly, 'B' shattered the amity of the gathering by announcing, 'I have invited Miriam to go with us.'

'Name of a dog!' exclaimed 'A' in fury. (It had been, I think, his climb in the first place.) 'You can't do that to us. Quite impossible to take a woman on a climb like this!'

'I'm not so sure of that, *mon vieux*,' retorted 'B', a little annoyed now himself. 'Bear in mind that you haven't met her yet. In any case, I will take her on my rope. You can have "C" on yours.'

'A', however, was far from mollified and the matter was settled finally only by 'B's' pointing out again that he had already asked me. No help for it, then. 'A' thereupon announced that he was going to invite Marianne. As retaliation this move fell rather flat, since no one objected to the presence of Marianne, one of France's best woman climbers. The result, however, was to make 'A's' rope on the whole slower, since in difficult rock-climbing, where the members of a rope must move one at a time, each pitch delays three longer than it does two.

You see, I have to call them 'A', 'B' and 'C' because I am not supposed to know about this rather warm dispute on my account. Among the French, however, gossip gets around as efficiently as anywhere and it is not surprising that this bit of it eventually reached me. But at the time I knew nothing, and when I made 'A's' acquaintance as we started to the hut all I noticed in his correct and courteous greeting was just a touch of formality. Shy, perhaps? The truth, that he was not too pleased to have me there, I was never allowed to suspect.

All went off in usual fashion until shortly after nine the following morning. We had reached a point on the climb where the gully we were mounting was closed in by a large overhang. Could we turn it on the left, up a small wall and then out still farther to the left over a bulge above? 'A' was leading and he tried. The wall went all right but not the bulge. He tried it again, but again he could not find a hold for his rope soles on the minute excrescences of the granite. So silly, I thought very privately to myself, to stick to those old-fashioned rope soles (though with them, in more years of experience than mine, he had accomplished a long series of extraordinary climbs). There were better things now, and it had never seemed to me that rope held well on this particular sort of rock. But it wouldn't have done, of course, for me to mention this.

76

Then 'A' asked 'B' if he would like to try. 'B', also rope-soled, worked on the problem, he too without success. 'A' tried again. Curiously enough, although I was ready to grant that both 'A' and 'B' were better climbers than I, this pitch from below did not look to me impossible and at a pause when everyone was just standing around, looking up, I asked, 'May I try it?'

'A' stepped aside instantly, without comment. If he was surprised, he didn't show it although, frankly, this was not the sort of remark that in those days the French expected from a woman. 'B's' expression was one of exaggerated nonchalance and unconcern, but with perhaps the faintest twitching at the corners of his mouth.

While it was the first climb of the season for 'A', 'B' and 'C', it wasn't for me; I had just come from some pretty sensational things with Angelo in the Dolomites. I cannot now remember what I was wearing on my feet, whether old (and therefore well-conditioned) *scarpe da gatto*, or just rubber sneakers; but whatever it was, it wasn't rope, my feet held, and I got up.

At the top of the bulge I found a niche where I could jam myself into some sort of security and look the situation over. We couldn't get back into the gully from here, at least not right away. But above my head rose slabs with a delicate tracery of small cracks and crevices—most delectable climbing. Still, it might be tricky, and I'd like to have my second man as close as possible. 'Venez jusqu'ici,' I shouted to 'B', who now came up with ease. It's odd how a rope from above facilitates a climb even when it provides not the slightest material support. There was not room for two of us in the niche; I had to leave before 'B' arrived. So off I went, enjoying immensely this small-hold, delicate climbing that is just my specialty. When I had climbed the full length of the rope without coming to any belay, 'B' had to follow, and we both climbed together perhaps another rope-length before we reached a place where it would have been possible to assure the rope, a splendid large platform. From here we could apparently continue directly up the peak.

But for two hours here we sat. ('B' subsequently sent me a 'copie fidèle de ma fiche d'ascension', showing 'Halte sur l'arête, 9h 40—11h 30.')

We chuckled a bit at first over the continuing efforts of the others to get up over the bulge, and then became genuinely concerned that we had dashed ahead, giving them not a single thought. Had this been a party of Americans, it would have been natural for me to consider the others, perhaps by suggesting before 'B' started that the second party tie their rope to his waist. But even had I thought of this that day, I surely would never have mentioned it. I had already overstepped the bounds and would not have offered an added insult to those Frenchmen, 'A' and 'C'.

How could we help now? Our rope was not nearly long enough to drop them an end, as they finally suggested. I did, indeed, climb back down towards them for the length of the rope, with 'B' holding it from the platform, and found the climbing surprisingly difficult. (Where the holds are small and hard to find, uphill is so much easier than down, since one's eyes are placed for uphill; with eyes down at the ankles, downhill would be easier.) But in any case, I couldn't go far enough to do any good, and frankly, I was afraid to have 'B' leave the platform; I didn't want to climb down any farther without a firm belay from above. One or two pitons here would have altered the situation completely but—and one can date our climb from this fact—not one of us in those days would have stooped to carry a piton. So we waited, lounging there on the commodious platform in the pleasant warm sun. Nobody was in any danger, of course. Although we two couldn't go back the way we had come, 'B' and I could presumably have found some other route down the mountain had it been necessary— as we subsequently did, after going to the summit.

Finally 'C' led the pitch—'C', whose reputation as a *glacié-riste* (ice specialist) was so dazzling that it had rather blinded me to his ability as a *varappeur* (rock-climber). The first thing 'A' did on reaching our platform was to hurry to me with the warmest sort of congratulations (a pitch always seems harder to one who is not leading); no formality now, no stiffness, and from then on we were the best of friends. He later proposed to me some *belles premières* (fine first ascents) in a more distant region, but it was never easy for me to arrange to get there. A missed opportunity which I regret, and it's too late now.

From the platform our regular leaders, 'B' and 'A', led the two ropes to the summit. On the descent, when we came within striking distance of the hut, 'B' spoke up plainly, if somewhat ungraciously, as follows: we would separate here. Since it was so nearly dark, the other three would have to spend a second night at the hut (for there was a little more rock-climbing below the hut on the way to the valley). We, however, being the faster party, could get down this pitch of rock-climbing before dark and reach the hotel in time for a good, if late, dinner. We had waited for them that day, but now that the difficulties were over we would go along. 'A' agreed whole-heartedly with this argument and in addition he was glad to have us go down to reassure his wife that all had gone well, and that his failure to return that night was not due to any accident.

But we had figured our times closely and this discussion itself had delayed our start by a minute or two; perhaps another five minutes went to searching through our rucksacks for every crumb and candle-end to leave with 'A's' party; in addition, since it was a cloudy evening, it got dark a few minutes earlier than we had counted on. All in all, adding up these trifles, it turned out that we—fast party that we thought ourselves—did not have time enough after all to get down the rocks before dark. And on the rocks we spent a cold and uncomfortable night. When it finally became pitch black we were still groping about. If only we had kept one candle for our lantern! 'B' had a match or two, but they were soon extinguished by the breeze after showing us merely that there were no boot scratches where we were, a thing which we had suspected anyhow. We were off the route and no amount of feeling around gave us any hint where to take the next step towards the valley.

Fortunately there was room to sit down where we were, on a rather narrow ledge of hard and uneven rock, our feet hanging over the drop. Rather carelessly we had hurried through a waterfall and now our damp clothes made a bad combination with the evening wind. We thought so longingly of the scraps of food we had left the others, who had no doubt been feasting on them in the nice warm hut. I also thought more than once of their blankets. From time to time I dozed off on my cramped position, but not for long. Most of the time I just sat there and watched the rotation of the earth. The clouds had cleared away and the stars came out, so many of them and so beautiful from this high perch. I know little of astronomy but I picked out certain groups of stars which gradually through the night moved across the sky. There is a big difference between knowing in theory that the earth turns and actually watching it do so. I felt that I was witnessing quite a stupendous thing!

At 4.40, before it was really light enough and in spite of our chilled and stiff muscles, we were up hunting for the route. We found the boot scratches about ten feet from where we had sat out the night. As we passed 'A's' hotel we spoke to the man who was sweeping the terrace before the guests were awake, 'Voulez-vous dire à Madame "A" . . .?' And that was what gave us away. Had we forgotten that errand, the others might not have known. But when they got down and Madame 'A' said how relieved she had been to get the message this morning, 'A' was a bit annoyed with the man for not telling her last night. He even hunted him up to inquire at what time we had come by. Then, indeed, laughter broke out on that terrace! And I must admit that 'C' and Marianne were still laughing when they joined us at the hotel—and for some time afterwards.

'B' was disappointed in our bivouac, he informed me later. I hadn't cried. It was understood that a girl cries on a bivouac; it was something any man had a right to expect.

Many years later, when talking with one of the Annapurna men, mention of their frightful bivouac in the crevasse high on

80

the mountain led me to tell of this one of ours. 'You bivou-
acked *below* the hut?' the Annapurna man, who knew the place
well, asked incredulously. 'B', still allegedly embarrassed by
this contretemps even after the passage of so many years,
remonstrated with me in exasperation, 'Of all the things you
might have said, couldn't you think of anything but that?'

V

The Bernese Oberland

I. CLIMBS IN 1929

In the spring of 1929 when I was making plans to climb in the Oberland, a region I had not yet visited, I remembered what Bob Underhill had told me about Adolf Rubi, a young lad he had once or twice taken as porter or second guide and had found to be an extraordinarily fine climber, both on rock and ice. He would become, Bob felt sure, one of the really outstanding guides. Now he was very young, not old enough to have a first-class guide's licence, and he had not yet done many of the big climbs. But in a few years . . .

Right now, I decided. A good climber was just what I wanted, and so much the better if he hadn't done the climbs; we would explore the routes together. I engaged Rubi and, even though he was a second-class guide, we ran off some first-class climbs that first season, most of which were as new to him as to me.

We chose for our first the northeast ridge of the Jungfrau, but when the telescope at the Jungfraujoch Hotel showed much ice on its rocks and the following morning dawned very cold, with a strong wind, we turned instead to the Mönch, which we ascended by its southwest ridge. Then down over the Nollen, that huge bulge of hard ice, long and steep, in the hanging glacier on the northwest face. Here we roped down by carving out little knobs of ice around which to place our rappels, b careful on our descent to hold the rope down close to the s of the ice lest it jump out of its shallow supporting g We were using 260 feet of rope and, in theory, when at the bottom of each rope-off I was supposed to c

Adolf Rubi of Grindelwald in his late twenties. Born 1905, qualified as second-class guide in 1926, as first-class in 1930. Ski champion of Switzerland in 1926, 1928, and 1929; member of Swiss Olympic Ski Team at St. Moritz in 1928; has a mantel decorated with over 30 ski cups and other trophies. He was a member of the Swiss Expedition to Kangchenjunga in 1949 and of an expedition to Kilimanjaro in 1959.

Adolf cutting out knobs of ice, so-called "mushrooms," for fixing the rope on rappels.

firm platform to stand in before Adolf started down. Actually, however, Adolf invariably arrived long before my platform was finished to my satisfaction. Five times we roped down before the slope eased off enough for us to proceed in ordinary fashion on our crampons, and even then it was only Adolf who thought it had done so. When I protested that my crampons did not hold because of the steepness, he suggested that I just let them slide—eventually they would catch on to something.

Next we did the northeast ridge of the Jungfrau, now in much better condition, and then the traverse of the Schreckhorn and Lauteraarhorn. The Schreckhorn we ascended by its southwest ridge and it was only while enjoying the marvellous views from its summit, at about nine o'clock, that we began to consider what our route of descent was to be. The regular route or the Andersongrat? Or perhaps, more ambitiously, to the Schrecksattel, over the Lauteraargrat, and down from the Lauteraarhorn by its southwest ridge direct to the Strahlegg Hut? This last plan would involve a lot of rock-climbing for one day, and might well require more hours than we had at our disposal, particularly since the southwest ridge of the Lauteraarhorn had not before been descended. However, compared with this last really stirring project, the other possibilities seemed mild and unexciting, and on it we embarked, Adolf having counted up the probable times and decided that if we really hurried we might get down shortly after dark. The long series of gendarmes along the Lauteraargrat offered us most entertaining climbing. 'It's a good thing you like them,' commented Adolf, 'because there are fifty more.' At that moment I began counting, but when I had reached twenty-seven I was just having too much fun to bother any longer. 'My watch must have stopped, it says only 1.10,' Adolf observed when we reached the summit of the Lauteraarhorn. Mine, however, agreed with his; our worries about time were over.

For this new descent Adolf went down first. Before I started climbing with him I had traversed the Grépon manless, and his opinion was that anyone who had roped off the Grand Gendarme on the Grépon without being held on a second rope never needed such protection on a rope-off again for the rest of her life, an idea to which he was still clinging twenty-four years later—on the Ago di Sciora, for instance—when it was really becoming time for him to give it up. I was interested on this occasion to watch Adolf's rappels, since most of the rocks around which he laid his rope looked to me as if they might come out. Loose they were, but when enough of them were used at once they could apparently be made to hold each other in. I remember particularly one rope-off over an overhang on the north side of the ridge. As I was sliding down, spinning around as one does when hanging free on a rope, I suddenly became aware of frantic shouts from Adolf beneath me. Stopping my descent in order to hear better, I finally made out the words, 'Don't let go of the rope!' In some astonishment I looked down at Adolf on his little platform far below, then beyond him down to the Schreckfirn, and shook with laughter. Why did he think I might want to?

A little after three we reached the bottom of the steep part. As far as I was concerned the climb could have ended here. It had been a splendid day, long to be remembered, and these last hours of unstimulating rock-climbing, unlike a relaxing stroll over alplands or even down a path, were a tiring anti-climax.

We had two more fine climbs that summer, the second ascent of the southwest ridge of the Wetterhorn, and the descent of the Jungfrau over the Silberhorn into the Trümletental. Second-class guide?

II. THE DREIECKHORN

To my taste, our best climb in the Oberland was the traverse of the southeast ridge of the Dreieckhorn on 29 August, 1930. As you look across the Aletsch Glacier from a little south of the Concordia Hut you see opposite a long rocky ridge bristling with innumerable slender spires. Although the three main summits, the Olmenhorn, the Klein Dreieckhorn, and the Gross Dreieckhorn, along with one or two of the individual gendarmes, had been climbed, the section of the ridge south of the Klein Dreieckhorn had never been followed throughout its length.

The long ridge of the Schreckhorn-Lauteraarhorn.

Climbing on the Dreieckhorn ridge.

Starting from the Concordia Hut at 3.30 in the morning, Adolf and I tramped down the Aletsch Glacier for almost two hours, with our eyes glued on that line of peaks as soon as there was light enough, selecting the best section of the ridge. At 5.20 we left the glacier and at last started uphill over scree slopes, patches of snow, and a band of steep but uncomplicated *roches moutonnées*, those glacier-scoured rocks. Here we were travelling unroped, with Adolf much of the time very far ahead. And only occasionally did I catch glimpses of him, showing the general direction to follow. After crossing the small glacier that lies along the northern base of the Olmenhorn, we attacked the final wall itself by a little subsidiary rib. At 8.40 we gained the main ridge just north of the Olmenhorn (to be exact, for those who like to check on the map, on the first peak north of Sattel 3215). This point marked the beginning of the higher and rougher part of the ridge, lying to the north; the southern section, which we cut off, looked to be more or less without interest. And we had, measured airline on the map, two miles of rock-climbing to the Gross Dreieckhorn, which was our projected goal. Although miles are hardly an appropriate or adequate measurement for mountain climbs, these two miles at least suggested that we were in for a long day. We put on the rope and began work in real earnest.

After a short distance we realized that we had undertaken not only a long but also a difficult rock-climb. All too soon Adolf pronounced his depressing conclusion: we could not possibly do this ridge in one day. Would I mind sleeping out on the rocks? A bivouac, I replied, was nothing to me, and I reminded him with some superiority that my experience with bivouacs was way ahead of his: I had spent one night out, Adolf none. And we began glancing down the side to find a sheltered spot for the night, a premature action, perhaps, since we still had almost twelve hours of daylight ahead of us. 'We can do a lot of rock-climbing in twelve hours,' observed Adolf, and subsequent events proved that he spoke the simple truth.

The first part of the climb, to the Klein Dreieckhorn, gave the best sport—and such sport it was! The whole ridge was a

85

series of great jagged towers, and we climbed up and over practically all of them. Occasionally, I suppose, we might have turned one on the side, but the rock there was more friable and insecure, and anyway it appealed to us as better fun to stick to the ridge. Most of the rock on this first section was splendid, the firmest granite I have found anywhere in the Oberland. The huge blocks presented the climbing problems characteristic of granite everywhere: cracks and chimneys like those on the Chamonix Aiguilles, and an occasional ridge to be climbed *à cheval* like the summit ridge of the Pointe Carmen in the Aiguilles du Diable. Intermingled with such, to vary this strong-arm type of climbing, more delicate problems presented themselves: steep slabs with slight roughnesses for the finger-tips, or detached flakes of rock with barely room to get a little finger-grip underneath. The day was warm and sunny, but still with that brisk and invigorating air that comes with elevation. Under perfect conditions like these, rock-climbing is to my mind the finest sport there is. Not only does it require co-ordination of muscle but also the exercise of sufficient intellect to solve the tactical problems at a glance, to choose unerringly the right hold the first time, in order to move swiftly as well as accurately and lightly over ground where no two consecutive pitches require the same technique. Two people are the perfect number for exhilarating rock-climbing, and we usually climbed together with whichever one of us ahead who happened to be there. Most often it was Adolf, but any time he was held up, as for instance to retrieve our rope after a rappel, I would seize the chance to get the lead. For occasionally, to descend a gendarme, we took off our climbing rope and roped down, not only where it was necessary but also where we thought it might save time to do so. For time was the opponent we were racing all day. The towers went on and on, and while we enjoyed each one of them we thought they would never end. We were climbing up and down rapidly, but our horizontal progress along the ridge seemed slow. Yet at 1.05, when we stopped for lunch, the Klein Dreieckhorn rose right ahead, separated from us by only a handful of small gendarmes.

Then, for the first time, Adolf began to wonder if perhaps we might finish the climb that day, after all. The ridge from the Klein to the Gross Dreieckhorn, which his brother Christian had been down, he knew to be easy. Perhaps by hurrying . . . Hurrying, indeed! What else had we been doing all day?

While I lingered on the summit of the Klein Dreieckhorn, with Adolf, who had started down its north ridge, impatiently held up a full rope-length ahead because he couldn't move until I did, I dug around in the rocks and discovered a bottle with a record of the first ascent of this peak by Julien Gallet with Joseph Kalbermatten and Christian Kaufmann Jr., in 1897.

A few gendarmes north of the Klein Dreieckhorn, the character of the rock seemed to change to the looser variety more usual in the Oberland, and consequently the towers became less steep and less difficult. But the ridge was still long. Although I don't think I have ever climbed much faster, it was 6.15 when we reached the summit of the Gross Dreieckhorn. We took just fifteen minutes to finish up our last food, while casting a quick glance at the lovely sunset colours. But we could see, too, that the lights were already on in the hotel at the Jungfraujoch; and we still had 3,600 feet of descent to the glacier by the ordinary route down the northeast ridge. The upper part of this ridge was snow, and although I should have preferred to follow the crest with comfortable steps cut for me, this did not appeal to Adolf at all. We should lose an extra hour, he protested, if he had to cut steps; better to walk right down the snowslope on the right. This I didn't like too well, for while the substance looked a lot like snow, there was really only an inch or two of snow over an ice foundation, and the slope at the top curved over so steeply that as far as I could see it might not have any bottom at all. Here, cramponless, I never enjoyed a really firm step, and since it seemed to me improbable that Adolf could hold me at any time, as he insisted he could, I was happier when, after thirty-five minutes, we were finally off that snow. But perhaps he could have held me after all, for later, in 1953, we met similar conditions in descending a short slush-covered ice slope on the side of the Tour Ronde above

Courmayeur. There were three of us to hold this time, my two boys and I, and Adolf, after asserting that no steps need be cut and that he could hold us all if necessary, had the opportunity to prove his statement. I fell, pulling the boys off one after the other, and Adolf did indeed hold us all. On that occasion, however, he suggested that the next time, when he might well be sliding with us, we aim our course towards a large rock below, two of us passing to one side and two to the other.

The rest of this Dreieckhorn ridge was rock-climbing, easy enough, but there was too much of it now that darkness was really coming on. Yet it would hardly do to get stuck out here, so near the end. So, running, jumping, sliding, we tore down, and covered some nine-tenths of the way in little more than an hour before it finally got so dark that we could see nothing more. At 8.20 we lighted the candle lantern, and what amazement that aroused (we learned later) in the Jungfraujoch Hotel! They thought that rock ridge an odd place to be climbing down at night. Adolf's father, waiting up for us across in the Concordia Hut where he was hut-keeper, was watching our lantern too, but he at least knew to whom it belonged. It is particularly hard to do rock-climbing downhill with a lantern away below in front of you, where practically all it accomplishes is to emphasize the great black shadows. This last tenth of the distance with the lantern took us longer than the first nine-tenths, when we had been travelling by the fading light of heaven.

At 9.40 we jumped the bergschrund. All that was left then was a weary plod across the Concordiaplatz to that little light shining in the window of the Concordia Hut. Since this section of the glacier was badly crevassed, we couldn't walk close together, and the result was that Adolf's lantern was so far away that it did me no good at all. I was too tired to care and just tramped along anywhere, half-asleep. I woke up for a moment when I found myself dangling in a crevasse, partially buried by the large amount of snow that had fallen in with me. The rope between Adolf and me had been taut, more from habit than from any intentional prudence on my part, and when I had first felt the snow giving way under my feet I had taken a turn of the rope around my hand almost without thinking, so that all those extra loops that I had been carrying had no chance to run out and drop me just that much farther down into the crevasse. In fact, I was hardly in at all and Adolf pulled me out with the greatest ease.

Adolf's father had the stove humming and the water boiling when we pulled in at 10.45, after slightly more than nineteen hours of strenuous going. Tea and hot lemonade tasted good, but I was too tired to do any serious eating. The following morning the walk up to the Jungfraujoch looked to me nearly impossible. 'Telegraph for the polar hounds,' I suggested to Adolf, who calls the huskies this, but he objected that entertaining tourists is all that is expected of them and I would have to walk. It took me five hours, which I feel sure must be a record. But our climb had been a good one, three times as much work—and fun—estimated Adolf, as the east ridge of the Jungfrau or the Lauteraargrat. And Adolf reports to me (in 1954) that it has never been repeated.

III. THE ENGELHÖRNER

The Lauteraargrat had first been traversed in 1902 by that extraordinary woman, Gertrude Bell, as outstanding in mountaineering as in the fields of exploration, archæology and diplomacy. Why not repeat some more of her climbs, so engagingly described in *The Letters of Gertrude Bell*?

The Engelhörner above Rosenlaui, delightful small limestone peaks, smaller-scale Dolomites, were a most welcome refuge for Miss Bell in 1901 and 1902, and for me in 1930, when snow on the higher peaks and bad weather interfered with bigger climbs. She to be sure had the best of them, for when she and the Fuhrers did their climbing in the region almost every rock they touched was virgin territory. 'The whole place up there is marked with chamois paths, no one, I expect, having ever been there before to disturb them.'* On August 23, 1930, Adolf and I undertook the ridge traverse over the Mittelgruppe and the

* *The Letters of Gertrude Bell*, vol. 1, p. 124.

Gross and Klein Simelistock, many parts of which Miss Bell
had accomplished for the first time, and which I had the fun of
leading all the way. There was one pitch, the *Egg*, or corner
on the Simelistock, just above the Simelisattel, where you climb
on finger- and toe-holds over a sizable overhanging bulge to
a big rock shoulder, leaning out backwards as you climb. In
such cases even where the angle of the overhang is slight, as it
was here, you still must use part of your strength just to hold
yourself on to the wall—not all of it can go into pulling yourself
up. I wasn't sure just how much I liked it. Yet, although
exposed, the pitch did not turn out to be so very difficult.
Adolf, down below, kept telling me soothingly that it was soon
going to be easier up above. This would have reassured me
much more if I hadn't known that Adolf had never been there
either and consequently knew no more than I did about what
was coming. There was another pitch, I think on the Gertrud-
spitze (named for Miss Bell), where I let Adolf take my rucksack. When I was well along above the difficulty he casually
remarked that the leader usually took a *courte-échelle* there (i.e.
got a start by climbing on to the shoulders of the second man).
That was a fine time to mention it, after I was already up, and
I said so. 'Why should I tell you a thing like that?' protested
Adolf. 'I was hoping you would fail, and then you would have
had to let me lead!'

IV. THE WELLIGRAT

When Gertrude Bell had been doing the Engelhörner peaks
she had had in mind other, bigger climbs in the Oberland, and
so had I—the same ones, the Welligrat and the northeast face
of the Finsteraarhorn. 'Between the two Wellhorns there is
an arête of rocks which has never been attempted—it is indeed
one of the four impossibles of the Oberland, and we intend to
do it and we think we can.'* They were indeed able to do it
and made the first traverse of the Welligrat on July 13, 1902.
Adolf and I repeated the climb on August 25, 1930, but instead
of returning to Rosenlaui from the Wellhorn as Miss Bell had

* *The Letters of Gertrude Bell*, vol. 1, p. 136.

On a gendarme in the Mittelgruppe of the Engelhörner.
Photo by Adolf Rubi.

done, we continued on to the south up over the Wellhorngrat and the Wettersattel (just below the summit of the Wetterhorn) and so down to the Gleckstein Hut above Grindelwald. Since all this mounted up to a long climb* and since I wanted to traverse the ridge in rubber soles instead of the nailed boots of the day, to increase speed we took along a porter from Rosenlaui for the major part of the course.

It was a little after five when we left Rosenlaui. For such a long climb we should definitely have started a lot earlier, but nobody had remembered to wake us up, and we had not set any alarm watch ourselves. And no matter how great the need for hurry, for the first few minutes I walk slowly. All the speed I make on a climb comes later. I pretend, of course, that this is intentional, that it is better for the circulation to start out gradually, but the real truth is that I simply do not feel energetic just after waking up, in the dark. And perhaps this morning, after the Engelhörner traverse, it took me even longer to get my second wind. My strolling along up the path, however, did not suit the porter at all. In Swiss German he complained pretty constantly to Adolf about it; Adolf would have to speak to me. I took it all in.

Although I had been exposed to Swiss German for several years, the idea had never occurred to me that it was one of those languages that one could learn to understand until quite suddenly, one day in the middle of the Aletsch Glacier, I *did* understand it. Adolf had just paused to exchange a few remarks with the guide of another party; it is the custom for Swiss guides when they meet in the mountains to chat with each other a moment on the characteristics of their respective tourists, and not all their remarks are complimentary. This time Adolf had said that here was Miss O'Brien, who had done

---

* The difference in elevation between Rosenlaui and the Wettersattel is 7,250 feet. In addition, we had to climb up again from several intermediate descents. At the time, I added these up and brought the total to nearly 10,000 feet of ascent, but now, working from a map, I cannot check this figure. It is true, however, that we did not follow the south ridge of the Wellhorn over its easy but numerous gendarmes all the way to Col 2961 but dropped down the east side to the Rosenlaui Glacier, losing elevation but saving time. From there over snow we joined Col 2961 at the base of the Wellhorngrat.

Our guide, Hermann Steuri, descending on the southwest ridge of the Wetterhorn.

the Grépon manless. Of course there were some key words there—O'Brien, Grépon, manless—that helped me get the idea. But after that I paid closer attention, and found there was nothing to it; from then on there were few secrets from me in Swiss German. Adolf's Oberland dialect was naturally the easiest, but even in Zermatt or the Engadine I could usually make out well enough what was going on. When I told Adolf one time that I understood him, he replied sadly, 'I know you do, and it is a great nuisance for me.' Later, in 1953, when I summarized for my son Bobby a conversation Adolf had had with another guide, he was to exclaim in mock exasperation, 'This is really too bad. I was talking my worst dialect on purpose so you wouldn't understand—my *very worst* dialect.' No language was left to him now for confidential communication, he said, except Hindustani, a few words of which he had learned on a trip to the Himalayas.

But to come back to the Welligrat. This porter was now criticizing Adolf's unprofessional conduct of the trip. A guide's business, he said, was to take charge of things, to walk in front and set the pace, and not to let a languid tourist, walking first, hold up the party this way. It was, moreover, quite fantastic for Adolf to suppose that he could do the Welligrat with a tourist who wasn't any better than this one. I thought Adolf's replies were a bit evasive and noncommittal. Although he may have agreed with the porter, there were difficulties in the way of his saying so. When forced to make a reply of some sort, he merely mumbled that he thought it would work out all right in the end.

At 7.40 we reached the beginning of the rock-climbing on the Vorder Wellhorn. We should have got there in two hours, the porter felt, and were thirty-five minutes late, as he had known we would be. Here I changed my boots for sneakers, and one hour later on the summit of the Vorder Wellhorn changed back again to nailed boots. One look at the ridge ahead of us and we knew that here was no rock-climbing that required rubber soles. Standards of difficulty change over the years; the Welligrat was not nearly so hard in 1930 as it had been in 1902.

92

But it was fun. We were roped with me in the lead, Adolf in the middle and the porter at the end. I was all ready now to fly along. The porter's complaints followed a new line: Adolf would simply have to speak to me, this was too fast; I would exhaust myself. Adolf still said nothing. When, finally, the porter objected that he himself could not possibly keep up at this rate Adolf spoke out firmly: he had found that nothing could be done about my pace, one way or the other; the porter would simply have to come along as rapidly as possible; after all, when the rope was taut, I should have to wait. The rope was not taut very often; occasionally, yes, but in general the porter climbed very well indeed and we all three romped along.

After traversing six little gendarmes we came to a big one which, from a distance, had looked most repelling. It was composed of great smooth slabs apparently set at a high angle and crowned with an overhang above. But looking at slabs straight on often steepens them, and when we came to grips with these they flattened out enough so that we could almost walk up, while the overhang was easily turned on the left. Beyond, the ridge became loose and friable and we had to take care, as we knocked down large blocks of rock on each side, not to go with them ourselves. Then came a sharp gap followed by two short but exposed chimneys which afforded the only bit of serious rock-climbing on the whole ridge. Miss Bell's party had put in almost an hour getting up these chimneys and the second two members succeeded only 'with the aid of an iron nail driven in at the worst place and of a double rope.'* (At that time, apparently, pitons were not so much in disfavour with English climbers as they later became!) Unless the rocks have changed, as they may have done, it is hard to understand why Miss Bell's party should have had such trouble with these chimneys, since their splendid first ascents in the Engelhörner were surely more difficult. We thought we saw two other possible routes besides the chimneys, and Adolf is still convinced that the one he chose, a bit around to the left, would have been the easiest.

* The Letters of Gertrude Bell, vol. 1, p. 137.

93

He never had time even to investigate it because he was roped to me and I, looking into Miss Bell's chimneys, had found them so much to my liking that I had gone right on up.

We were on the summit of the Wellhorn in less than three hours. The rest of the climb was more or less routine until we were off the Wellhorngrat at about half-past three. The porter having gone home to Rosenlaui, Adolf and I started the long trudge over the glacier up to the Wettersattel. The sun had been beating down on this snow all day long and now, late in the afternoon, it was heavy with water and so soft that we sank down to our knees. I stepped aside unobtrusively for Adolf to go ahead, hoping he would do this automatically, without noticing that we were changing places. But it didn't work. Dramatically, he stood stock still. His amazement, if somewhat feigned, was boundless. 'I thought you wanted to lead this climb!' After about ten steps, with the sweat pouring down his face, he stopped and tried again, 'It doesn't count at all, you know, if you don't lead *all the way*!' But just following, for that last hour and a half, was quite hard enough for me. Perhaps because it was so hot, with not even a slight breeze to invigorate us, or perhaps because it was the last thousand feet of ascent, and so many others had gone before, this stretch was most arduous. 'One can always count on Rubi to choose short and easy climbs suitable for a lady,' was running through my head. An Englishman who had brought his wife out to the Alps for a first season had written this in Adolf's guide's book. I'm not sure that Adolf liked it very well, or perhaps he merely tired of hearing me quote it. So often, however, as for instance here, or in connection with the Dreieckhorn or the Finsteraarhorn to come, it seemed such an apposite remark.

We reached the Gleckstein Hut at 7.15—I mean I did, Adolf had already been there twenty-five minutes—just in time for a leisurely supper and a fine night's sleep. Once again Adolf was astonished, and this time genuinely: he had assumed, as of course, that we would go on down to Grindelwald that night. This problem, however, was easily resolved to the satisfaction of both of us: I would go down alone the next morning, while

Adolf went that night, after telling me the best route by which to cross the Ober Grindelwald Glacier on the way.

V. FINSTERAARHORN, NORTHEAST FACE. THE ONLY GRIM CHAPTER

The prize story in *The Letters of Gertrude Bell* is the one describing her attempt on the northeast face of the Finsteraarhorn. Miss Bell and her guides, Ulrich and Heinrich Fuhrer, were the first to attempt that great wall which rises over 3,000 feet from its base on the Finsteraarfirn. They chose a small rib that runs straight up the face almost to the summit. On July 31, 1902, they reached a point about two-thirds of the way up the mountain; here they were overtaken by such bad weather that there was no question of their being able to continue the climb. Miss Bell's account of the descent—the two days' climbing in thunderstorms and snowstorms down the precipitous ice-sheathed rocks, having to rope down almost all the way with ropes stiff with ice, and the two nights, the first one spent tied on to the rocks of the great wall, and the second huddled together in pouring rain on the glacier below, in all mountaineering history one of the great feats of endurance and fortitude—is a magnificent story. And yet the tale is written with a simplicity and light-hearted courage that clearly under-emphasize the horrors of the trip.

Since then the wall had been climbed twice: the first time in 1904, by Gustav Hasler and Fritz Amatter, with a bivouac about 500 feet above the bergschrund, and the second time in 1906, by Val Fynn and Brüderlin, with one intentional bivouac at the start, slightly higher than the Hasler-Amatter bivouac, and another—indubitably much less welcome—just under the summit. Although Hasler observed, concerning this climb, 'A bivouac will always be necessary,'* the optimistic Adolf and I decided to try it without one. The Strahlegg Hut had been built since the earlier ascents and we thought that the four hours or so of extra climbing from there over the Finsteraarjoch to the base of the wall would be less fatiguing as a preliminary to

* *Alpine Journal*, XXXIV, p. 279.

the climb than a night spent out on the rocks. We were then in the month of September, when the nights are a bit longer and colder than earlier in the season, and a bivouac would have been quite uncomfortable. And finally, we had been making pretty good time on our climbs.

Adolf, his younger brother Fritz as porter, and I reached the Strahlegg Hut early, shortly after two, on the afternoon of September 2, 1930, planning to have a good rest before our climb. After a large meal we retired to the bunks, where we dozed from 3.30 to 6.30. We tried to rest again after a light tea, but with no success; we had had enough sleep and I, for one, was becoming excited. At 11 I did not want anything more to eat, but by overlooking the fact that this was 'breakfast' and pretending to myself that it was refreshments at an evening party, I managed to get a little something down. We wrote in the hut book, 'Left Strahlegg Hut at 12 for the Finsteraarhorn by the E. face.' But it wasn't quite 12! After a little gay banter on the subject of whether, if you wish to do a climb in one day, it is ethical to start the day before, and one more cup of tea, we actually left the hut at exactly midnight.

We started up the regular route to the Finsteraarjoch, with Adolf cutting a few steps here and there where the ice of the glacier was steep. Just as we were turning a rock corner on the lower slopes of the Strahlegghörner, down came a fall of stones. We dashed for shelter. The stones were small, hadn't fallen far, and injured no one. I came out of it with nothing more than one sore finger and quite a collection of gravel and pebbles down my neck; they stuck for a while at my waist, and finally fell out of the bottom of my trousers when I took off my boots in the Finsteraarhorn Hut more than twenty hours later. But although the physical damage was slight, this was the first in a long series of events which that day nearly wore through my rather fragile courage. I have always been afraid of objective dangers (those arising from external circumstances) and in particular of falling stones.

We decided to turn to the right; farther out on the glacier away from the rock walls it would be safer from falling stones.

But at midnight, by the light of just one small candle lantern, you cannot always be sure of what you are getting into. People coming up in daylight the next morning saw our tracks and wondered what sort of idiots would walk right out into that maze of crevasses. We lost a good half-hour in our wanderings here.

As we approached the pass, the Finsteraarjoch, we met an icy, penetrating wind that was to be with us all day long. When over the other side, we dropped down a bit and crossed the glacier, the Finsteraarfirn, skirting along under the great face of the Finsteraarhorn. It was too dark to see much—just a stupendous mass looming up menacingly above our heads. By 3.50 we had reached the place where we should have to cross the bergschrund, but for an hour there would not be light enough to do so. We sat down to wait in a slight depression which we thought might give us as much shelter from the wind as anything in the neighbourhood, although stones from the wall above could have fallen on us here as well as not. But the shelter was far from adequate and in only a few minutes we were miserable from the intense cold, and aghast to think what a bivouac would have been like anywhere around here that night. By 4.30 we had had enough; we would start on at once and try to cross the bergschrund in the dark. In any case it would be light before we got to the rocks.

The earlier parties had not reported any trouble with the bergschrund (that large crevasse where the main part of the glacier, in moving down, splits away from the ice adhering to the rock mass of the mountain), but they had crossed it on July 16, July 31, and August 12. Now in September, after many days of fine hot weather, the bergschrund presented a formidable appearance, wide open and with the upper wall towering high above the lower. Along its whole length where we wanted to get on to the mountain we found just one spot where a crossing looked possible. Exactly at the foot of the main gully, between Miss Bell's rib and the other prominent rib to the south of it, the stones draining down the face had worn a groove which cut down through the ice of the overhanging

97

upper lip, and had piled themselves up into a substantial cone on the lip below. By standing on the apex of the cone we thought it would be possible to reach with our ice-axes the ice above, cut holds there, and pull ourselves up.

Now would have been the time to give up the climb, but at the moment that would have seemed, I think, rather silly. A dangerous place this admittedly was, draining as it did all the stones falling from a considerable portion of the 3,000-foot face, but we should be there only a short while, and the chances of stones falling so early in the morning, in such cold weather, were slight. Later in the day, after the sun had risen and melted the ice that held the stones in place, it would have been suicide to go near the spot, but not now. So I did not say then and there that I would go no farther, although afterwards, and more than once, I was to wish that I had done so. Even today that climb remains a very unpleasant memory. It is the only climb I have ever done which I cannot think about with pleasure. Not that this was the only occasion in the mountains when I have ever been frightened, but it was the occasion when I was most badly frightened, and for the longest period. I may as well admit that I haven't the kind of courage it takes to do such climbs as that. Fun, to my mind, is the only reason for climbing mountains, and the northeast face of the Finsteraarhorn was not fun.

Standing on top of the cone, Adolf could reach up with his axe across the great gaping bergschrund to the groove in the upper lip, chop out some nicks for holds, and pull himself up. Above, up the nearly vertical ice groove, he had to continue to chop steps and handholds, and while he was doing this in the dark, down came a fall of stones. Fritz and I rushed to shelter, to a spot on the edge of the lower lip of the bergschrund where the upper lip somewhat covered it, but Adolf could not move. I experienced a horrible sickening feeling, listening to those stones whistling by, and knowing that Adolf was probably directly in their path. But he was not hurt, for when the sounds of the stones stopped the chopping of the ice-axe began again, and the rope ran out in its usual little jerks as he worked on up,

98

one step above another. Finally what was left of the rope was pulled taut, a signal that I was to go. It was a distasteful moment, this stepping out into the line of fire, but with nervous haste I scrambled up the cone rapidly so that we could all get to a safer place in the least possible time. Standing on the tip, my fingers could hardly reach across the gap to the upper wall of the bergschrund. I wasted no time but, holding my ice-axe above my head, with one good sharp blow I drove its pick into the ice and hauled myself up, all the time thinking of just one thing: the stones that might come down at any moment. Once in the groove above, I found it steep and still too dark to make out very well just where the steps were that Adolf had cut. By feel I found them and scrambled up rapidly, in apprehension. As soon as I emerged above the lip I was able to make out, ahead, a line of steps leading to the left up out of the groove. I don't think many things in life have brought me more relief than the sight of that route of escape! But before I could quite reach the steps the rope tightened below me; Fritz would have to come up before I could go farther. Then down the gully came another fall of stones. Flattening myself against the slope, I threw my rucksack and my arms above my head and just waited; there was nothing else I could do. Although a great many stones hit me, they all seemed to be small ones, and travelling slowly; they had not fallen very far. Then came a shout from Adolf above, 'Stones are falling!' A keen fear swept over me, that now there were big ones coming too, but at any rate no big ones hit me, only the same small ones. When Adolf shouted urgently to get out of the couloir as fast as possible, I took it to mean that Fritz had now come up part way and I had enough slack in the rope below to move on. But to do that I should have to take my arms down off my head—and how I hated to do so!

When we were all three out of the groove, up to the left, we were much safer, of course, but still not completely so. We hurried on up, quickly crossing the snow, and soon reached easy, broken rocks. It was beginning to get light, the face of the mountain rose above us ominously, and the more I saw of it the less I liked it. The rock looked so loose and the whole mass of it so oppressive that it almost seemed to overhang—an illusion, of course. We climbed up easily for about half an hour, until we found a good place to cross the big central gully back again to the right. First taking a careful look around, each one of us separately hurried across. We finally reached the shelter of a big red gendarme, the bottom gendarme on the long rib or buttress that we were to follow up the major part of the face. All these alarms of falling stones had made me, quite literally, sick, hardly a creditable way to react to danger and fear, and certainly not a helpful or useful one. But in spite of it my leg and arm muscles could continue to function and up to now, in my desperate haste to get to the ridge where I expected shelter, I had ignored this malaise; now, when we were at last in comparative safety, it should have left me, but instead hung on for hours as I dragged myself slowly and wretchedly up those easy rocks. At eight o'clock we stopped on the sheltered side of the ridge, in the sun. 'Sleep for an hour if it will make you feel better,' suggested Adolf.

Adolf told me some days later that he thought there had been one time when I had wanted to go back. One time! There had hardly been a moment when I did not wish myself off that face, but the thought of crossing the main couloir with all those stones cannonading down it, and getting over that bergschrund again, kept me from mentioning it. And also, there was the hope that the worst was over, that now, on the ridge which it had cost us so much anxiety to reach, things might be better than they looked. Finally, I have to admit, the climb was beginning to present a certain challenge.

In half an hour we started on again. It was 8.30 and in this first four hours we had covered half the distance up the wall. The second half was to take us nine hours more. Around nine or ten I began gradually to feel a little better and the time finally came when I asked myself with a start, and some incredulity, if it could possibly be that I was enjoying this climb after all! This did seem like an odd idea, and in any case the feeling didn't last long.

100

The rib was not actually a continuous and well-defined ridge, elevated above the rest of the wall, but consisted rather of a series of gendarmes or towers on the face, which got increasingly steeper the higher we rose. After surmounting one of these towers we would be confronted with the sheer, almost vertical lower wall of the next. To our left was the couloir, which we followed, I think, rather less than the other parties had. Not only was it continually raked by falling stones, but in that September its bed was hard ice. Hasler and Amatter had found some snow there, brittle and not trustworthy, but still easier and quicker to cut up than ice. After our climb Adolf and I went to see Amatter in order to compare notes with him. Although he had done the climb twenty-six years earlier he had not forgotten it! Of the ridge, he observed that although it was well marked on the Siegfried map, it seemed to be considerably better marked there than on the mountain. Not until 1951 did I meet Gustav Hasler for the first time, but I found that he too still remembered the experience of this climb well, even after the lapse of forty-seven years.

We kept to the rib. The exasperating obstacle was that the rock, although very steep, was so breakable. Not a hold could be trusted to stay in place. We found no first-class rock-climbing requiring delicate work on solid rock—good clean fun of the kind I like. Only twice that day did I need to take off my mittens (woollen mittens with leather covers, like a ski mitten). And all day long it was extremely cold, with a bitter wind. We wore all the clothes we had, and whenever there was a choice of route we took the south side, to be in the sun. But at one in the afternoon the sun set for us for good, on that northeast face, and from then on the cold was bitter and unrelieved.

The hardest pitch on the ridge was a great slab rising steeply, with a small chimney to the left of it. The chimney was icy and overhanging at the bottom; the take-off did not look good. The slab I thought could be climbed, but somewhere or other we should have to traverse into the chimney in order to finish, since the slab itself was closed at the top by a big overhang. From below I could see no way to make this traverse. We might have gone considerably farther to the left, into the main gully, which here lay just under the final precipitous summit wall. But the danger from falling stones would have been great. So before deciding on the gully route, Adolf went first to look around the edge of the slab to the right. He was gone a distressingly long time. Because of the wind, and the corner, and the distance, we could not hear each other and I had to guess what was going on. Adolf was gone so long and the rope ran out so slowly, with such long periods of time when it moved not at all, that I became most uneasy. Although the leader of course has the worst of it, he isn't the only one who suffers when he is in a bad spot, and he at least knows how things are going. How I envied Fritz his stolidity and apparent unconcern! Adolf was to refer to this pitch later as the place where he almost fell off. But at last he conquered it, a magnificent job, and arrived on the tower above us.

We were not on any account to go the way he had taken, he shouted down, but to come straight up. Straight up! I tried the slab and it did go, even though I had to take off my mittens here, for the first time that day. But although I studied the wall every step of the way, trying to get across to the chimney on the left, I could not find any possible route. So I kept on going straight up and up, on small and crumbly holds, until I was right under the final overhang, and still I had found no way of traversing to the chimney. I should have to swing across on the rope. But that's the sort of thing you must not do unless the man above is prepared for it. And on this face particularly it was never safe to assume that anybody was firmly anchored. Clinging precariously on this wall of friable rock, I shouted up to Adolf to explain my plans, but the wind was so high and he was so far away above the overhang that he could not understand. I was getting close to something like despair when finally Adolf shouted, 'Shall I pull?' That was better; if he was in a position to pull, he would also be able to hold a pendulum. I took a turn of the rope around my right hand as high up as I could reach, shouted back, 'Yes!' and pushed off vigorously with my feet. It worked beautifully. I swung even

The Finsteraarhorn. ABOVE: The northeast face is in profile to the left, the glacier of our approach in the right foreground. BELOW: Gendarmes on the rib we followed up the northeast face. OVERLEAF: The top part of the northeast face of the Finsteraarhorn.

farther than I had thought I could and, what's more, did not swing back again, but quickly and effectively caught my left toe in the chimney itself and an instant later grabbed a hold with my left hand. To allay Adolf's undoubted surprise I shouted up to him that everything was all right, as indeed it was. The rest of the chimney was easy and I soon joined Adolf. Fritz came directly up the chimney all the way, assisted at the beginning by Adolf's rope.

And so in time we came to Hasler's 'Great Grey Tower'. This repulsive sheer wall rose above us, effectively and definitively barring the way. Gertrude Bell and her guides had turned back about here. A few feet below, Hasler had found a rope sling that could have belonged to no party but theirs. We looked, but it was impossible to turn this tower on the right. We did what the other two parties had done—and I don't believe any other course is possible here: we dropped down into the small couloir on the left and then climbed up that. The trough of this nearly vertical little gully was filled with ice, a brittle, waterfall-type of ice that shattered when struck with the axe, and its sidewalls were steep and untrustworthy, their loose rock thinly glazed with ice. I think perhaps we joined this couloir somewhat lower down than Hasler reported, for as I watched Adolf he roped down 60–70 feet and then climbed down about fifteen feet more before reaching the gully, whereupon he worked his way up, chopping questionable nicks for his toes between the ice and the rock.

Perhaps 250 feet higher we could traverse to the right to gain the ridge again. But we had gone about as far as we could on the ridge. Above, it merged into the perpendicular final rock wall of the mountain. From here up was the steepest and most difficult section of all. The other two parties had followed the main couloir, which here narrows and steepens, and had then traversed to the left to reach the summit ridge slightly to the left of the highest point, and both had reported exceptional difficulty. But the couloir, on this occasion in ice instead of snow, was much too long to cut up safely, exposed as it was to falling stones and also to falling blocks of ice and snow from

103

the cornices of the summit ridge, which here overhung. We went to the right. Adolf says that if he were going to do the climb again—which he is not, don't misunderstand—he would take the same route, although it turned out to be an extraordinarily difficult one. This was the section to which Adolf was referring when he said, 'conditions so bad that it approaches the limits of possibility, and for over 100 metres was just flirting with death.'* He tells me now that the few parties who have made this climb subsequently have all followed this route of his to the right. They have reported finding, however, much less ice than we did; apparently conditions on the day of our climb were exceptionally bad. And then, of course, we had no pitons.

On the wall to the right, just below us, lay a sheet of ice and an unbroken drop of perhaps a thousand feet. Above the ice sheet, about 100 feet away, we could make out a small shallow chimney running upwards. If we could get into it by a traverse along the almost vertical wall of ice-glazed rocks just above the ice sheet, it might take us up. . . .

Adolf lengthened the rope between us by tying on the *corde de rappel*, gave his rucksack to Fritz, and started out to see if he could make it. I doubt if I have ever experienced in the mountains any period of suspense more taut than this one as I watched Adolf slowly working his way across. What joy I felt when he arrived safely in the chimney! After he had struggled up this for sixty or seventy feet he reached a little stance where he was reasonably firm and I could come. I have never felt more insecure on any passage. Ordinarily you test each hold by a good tug before you put your weight on it, but it didn't do to practise that here. Too many of the holds came out, bringing large chunks of the wall with them. I simply used them, as delicately and gently, and as rapidly, as I could, loose though I knew them to be. If I didn't disturb them too violently, perhaps the ice would hold them in just long enough for me to get on to the next one. I had to work quickly not only on account of the insecurity of the holds; in addition a film of ice covered almost everything and, my mittens being off here for the second

* *Alpine Journal*, XLII, p. 339.

time, my fingers were getting chilled and dangerously numb. And so I edged along sideways, faster than I liked, using holds that were only half-way secure and hoping that all of them wouldn't give way at once. I felt some astonishment when I reached the chimney without having fallen off.

Since the rope from me to Fritz was much shorter than the one (or two, rather) from Adolf to me, I could not get all the way up to Adolf's position before Fritz's rope became taut, and had to stop when only a few feet up the chimney. I had no firm standing place, just a couple of insignificant toe-holds on the loose rocks. Although I could balance here after a fashion, with my hands free to take in Fritz's rope while he came across that difficult traverse, Adolf above would have to hold us both if anything happened. And that's exactly what he *did* have to do a moment later.

Although I couldn't see Fritz, I knew—psychically, perhaps!— that he was going to fall off a split second before he did so, and had just time to take a quick turn of his rope around my right hand. Otherwise I am sure I should not have been able to hold it. At the same time I took a turn of the rope above my head around my left hand. This was not strictly necessary because of course the rope was tied to my waist anyway, but it prevented a jerk where the rope went around my body, and perhaps gave a certain amount of spring to the whole system. Fritz took a really stupendous fall. Since I was not much above him, and far out to the side, he executed a long-radius pendulum, fast and far, before finally coming to rest on the perpendicular ice slope below our chimney, out of sight of both of us. The force of his fall pulled me out away from the wall, and his additional weight on the rope so stretched the section from Adolf to me that when the system finally settled into equilibrium, although my toes were still on their small holds, my body was nearly horizontal. Both my hands, however, were still holding their ropes.

It took a minute or two, I think, for Adolf and me to get our breath. Probably due to the fact that he had slid over relatively smooth ice, and not jagged rocks, Fritz had not suffered any serious physical injury from his fall, but we had no way of knowing this at the time, since he did not answer in any way when we called down to him. Adolf shouted to me to tell Fritz to climb up, but this he obviously could not do. There were no holds on the glare ice where he was, and I was not even sure that he was in contact with it. Then Fritz must climb up the rope, said Adolf. But apparently Fritz was somewhat stunned; he had not spoken or moved, and there was no way of knowing whether he heard what we said. The only thing left, declared Adolf finally, was for me to pull him up. If the situation hadn't been so grim that suggestion would have struck me as fairly funny. Fritz probably weighed forty or fifty pounds more than I did and I couldn't lift him at all. Privately, I had thought that I was doing rather well just to hold him.

Of course, in the end it was Adolf who had to do everything. He found some sort of rock projection around which to tie the rope on which he was holding both Fritz and me, and I don't believe it was easy either to find a suitable place or to do the actual tying with our weight still on the rope. Then Adolf climbed down, using the rope to me as a hand-hold. That manœuvre brought the weight of all three of us on the same rope—my thin alpine line!—and if it had cut, or come off whatever it was tied to, that would have put an end to three climbers. But it was well tied and it was a good rope; I made a practice of buying new climbing ropes each season in those days, before nylon came in. When Adolf got down to where he could reach the rope below me and get a stance for himself, he pulled Fritz up, and that wasn't so quick and easy as it sounds, either. Fritz still seemed dazed, and when after a moment's rest Adolf and I, intensely eager to see if this route was going to take us to the summit, were ready to start on, we still couldn't seem to rouse Fritz. He simply sat there, staring straight ahead with vague and unseeing eyes, apparently not aware of anything we said or did. At least I could carry his pack for him, but as I started to lift it off his shoulders, this action of mine (an insult, perhaps?) seemed to get through to him and he resisted it vaguely. Gradually his eyes focused and he gave me

106

to understand that no young lady was going to carry his pack. He finished the trip most creditably indeed. In some contemporary accounts of it, I omitted mentioning the fact that Fritz fell off. But quite without reason, for to fall off that traverse while carrying two packs would be no discredit to anybody.

From here to the summit ridge was a very short distance, not much more than 300 feet. The going was almost entirely up steep ice with small rocks sticking out here and there. We should have liked to use these rocks, but time after time it developed that they were held in position only by the ice itself and any chopping intended to fashion them into holds merely dislodged them. Getting up was in consequence delicate work. On the first pitch, after Adolf had gone the whole length of the 130-foot rope between us without finding any place to stop, he had to balance gingerly on his steps in the steep ice, take off his rucksack, get out our third rope again, tie it to the first, and proceed perhaps fifty feet farther to an adequate stopping place. From there he could see the ridge.

We reached the summit ridge at a little col some 200 feet northwest of the top. Here we were on the ordinary route, a broad, gently-rising ridge of no difficulty whatever. At 5.30 we reached the summit. I felt relief, of course, enormous relief to be at last off that wall, but little of the elation and joy that usually come at the end of a good climb. Adolf's hands were torn and bleeding; the next day five of his fingers still needed to be bandaged. Think nothing of it, said Adolf's father later; he had been at the Finsteraarhorn Hut in 1906 when Val Fynn and Brüderlin had arrived there after their ascent of the face, and with their two nights of bivouac, and they, too, to put it mildly, had been scratched up!

VI
Skiing

I. PIONEERING IN NEW ENGLAND

When I first heard of skiing, as a student at Bryn Mawr some time before 1920, I regretted exceedingly that I was too old to take up such a very fine-sounding sport. Fortunately now, nearly forty years later, I no longer consider myself too old to ski.

In the early 'twenties my brother Lincoln and I had some skis in the house in Dedham, Massachusetts—big, heavy yellow boards, with toe-straps at first and later with miscellaneous leather-strap bindings—and we used to slide along the woods roads, often pulled by our horse Hannibal. Hannibal liked the game well enough too, but often wanted to go faster than we did. Link, *on* a horse, was very skilful; behind, on skis, he occasionally found he had inadequate braking power to cope with a big strong hunter like Hannibal, and we'd be left in a heap in the snow while Hannibal took off for home and the stable.

What a controversy there was over bindings versus toe-straps! It was quite daring to have bindings. I liked them better myself; they gave better control, it seemed to me, over the skis. But I belonged to a small minority. When the argument raged on this point it was my custom to inquire, 'Would you like to have your ice skates fastened on merely by toe-straps?' But it was always proved that a ski bore no resemblance to a skate; it was merely a different form of toboggan for sliding down a hill. Anybody could see that toe-straps were safer; in case of a fall the ski would come off and there was less likelihood of

108

breaking a leg. Come to think of it, this may still be true—look at all the people today inventing 'safety bindings' aimed to permit just that—but as I glance around the ski hills from Mont Tremblant to Aspen, bindings seem to have won out. So strong, however, was my early conviction that I wanted my skis fastened to my feet, and so vigorously did I have to do battle for this conviction, that today I refuse even to try safety bindings.

Our clothes, too, in those early days were not so uniform as they are now. At first, naturally, we used our woollen skirts and winter coats, but it became evident at once that this was impractical. One of my Bryn Mawr classmates whispered to me after a winter holiday at home in New England, 'Don't tell Louise, but my brothers call her "the girl who doesn't wear bloomers".' It was unheard of, in the New England of those days, not to wear bloomers underneath. No one would have known that styles were different in Atlanta if it hadn't been for skiing. Then we put on knickerbockers with long, snow-catching woollen stockings to the knee. In 1927 I read in *Vogue* that *chic* Europeans were skiing in long trousers. Since no such thing could be bought in Boston for women at that time, I made myself a pair, the first I had ever seen, like the picture in *Vogue*, fashionably full at the ankle, but not so floppy as they got later. I don't remember how *chic* I felt, but I do remember feeling extraordinarily conspicuous the first few times I walked through the North Station in Boston in those long trousers. Evidently I wasn't the only person who hadn't yet seen them.

It was about that time that Arthur Comey invented some ski trousers that he could take off without removing his skis. 'But why do you want to?' inquired my mother, to whom he was demonstrating this. It developed that they were a second pair, for extra protection in rough weather.

In 1925 I got my first good skis. Park Carpenter, a fellow-member of the Appalachian Mountain Club who had been working in Norway, arranged to have Norwegian skis shipped over for a group of us, long, heavy hickory skis with slotted

109

Huitfeldt bindings. These we always called our 'gold-plates', having reference to their total cost when finally imported into the United States. I don't believe, at that, they were so gold-plated as the skis we buy nowadays.

In the winter evenings and on week-ends when there was snow around Boston we'd have our skiing parties. Friends would come to dinner and afterwards we'd ski on dim golf courses or along really dark woods roads. The style we were aiming at was Norwegian. Standing proudly upright with one foot a little ahead of the other—it didn't matter which one—we'd slide directly down the hill. In theory we'd do a stop telemark at the bottom, but many of us stopped in simpler ways.

Soon came the period of learning to ski out of books. Arnold Lunn's *Ski-ing for Beginners* and Caulfeild's *Ski-ing Turns* went with us on every week-end trip. The latter, in a pocket at the back, had a series of cards with pictures illustrating the turns. I can remember Robert Underhill standing on the brow of a hill, a slope of unbroken snow in front of him, running through the cards and deciding that the open christie looked like an easy one to learn first.

It wasn't until 1929, when Otto Schniebs arrived in Boston, that we had an experienced ski-teacher, and by that time we had already done a great deal of skiing. Otto brought news of a newly-invented style, the Arlberg, characterized mainly by a deep crouch. I never made much progress in any style of skiing. In late years the pretty French style has attracted me, but if I don't wholeheartedly share my husband's conviction that at our age we are no longer capable of learning anything whatever, still so far I have taken only one lesson in it. The main reason, I suppose, why I have never acquired any particular skiing style is that learning ski-technique has always seemed to me so much less interesting than just taking off and going places on skis.

And go places we certainly did, sometimes as an Appalachian Mountain Club group or, more often, Arthur Comey, Robert Underhill and I alone. Since our New England mountains are densely forested and no ski trails were opened up until much

110

Climbing Mt. Chocorua
with Arthur Comey.

Arthur Comey climbing the roof on skis in order to practice jumping off the other side.

later, we hunted out every possible mountain road and summer walking trail and, of course, a great many impossible ones. The carriage roads on Mt Washington and Moosilauke were obvious. So were all old lumber roads through the White Mountains, and many of the narrow climbing trails that had been cut for summer use. I believe somewhere in Sir Arnold Lunn's published works there is an admonition not to ski within five feet of a tree. This we found most hilariously funny, there being hardly any spot on the places we skied where it was possible to get as much as five feet away from a tree.

We never met any other skiers. I first skied up Moosilauke, where crowds of Dartmouth skiers now disport themselves, with Arthur Comey, whose parting words at the bottom as he forged up ahead through the unbroken powder were, 'You'd better turn around when you meet me coming down.' I didn't see him again, or anybody else, for several hours. But I didn't turn around when I met him; I went on myself to the top first. And I remember Arthur, too, at the foot of Mt Hale, watch in hand, practically leaping for joy at his estimates having proved so accurate. He had prophesied to himself when he got down, 'Robert will be here in two minutes. Then we'll both sit down and wait twenty minutes for Miriam.' It had turned out just that way.

Arthur owned a summer cottage near Mt Chocorua in New Hampshire, which was our headquarters for several strenuous winter trips. At first we took the train to the nearest station and skied in the six miles to the cottage; later we were able to get nearer and nearer by car. Although we covered most of the summer climbing trails in the region, one trip in particular stands out. From Arthur's house we climbed Chocorua by the old Liberty Trail (not the ski trail which was built later), skied across the windswept summit on practically bare ice—no steel edges in those days—then down the other side of the mountain to the Albany Intervale and returned to Arthur's over the Bolles Trail, which crosses a col between Chocorua and the next mountain. It was seventeen miles, but the outstanding circumstance of the trip was that a previous heavy sleet storm had bent over the birches, whose tips were then solidly frozen into the snow. For miles we crawled, almost lying down on our skis, under those tangles of looped-over birches. Occasionally we'd come out and try to climb over the tops, but that was harder. We reached the house at 1.10 the next morning.

We even planned once, but never carried out, a twenty-mile ski trip up Mt Washington (6,288 feet, the highest summit in New England), and then down the Davis Path, a winding summer trail that traverses the half-dozen minor summits of the long, southerly Montalban Ridge of Mt Washington. It is so narrow that we probably should not have been able to find it at all in the winter. Although we started twice, we were turned back each time by storms. Bob had previously been editor of *Appalachia* for seven years, and his attitude, in writing up the accidents and deaths in the White Mountains, was that the people involved were invariably fools. By persisting in the face of bad weather, not having proper equipment and clothing (e.g., woollen underwear), etc., they richly deserved whatever they got. One March day on our way to the Davis Path, as we struggled up the Carriage Road on Mt Washington against a frightful wind with a storm obviously coming up, with Bob shivering in his cotton underwear and the back of his neck frozen because he had no parka, Peter Chase (who is still skiing with us this winter in his seventy-fourth year) remarked, 'I don't know why I keep on. I should really like to survive this day, if only to read in *Appalachia* what Marjorie Hurd [the subsequent editor] has to say about the death on Mt Washington of Robert Underhill.' That was the signal for turning back.

All these years I was really master of only three ski manœuvres: (1) I could do a kick-turn; (2) I could snowplough; and (3) I could ride my sticks. And really, for the trips we took, that was a practical and adequate technique, with occasionally a rudimentary telemark in deep snow. Even had I known a parallel christie, it would have been less use to me on a steep and narrow woods trail than my ability to sink down into a deep, relaxed snowplough, and hold it mile after mile to the foot of the mountain. It is a pity, though, that these manœuvres which I spent so many years in mastering so thoroughly, and which, if I may be permitted a bit of boasting, I can still do today uncommonly well, add so little to my prestige on the ski slopes and occasion, to tell the truth, nothing more than lifted eyebrows.

And all these years, too, we were learning to handle all the varieties of snow that nature provided: powder, crust (hard or breakable), wind-packed, ice, corn snow—all the snow surfaces there are except just one, the hard-packed polished *piste*. I had skied a great many years before I ever saw a modern ski-trail surface. In a way, of course, it is great fun to rattle down the smooth hard modern trails, but I still feel more at home with unbroken snow in front of me, and not so many people running into me from behind. Of recent years most resorts in North America have their ski patrols in charge of safety, with lads trained in first-aid and in tobogganing the injured down the mountain. These are admirable organizations that have done much to reduce the accident rate. That the ski patrol should close a trail because of avalanche danger, or because they want to save the snow-cover for a race, I can concede. But it is not so easy for me to accept gracefully the closing of a beautiful powder-snow trail because it is not 'broken-out' and the deep snow will not be safe to ski until it has been packed! In any case, it shows how far we have come from the early days.

II. IN THE FRENCH ALPS

The winter of 1928–29 I spent in Paris, supposedly studying, but I got in quite a bit of skiing, too, mostly with my French climbing friends of the Groupe de Haute Montagne. At Christmas a group of us went to Morzine in the French Alps of Savoy, south-east of Annemasse. We practised our turns on the Arête de Plenay, nice, mostly open slopes to the west of the village, and the turns we were practising were still telemarks. Three of our best friends among the Chamonix guides, Armand Charlet, the most renowned of all the French guides, Camille Tournier and Georges Cachat, skied over for a surprise visit.

There was a very pleasant comradeship between the best of the Chamonix guides and the G.H.M. members, mountaineers all. The next morning when Armand, Camille and Georges started back to Chamonix over the Col de Jouxplane and Samoëns, we went with them as far as the Chalets de Nion, and three of us, Jean Matter, the best skier of us all and later president of the French Ski Federation, Maurice Bernard and I skied on up through beautiful powder snow to the Pointe d'Angolon, following the ridge as far as skis could go. To our right rose the Chamonix giants, all shining white; to our left lay the Lake of Geneva under a sea of clouds.

On Christmas Day Matter, Bernard, Henry de Ségogne, one of France's foremost mountaineers and a founder of the G.H.M., and I skied up the Pointe de l'Aiguille, starting out before daylight by sleigh up the valley as far as Charny. In the golden light of early dawn, as we cut through the cold, fine powder snow on our upward zig-zags with Henry singing 'Il est né, ce divin Enfant', a Christmas carol I had learned at school in Boston, it seemed like a very fine Christmas Day indeed.

At Chamonix after the Morzine trip, and again in February, with Armand Charlet or Georges Cachat, I roamed the lower mountains on skis, to the Lognon and the Col de Balme, to the Col du Brévent and the Col Cornu in the Aiguilles Rouges, to the Requin Hut. On the February trip Armand and I drew up some really impressive projects of first ski ascents, but three continuous days of storm snuffed them out. All that fresh snow made the avalanche danger too extreme. I don't mind admitting now that we planned to climb Mont Blanc itself on skis later in the season, but circumstances never worked out right. It is always pleasant to have plenty of fine schemes on the agenda, and if one gets to carry out half of them, it's an excellent average. Another unrealized project was a ski traverse of the French Alps, from Briançon to Chamonix, with Marguérite Leleu, just the two of us, manless. This was Marguérite's idea, and a good one.

In February some of us G.H.M. skiers had a long week-end in the Jura, near Mont d'Or, and at the end of March we took off again for the Tarentaise. My Buick, which I had over in Paris, was equipped with chains, naturally enough for a New England car. These seemed to be curiosities in a country where chains are rarely needed, but they did help in getting up into the mountains for skiing. Not that we (Micheline and François Morin and I) got to Tignes, on the road to Val d'Isère, the first night by car. Not only was the road still officially closed for the winter, but it was the season, we were told at Les Pigettes, for the large icicle overhanging the road to fall. We would do better to leave the car there and sneak by quietly on foot. This we did, with skis and rucksacks, walking attentively, and one by one, under the icicle. Two days later, when the icicle had in fact fallen and we walked back down to get the car, men were still shoveling away the debris. Mich and I speculated on how many people they would uncover underneath.

At the Hotel de la Grande Motte (soon, with the whole village of Tignes, to be deep under water, due to the construction of a dam), we found the only other guests were four delightful Belgian skiers, who set to at once, even though the hour was late, to repair something amiss with my ski bindings. One of them was Count Xavier de Grunne, who was to die so tragically, after years in a German prison camp, just a few weeks before the liberation.

Our best ski tour from Tignes was the ascent of the Aiguille Percée (9,059 feet). Mich and I, and André Vercken, a good skier but a novice mountaineer, left Tignes at 4.20 a.m. and managed to travel up the picturesque valley as far as the Lac de Tignes on our skis fitted with skins, although the snow underneath was icy hard. Later, before we came down, the surface would melt into beautiful spring snow. Beyond the lake, where the terrain was steeper, we took off our skis and towed them. It's been years, in these days of chair-lifts and T-bars, since I've seen skis with holes bored in the tips for fastening the tow ropes, but we all had them then. The final rock-climb was short, but exhilarating. Not realizing that the route was to start up a couloir on the north side of the peak, filled with masses of unconsolidated powder snow, light and feathery and oh! so cold,

we had left our coats and mittens somewhat below. A mistake!
I floundered about in this snowy couloir, plunging my arms to
the shoulders into the snow, feeling around for something solid
to hold to. Every few steps I'd have to pause and slip my
aching hands inside my clothes for a moment's warmth. Fortunately, although steep, the gully was short, and in 40 or 50
feet we were out on the rocks. The final ridge up to the summit
was a bit airy and the rock none too firm, but it was a delightful
change from the snow-filled couloir. Here André, who was on
his second rock-climb, tore a great triangular hole in each
trouser leg, which gave him a bit of trouble on the descent by
filling up with snow. We had a marvellous run down, on perfect
spring snow, 3,600 feet to Tignes.

Two days later I met my old comrades Matter, Bernard and
Ségogne at Nancroît-sur-Peisy in the valley to the south of
Tignes, and with the first two—Henry was ill—climbed the
Aiguille du Saint Esprit (the Needle of the Holy Ghost), a more
serious undertaking than the little Aiguille Percée. Leaving the
Refuge du Pourri (5,632 feet) just before 3 a.m., we climbed
briskly, for the cold was intense, up towards the Grand Col,
towing our skis and with our crampons biting well into the
frozen surface. When, on the plateau slightly below the col,
we ran into patches of powder snow into which we sank deeply,
we put on our skis and sealskins. The cold and the wind were
increasing. We reached the Grand Col (some 4,000 feet above
the hut) at 5.45 and paused only a minute to drink a raw egg
apiece and leave our skis, since from here on our route lay up
over a steep glacier across which the wind was howling. At
least our packs were lighter for this part of the trip. We left
the food and the canteen of tea, now solidly frozen, with the
skis at the col; our crampons were on our feet, our axes in our
hands, the rope around our waists. Every item of clothing we
put on. Although I already wore a woollen cap and parka, I
wrapped a woollen scarf around my head and face, leaving just
a crack to look out. The violent wind was blowing fine particles
of ice that stung as they hit our faces. Over my ski boots I drew
a pair of socks of my own invention, which I had knitted of

five strands of heavy wool simultaneously. Wearing these between my boots and my crampons did a good deal to keep my
feet from freezing. But in spite of everything we were cold;
in spite, too, of very vigorous exertion as we struggled up,
stamping footholds in the deep drifted snow up a very precipitous slope, sometimes sinking in to our waists. The bergschrund
gave a little trouble, but was overcome by Matter very skilfully,
although from below his manœuvres looked more like swimming
than anything else. When my turn came to crawl past those
sinister-looking black holes in the deep white snow I was
thankful indeed for a rope from above. And more than once
I crouched down against the slope to allow a violent gust of
wind to pass. We arrived on the summit (11,063 feet) at about
9.30 and with unanimity gave up our original notion of continuing along the ridge to the Pourri, some 1,400 feet higher. The
weather was bad, there had been no sun, and thick black clouds
were already grazing the summit of the Pourri. It was no place
for us. Anyway, we had had a fair amount of exercise for the
day.

When we turned around almost at once, prepared to follow
our tracks back down, not a track was to be seen. The wind
had filled them all in, sweeping the slope clear almost as fast
as we had come up. Plunging down, I thought of André and
the holes in his trousers on the Aiguille Percée. This would be
no time or place to open up any holes in mine, and I took some
pains to keep my crampons—ten sharp spikes on each foot—
from coming into contact with the legs of my ski trousers.
Sheltered at the col, we waited a bit in hopes that a little touch
of sun would melt the surface of the snow enough for us to ski
down easily, meanwhile munching away on the food we had
left there, which was now frozen solid. Some time was needed
to warm it up in our mouths enough to chew and swallow.

But the snow stayed hard and at 11.20 we put on our skis
and started down, very carefully, in a series of gentle traverses
with kick turns. Sometimes the edges of the skis would bite
into the icy surface enough to hold, and sometimes not. I lost
altitude faster in the second case but my companions protested

vigorously. Matter, in particular, was all for having things done properly. As we descended, the going improved, although Bernard insisted that the powder snow we had fallen into on our way up had turned to ice. Our main difficulty now was with the lighting. The entire sky was covered with clouds, producing a completely diffuse illumination. Sky, powder snow, ice, up-hill, downhill, all looked exactly alike to us—a sort of insubstantial whitish mist. Only the changing motion of the skis as they ran smack into a bank or dropped off into thin air, indicated the nature of the ground.

But lower down the going got distinctly better. For the last 4,000 feet down to Nancroît the snow was splendid and we enjoyed a wonderful run. Towards the end, it is true, we met more and more patches of bare ground, but it is surprising how much grass and flowers you can ski right over if you adjust your balance to the checking of speed when you hit the grass and the acceleration when you leave it on the other side.

A brief trip to Chamonix with Dr. Robert Merle d'Aubigné in the middle of May finished up my skiing for that year. (On my first trip to Paris after the war I heard the following story about this gentleman. When the Gestapo came to arrest him, during the occupation of Paris, for his medical care of members of the Underground, he met them on the stairway of his apartment house. Having been warned of their approach, he was at that moment attempting to escape. When they asked him if he could direct them to the flat of Dr. Merle d'Aubigné he replied courteously—and with some presence of mind—that it was three flights higher up. They thanked him and continued up; he walked down and outside to safety!) With a base at the Requin Hut, we skied one day to the Col du Géant (11,055 feet) and the next day to the Col du Midi (11,630 feet). The Géant icefall we found, naturally, much more snow-covered than it is in summer, but just the same we worked our way up and down through its séracs and crevasses with some circumspection. And what a view from the col! All Italy, beneath us to the south, was covered by a sea of clouds that sparkled and glittered in the brilliant sunshine. Here and there a jagged, snow-hung peak, rising up above the level, floated on the mists. It used to be that only mountain climbers knew the real beauty of clouds as they should be seen—from above.

The next day our trip to the Col du Midi and back, and then down the Mer de Glace to Chamonix to catch the 3.30 train to Paris, did not leave us enough time to satisfy our inflated appetites. How disgusted were our companions in the compartment when, famishing, we turned out our rucksacks and ate up every last dirty little crumb that had been collecting there all the season.

III. THE ARLBERG

The next year (1930), in early March, Avis Newhall and I sailed for Europe on the 'French Island' (as a French cook of my family's called the *Ile de France*). A few days later, in Paris, we found our French skiing friends planning to start that same evening for the Arlberg, in order to look into the new ski system there. They had made reservations for Avis and me, too, on the Arlberg-Orient Express and at the hotel at Zürs. Although this came as a surprise to us, naturally we went right along. And naturally, too, we had a gay time with the old crowd. Henry de Ségogne brought me up to date at once on the current state of everyone's love affairs. ('My ears were flapping,' said Avis, after listening in.) Two members of the party, he reported, were being brought together with a definite purpose in mind and we should give them every opportunity to be alone. (Unfortunately this did not work out!) In the evenings we had some pretty wild bridge games. Since Ségogne and Matter held that the glory of France required that two French men should beat two American girls, they were willing to overbid their hands indefinitely to this end. To clean them up, all Avis and I had to do was be a bit conservative, and double.

But what about this Arlberg system? For a couple of years now we had been reading many an article, pro and con, in the *British Ski Year Book* and the Continental mountaineering journals. Here we were at last in the Arlberg, at one of its official schools, and we should see for ourselves. But perhaps my conclusions about the Arlberg system of skiing were overshadowed by my reaction to the school itself, which was not a felicitous one. We just did not hit it off; there was no mutual love at first sight.

It was my first experience at a regular organized ski school and it soured me for life on ski schools in general. The rigidity, the German thoroughness, the insistence on perfection in every minutest detail, oppressed me. There were 600 students at the Zürs Ski School when we were there. The classes were too large —as they often are—and too much of our time was spent watching each other ski badly. Even though we soon discovered that we could avoid the crowds by taking private lessons (at one-twelfth what they cost today in the United States), the same teaching methods prevailed there too. All of us except Matter, who was already an accomplished skier and was placed at once in a high class, started in the snowplough division. Through this we passed relatively quickly—after all, hadn't we been successfully snowploughing for years? But I bogged down definitively in Class IV-b, where the course of study was the pure Arlberg *Stemmbogen* or stem turn. Day after day that stem turn had to be done to absolute perfection in every type of snow, on every degree of slope, before I could progress to the stem christiana. I got bored with it. It is not a turn for which there is any great use in real life anyway. (I am told that the so-called 'Arlberg' schools in the U.S.A. today slide over it more sketchily, as well they may.) Curiously enough, however, I discovered in later years that I had actually learned the Arlberg stem turn fairly well, and this knowledge was to contribute heavily to my getting through the Ski Club of Great Britain's third-class test in 1938. My husband alleges that since at that time I could not do a christie and since he has never been able to do a stem turn, we both passed the test on my stems and his christies.

And then at heart I was a mountaineer. Class IV-b did occasionally go on tours, and I went on one with them up an

A ski class at Zürs, ABOVE: assembling, and RIGHT: starting on a trip.

The Eismeer Run, ABOVE: near the top,
and BELOW: approaching Grindelwald.

insignificant hummock somewhere, a ghastly affair of inter-minable waiting around. When I heard that Matter's class were going up the Valluga I recognized that as the sort of thing I should prefer to be doing. Since the Valluga (slightly over 9,000 feet), although the top ski tour of the Zürs Ski School and a fine run, was still not so high or so difficult as ski tours that Matter had already taken me on himself, he thought I should be able to handle it—as did I, naturally. But even though he assured the authorities that he would personally be responsible for me, leaving his class if necessary, it was impossible for me to go. A member of Class IV-b, they asserted unequivocally, would be completely incapable of doing the Valluga. (They were wrong in this; for ski-mountaineering it is much more important to be an experienced mountaineer than a polished skier.) I was, I'll admit, more than a bit put out, and decided that instead of taking so many *Stemmbogen* lessons I would hire myself a guide to take me up some mountains independently of the ski school. But there were no guides available. Every one was also a ski-teacher, and they were all needed in the school. The best I could find was a little boy, perhaps fourteen years old, who worked in the ski repair shop. He was permitted to take me, not up the Valluga, but up some little hill in back of the town. When we reached the summit, in less than two hours, the child told me that there was a nice run, longer and harder than the run back to Zürs, down to Lech, where we could hire a sled to pull us back home. He had been specifically instructed not to go down that way, but he knew the route. . . . Of course, I took his hint and we went that way. It was a nice run but still a pretty small affair.

In later years I have had an occasional happier contact with a ski school, particularly with the one at Franconia, New Hampshire, where Fletcher (Curly) Brown made an all-out attempt to modernize my style. But when Curly urged, 'A little more *dash*, Mrs. Underhill,' I countered with the query, 'How old is your mother?' and found, as I had suspected, that her age and mine were pretty much the same. That silenced him, as I thought it would. Curly himself is racing in the

121

Veterans' Class now and I am still skiing without any particular dash. Curly is the one who explained to me why teaching ruins a man's own skiing. 'You talk all day long about control, until by and by you begin to wonder yourself if there may be something in it—and then your skiing's ruined.'

IV. THE OBERLAND AND ZERMATT

All that time at Zürs I was plotting some schemes with Adolf Rubi, the Grindelwald guide with whom I had climbed in the summer, and who had been for two years the ski champion of Switzerland. We had discussed climbing a few peaks on skis some spring. It was a comfort to me, in this time of frustration in the Arlberg, when the Zürs school would not let me up the Valluga, to receive a letter from the ski champion of Switzerland containing the following: 'I feel sorry you find skiing so difficult, especially the törns, but you can't be worse enough that I would not take you out.'

Over in Grindelwald a bit later, Adolf, since he had never yet seen me with skis on my feet, suggested that before starting in on serious ski mountaineering we do 'a little practice run' to see if I could ski. This seemed eminently reasonable, but the little practice run he took me, a 7,000-foot descent from the Eismeer Station on the Jungfrau Railway down the glaciers to Grindelwald, would not, I feel sure, have been picked out by the Zürs Ski School as appropriate for a member of Class IV-b. Perhaps it was better luck than Adolf deserved that we got down all right. In the first place it was roped skiing, which I had never done, and in the second place, since there were only the two of us on the run that day, with no previous tracks, and since Adolf obviously had to hold the rope from behind, I was the one who threaded the route and tested the snowbridges through the short but steep icefall on the Grindelwald Fiescherfirn. But roped skiing turned out to be easier than I expected. Frankly, it's not much of a trick for the one who goes first; it's the second man, behind, doing his turns while always holding the rope at exactly the right tension, who has to be good. But since Adolf *was* good, there was no difficulty. In any case, I

122

don't believe I went at a speed that put much of a strain on him. In dealing with icefalls, crevasses and snowbridges, form is of less importance than control and a slow, cautious pace does no harm. It is the dash-and-crash skiers, on the contrary, who are more likely to get into trouble; many a snowbridge will hold up under gentle treatment but will vanish into the icy blue depths of the crevasse if you sit down on it suddenly and vigorously. It was a magnificent run all the way, beginning with the moment when, from the tunnel in the rock under the Eismeer Station that debouched on to the rock wall, we lowered ourselves, skis and sticks in our arms, down a rope to the glacier below. Here, in the cold shadow of the great wall of the Eiger, where the sun rarely if ever hits, the powder snow was unbelievably dry, fluffy and deep. Adolf mentioned casually, as we harnessed up, that if I fell down in this snow I'd never be able to get up on my skis again! As we sailed into Grindelwald, really quite early, 'Yes,' said Adolf, 'I will take you anywhere you want to go in the mountains, anywhere at all. But please don't ski around the hotel here, where people might see you.'

Avis, who had been off on some musical errand of her own, now turned up again, and with Adolf and his older brother Christian (who later became head of all the Swiss ski schools) we had a very delightful trip over the Lötschenlücke. (During this trip I had a bet on with Christian: I was to receive some substantial prize if I succeeded in pulling Adolf over. I never could.) From the Jungfraujoch to the Concordiaplatz was a pleasant run downhill; from there to the Egon von Steiger Hut, a hot climb up. The next day the weather was thick with clouds and snow and we ventured out only in the afternoon to climb the Ebnefluh in a snowstorm that was mild at the start and heavy when we got back to the hut. 'Just look at all you can't see!' remarked Avis. The following morning, too, it was still snowing, but, on two ropes of two, we went down the Lötschental anyway, catching only tantalizing glimpses of a very charming region. Starting out from the hut, Adolf remarked that he hoped Christian would not go close under the slopes of the Sattelhorn opposite, where there was danger of avalanches, because 'my brother is carrying my ice-axe.' When we got back to Scheidegg the following day, after having spent the night at Christian's house in Wengen, it was still snowing, and I find a note in my papers that there were three feet of new snow! It was on some such occasion as this that Adolf, looking out in the morning on a great accumulation of new snow, remarked, 'Either you learn the telemark in the first ten minutes, or we are stuck here until spring.' So then and there I finished up learning the telemark, and so thoroughly that I can still do it today, and frequently do. I like the turn and find it very pleasant to wander down at leisure away from the crowds on the beaten tracks. Granted that it is not a high-speed turn, I am in no particular hurry. Few who see it now know what I am doing. And as for all this fuss about not being able to do a telemark with modern bindings because they do not permit the heel of the boot to rise off the ski, why, all you have to do is simply loosen your boot lacings a bit, thus permitting the heel of your foot (which is after all the essential thing) to rise up a little inside the boot. I had supposed that this trick was known to me alone until I learned that a member of the Association of Canadian Ski Teachers (who now look a bit more kindly on the telemark), not being able to do the turn with his *longues lanières*, unlaced his boots to such an extent that one of them came off and ski and boot together sailed down the mountain. This is perhaps carrying things a bit far.

On April 10 Johnny Holden arrived. Johnny is now Commissioner of Education for the State of Vermont, but in those days he was only a Harvard graduate student looking forward, he said, to a lifetime of teaching a one-room school somewhere in rural Vermont. That winter he was studying in Germany and in this, his Easter holiday, he wanted to get in all the skiing possible. We set out to accommodate him as best we could. Five of us, Christian, Adolf, Avis, Johnny and I, skied from the Jungfraujoch down to the Place de la Concorde, as John called it, and up over the Grünhornlücke to the Finsteraarhorn Hut. The following day it was snowing, but we couldn't let that detain us. We climbed the Finsteraarhorn (14,026 feet), but only part

ABOVE: In the Lötschenlücke.

Snow falling on a village in the Lötschen Valley.

ABOVE: The Finsteraarhorn in winter. BELOW: Putting climbing skins on our skis in preparation for the ascent of the Finsteraarhorn.

of the way on skis. On the final ridge, from the Hugisattel to the summit, the weather was really very bad. We roped up for this part, with me in the lead, and John has a picture of me climbing crouched almost flat against the rocks to keep from being blown over. On the descent, on skis again, Christian carefully and properly shepherded Avis down on a rope; Adolf, who had to cope with both Johnny and me, was letting us run loose. When Christian spoke sternly to his little brother about crevasses, Adolf devised this solution: we would all three take hold of the rope behind Avis and let Christian hold the whole party if need be. From the Finsteraarhorn Hut we got back over to the Concordia Hut for the night. The next morning—how repetitious this is—it was still snowing hard. Adolf and Christian worked out a different system of roping, one more acceptable to Christian, for our trip down the Aletsch Glacier: Adolf and Christian would rope together, Adolf going first and sniffing out the route. The rest of us would follow behind exactly in their tracks, the theory being that if they got by all right without falling into a crevasse probably we could too. This scheme worked well. Once Adolf, however, who was cautiously feeling his way ahead, suddenly disappeared from sight: one moment he was there, the next moment he was not. Simultaneously Christian swung his skis sideways and leaned back on a very taut rope. So poor was the visibility in this snowstorm that Adolf had simply walked off the edge of a big block of ice some fifteen feet high.

Some guideless skiers, Swiss boys, came along behind on our tracks, but they skied so much faster than I that they were continually getting ahead of me. Adolf spoke plainly to them: they might go ahead, or they were welcome to follow behind, but they must not come between the members of our party; it was essential in this weather that we keep close together. Adolf and Christian chose the route down the glacier and over the Riederfurka, under most difficult conditions, with very great skill. Although we missed the train at Mörel, we got to Brigue that night by car; but all we could manage the next day was St Niklaus, which was as far as the Zermatt train went.

In those days Zermatt was an isolated little village in the winter and not the teeming resort it is today, with train service, open hotels, ski-lifts, and so on.

That afternoon in St Niklaus we all walked up to call on Franz Josef Biner, Bob Underhill's guide, and a good friend of all of us, in his chalet on the mountainside a few hundred feet above the village, and after dinner he walked down to return our call. St Niklaus, of course, was the home of the greatest guides in the Valais, and from there had come the largest number of renowned guides in the world. Besides Biner, Josef Knubel, several Pollingers and others dropped in to see us. It was a memorable evening. The talk ranged far and wide, over the whole world wherever there were mountains. These guides had climbed all over Europe, in the Andes, in the Himalayas.

Fortunately we were all sitting around the kitchen stove. There was no heat in the hotel except in the kitchen. The cold, dank stone walls of the bedrooms, unopened and unused all through the winter months, gave out a more penetrating chill than even the outdoors. John and I had been trifling with colds and that night in St Niklaus they really settled in for good.

Early the next morning a Seiler sleigh from Zermatt, with two beautiful dashing horses, trotted into town with a great flourish to get us. What a splendid equipage! It was a question which gleamed more brightly, the harness or the horses, who were all polished up too. We enjoyed the three-hour ride up the valley, which seemed much more adventurous than merely going up on the train, and were much impressed to find that for some distance the road had been dug out through the débris of an enormous avalanche. In Zermatt we were the only guests at the Confiserie Seiler, the tea room where all those great trays of cakes used to be laid out in the summer-time. The Confiserie was the only hotel open, but don't think for a moment that the food and service were not fully as good as they would have been at the more elaborate of the Seiler hotels. However, we did miss the orchestra.

For two days, with weather 'clearing at times', we took moderate ski tours—to the Schwarzsee, Staffelalp, etc.—but on

126

OPPOSITE and OVERLEAF: Skiing on the Boden and Gorner Glaciers, with Adolf Rubi and Simon Julen, on our way to the Bétemps Hut on Monte Rosa.

ABOVE: On the Gorner Glacier. *Photo by John Holden.* LEFT: John Holden drying his clothes at the Bétemps Hut.

the 18th we had to start for Monte Rosa, as John's time was nearly up. That first day was magnificent, brilliant with sunshine as we skied up the valley and then up the Boden and Gorner Glaciers to the Bétemps Hut. (The Gornergrat train was, of course, not running.) The snow and the slopes were so alluring that we had a lot of trouble restraining John from turning around for a little run back down now and then. My cold was not over but I had started anyway; there are very few diseases one cannot cure by a good ski trip. Unfortunately, however, this happened to be one of the few, and the next morning there was no question of my climbing the mountain; the only question was whether I should be able to get back down to Zermatt. But, shepherded patiently and competently by Simon Julen, who was just a young lad and a porter at that time, I managed to get up to Rotenboden and down the Gugel Ridge. It's curious, but fortunate, that one's muscles will continue to do the things they are used to doing, even when one's head is hardly aware of it. Back at the Confiserie Seiler in midmorning, I fell into bed and slept until the others returned from Monte Rosa the following forenoon. They reported that they had had a fine trip to the summit and down, even though they hadn't seen anything that was more than a few feet from their noses. Avis, who carried her valuables in her trousers pocket, reported that she had slid down much of the way on her letter of credit.

We now had to eat lunch quickly and make the 3.20 train at St. Niklaus. Our plan had been to ski back, since it was all downhill, but quite soon after leaving Zermatt we found that in the few days since we had come up the road had turned to mud, so that it was necessary to take off our skis and walk. Run, rather. It was not the first time, said Avis, that she had run for a train, but it was the first time she had run twelve miles for one.

V. PIZ BERNINA AND PIZ PALÜ

After a trip to Amsterdam to get my Buick, which had been stored there since the preceding summer, I reached Grindelwald again. On May 7 we—Avis, Adolf and I—left there for the Engadine. I had taught Adolf to drive the car, which was a clever move on my part since he then took over, apparently with pleasure, all the little chores—garaging, chains, greasing, tyre changing, and even added washing on his own. We now had both chauffeur and courier as well as guide, ski-teacher and friend all rolled into one. The only flaw, and a slight one, was that Adolf had no driving licence, and could not get one in a car carrying a Dutch registration, as mine did. As a citizen of Canton Bern, Adolf must take the driving examination in a car registered likewise in Canton Bern. But that did not worry me too much, since I felt that few Swiss would quibble with the ski champion of Switzerland over a driving licence; as it turned out, the question never came up, even on the afternoon when Adolf took the Pontresina policeman for a little ride. (I just hope that the statute of limitations applies in this case.)

The passes into the Engadine, all of them high, were still closed by the winter's snows, but a simple telephone call by Adolf to the station master at Preda, to the effect that Adolf Rubi wished to take his car through the Albula Tunnel, fixed everything up. At Preda a flat car was waiting for us, drawn up beside a ramp up which we backed the car, blocks of wood were adjusted under the tyres, and that's all there was to it. The train arrived, coupled our flat car on at the end—it was otherwise a passenger train—and pulled it through the tunnel to Bevers.

In Pontresina our aim was to make ski ascents of Piz Bernina (13,295 feet) and Piz Palü (12,835 feet), but we did not accomplish this without some struggle. Adolf is of the opinion that the tale of our difficulties had better, even now, be left untold (as it has been for twenty-five years) for several reasons: the practice of ski-mountaineering in the Engadine has developed so extensively in those years that what happened then could not conceivably happen today; he has many friends in the Engadine now whose feelings he would not want hurt; and (final, clinching argument) how does one ever know, says Adolf, when one may not find oneself deep down in some Engadine crevasse and need the help of the local guides to pull one up?

128

In spite of all these reasons for keeping quiet, I think twenty-five years of silence is enough. Our troubles came from the fact that ski-mountaineering was in its early stages then, and ski ascents of the Bernina and Palü looked more formidable than they do now. Then there is that widespread attitude—you can find it here and there today as well as you could in the Engadine in 1930: people often feel that there is something very special about 'their' peaks that makes them peculiarly fine and difficult, and are reluctant to admit that an outsider 'who doesn't know the way' may be able to climb them, not realizing that the mark of an expert mountaineer, guide or amateur, is such a mastery of the general principles of mountain strategy and technique that it makes little difference whether he has seen the peak before or not. Adolf was, of course, an expert of very great experience, and thoroughly capable of doing these climbs.

In the first place, the weather was bad (nobody's fault, that!). The weather had been bad for weeks in the Oberland, and we found the same situation here. Adolf and I wished that the boys in Zürich who sent out the weather forecasts would think up some new ones; we got awfully tired of seeing 'Stark bewölkt; Niederschläge' used over and over, with merely a change in date. But there was occasionally a clear morning, and in order to take advantage of it we must go to the hut in the afternoon, any afternoon, even if the weather was bad. This looked obvious to us, but not to many other people. We had engaged by telephone from Grindelwald the man Adolf considered the best Pontresina guide to make a fourth with us, but now he flatly refused to come. 'In *this* region one must have perfectly settled weather before doing big climbs.' But we still wanted a porter or a second guide even though Avis decided she would not go either; since the prevailing opinion seemed to be that Adolf and I were a pair of idiots, she felt there might be something in it. We were told that there was a law or regulation in the Engadine that one guide alone might not take a tourist on one of the big climbs. I wonder now if this was really so, considering how frequently the supposed rule was broken in the summer by outside guides. But in any case, since we thought it was true, and since it wasn't a bad idea anyway to have more than two people in the party, we tried to get a porter to go with us. Yet for a long time not a porter or a guide could we get.

We planned to climb Piz Palü first and hope for better weather later for the higher Bernina. We would go from the Diavolezza Hut, owned by the proprietor of the inn at Bernina-häuser, who, we had been told, would send a man with us to open the hut and also to accompany us on the climb. But when we got to Berninahäuser the proprietor refused definitively to allow a man to go with us; he refused to lend us a key to the hut or to permit us the use of it in any way.

Since it was then 3 o'clock on a bad, snowy afternoon, I don't think either of us really expected to climb a peak the next day anyway, but we kept on pretending that we did, and the next best bet, since the Diavolezza route was out, was to walk back to the station below, Morteratschgletscher, ski from there up to the Boval Hut (8,068 feet), which we knew was open, and aim for the Bernina. There was a company of moving-picture actors at the Boval Hut, some of whom Adolf knew, and he felt sure he would be able to persuade one of them to accompany us. At the Morteratschgletscher station-restaurant, in fact, we found some of the movie people, including a guide Lehner from Zermatt, who, not in the slightest in awe of the Bernina, said he would be delighted to go with us.

That night at the hut, which had sleeping accommodations for forty people, there were sixty-two. The hut-keeper very kindly gave me, the only woman, his private room and five blankets, which was much more than my share, while he went out and slept on the floor. (When Adolf went into the kitchen at 4 the next morning to start our breakfast there were so many people sleeping on the floor he had great difficulty in getting to the stove.)

The movie people were out that evening with magnesium-flare torches, filming a 'rescue party' among the crevasses just below the hut, and it was very beautiful and striking to watch. When they came in, Lehner reported that the movie director, not wishing to lose a good guide on such an enterprise, refused to let him go with us up the Bernina. He added, however, that there were several young Pontresina guides among the extras at the hut and we could surely get somebody. But could we? The discussion grew quite heated as the local guides told Adolf they would have nothing to do with the project, and that he himself had undoubtedly never seen such a big climb. To them the situation looked highly unreasonable: here was a 'foreign' guide, who made no secret of the fact that he had never done the Bernina, summer or winter, who obviously did not know the way, who had no crampons, who declared that he wanted a second guide merely to comply with the law and that he did not really need him. A prize piece of effrontery was that he thought he could take a woman on a climb like that. There was a fair amount of conversation on this woman question, all in Swiss-German which the other guides did not know that I understood. Tempers were getting pretty hot. The two most likely guides refused on the ground that they had no crampons, although there were many extra pairs of crampons in the hut that they presumably might have borrowed had they so wished. Adolf's remark, that he didn't think crampons would be needed on a simple snow climb like the Bernina, naturally enough enraged the Pontresina guides, and I don't know that I blame them. Finally Adolf, in an abnormally sweet and gentle tone, which I recognized as a symptom of fury, argued like this: We don't know that we can get up without crampons but we should like to go and see. We will pay you just the same. Will you come with us and try? The answer was no. This was the end of the argument. With no change in expression, completely absorbed in waxing a ski and rubbing each square centimetre intently and meticulously, Adolf spoke not a word more until the guides had moved away. In the twenty-eight years I've known him this was the only time I have ever seen the good-natured and equable Adolf really angry, but this time he definitely was. To me, with his voice almost choking, he murmured, 'I'll show them. If only the weather is half decent, I'll show them whether I can climb their Piz Bernina.' When I ventured to remind him that we still seemed to be only two people, he replied with great surprise that the solution of that problem was very simple: we would climb as friends, I paying him nothing, and as two guideless climbers (!) we should not be violating any regulation.

But then, most astonishingly, the young kitchen boy, who had been taking this all in, offered to go with us. His jobs at the hut were washing dishes, grating cheese for the macaroni, etc., but he had a guide's licence, badge, and everything. He said that of course we should not be able to climb the Piz Bernina, but that if we wanted to go out and ski around the glacier a little he would come along with us. I am sorry I cannot remember his name. He was a very pleasant lad and a splendid skier. If he wasn't quite so experienced as a mountaineer, yet he did well enough. He had done the Bernina once before in the summer and had some general notions of the route, and while on easy going he willingly took his share of breaking trail, on difficult parts he sensibly left the leading to Adolf. Naturally I shouldn't be telling this story at all if we hadn't reached the summit successfully. The weather, although never very good, was not dangerous—just a sort of April-shower weather, with clouds all day, snow the first five hours, and slight snow flurries every now and then after that. Adolf kept pointing out that it was really quite perfect, cool weather for climbing; not only were we not bothered by a hot sun beating down but at this temperature the snow was hard and crisp, the danger from avalanches nil. Cool it was without any doubt. Cool enough, at any rate, to freeze Adolf's ears. We all had woollen scarves tied around our heads, over our regular hats, and I had mine anchored with safety-pins to my beret. The whole arrangement shortly became rigid with ice, resembling a medieval helmet, but this made it an even better protection from the wind. Mine stayed in place, but Adolf's rotated a bit, opening up just a crack leading to the front of one ear and the back of the other, which then froze. I carried three pairs of truck-drivers' sheep-skin mittens, with the fur side inside; when one became damp, I put on a dry pair. It was so cool that for twelve hours we did not stop, practically speaking, except for a minute or two to

swallow a gulp of tea from a thermos and to stuff some food in
our pockets to eat on the move. We started from the Boval
Hut at 5 a.m., left our skis about 11 at the beginning of the
final rock ridge, reached the Italian summit at 11.50 and the
Swiss summit at 12.15. The last part up the narrow rock ridge
was good fun. The rocks were loaded with snow and here and
there bore beautiful curving-over cornices. Just once the mists
rolled away for a moment and we glimpsed a glorious view down
into the Tschierva Valley. I should have liked to see more, but
when it comes to mountain weather you take what you can get.
When we reached the summit, not the least jubilant member of
the party was our second guide. And his admiration for Adolf
was boundless: 'How could you, a foreign guide, do this?
Donnerwetter!' When his remarks, in Swiss-German, got
around to the woman, I thought it was my cue to tell him (in
regular German, as though my remark had no connection with
anything said before) that this was 'meine erste Tour im
Hochgebirge.' But he was not taken in.

On the descent of the snow-covered rock ridge Adolf held the
rope for the second guide and let me climb unheld. Mountain
climbers will recognize this as an unorthodox arrangement.
When we once got our skis on at the foot of the ridge our
troubles burst upon us. In the first place, the lighting was so
bad that we couldn't see what snow conditions we had to deal
with; but perhaps this was a blessing, since they were the worst
I have ever experienced, and varied abruptly from yard to yard.
And then we were skiing three people on the rope, which is
much more difficult than two. Here, for the first and only time
in all the years we climbed together, I succeeded, once, in
pulling Adolf over. At the start the snow was hard and icy,
with unexpected drifts now and then of deep, soft powder.
When we began to get used to that we met, in addition, a great
deal of breakable crust. Through this we ran with our skis
about a foot under the surface and the crust breaking against
our legs enough to slow us down. Then there were ice ridges
sticking up, crevasses, and icefalls. The main complication was
that conditions would change every few yards, invisibly, and

that brought on a good many falls. On other runs Adolf had frequently found my pace a little too slow to suit him, but here he was a marvel of patience, admitting that the snow was indeed difficult and allowing me to take my time; the only thing that mattered, he said, was not to get hurt. It took us nearly three hours to get back to the hut.

Three days later, although it was still cloudy and snowing off and on, the same three of us climbed Piz Palü, also from the Boval Hut. The snow was heavy and the conditions, although not quite so bad, were in general much like those on the Bernina.

VI. MONTE ROSA, FROM ITALY TO SWITZERLAND

From the Engadine we could so easily drop down into Italy and approach Monte Rosa from the south that it occurred to me to ski up it from that side and perhaps down into Switzerland afterwards. Adolf was delighted with this project, not only for itself alone but also because it postponed still longer the laborious job that awaited him at home, splitting shingles for the roof. Avis, who had already done Monte Rosa in April, offered to take the car through the Simplon Tunnel and meet us on the Swiss side.

The only obstacle in the way of this scheme, and it was admittedly a major one, was that at this time the Italians were refusing to permit anyone to cross their frontier except at an authorized station, manned by customs and immigration officials. The former free-and-easy wandering across international boundaries by mountain climbers was now definitely out, as far as the Italian frontier was concerned. Troops, the picturesque *bersaglieri* with the coq feathers on their hats, were stationed in mountain villages along the frontier, keeping an eye on the mountains. There had been incidents of climbers being arrested or even fired at by these guards. If we were to cross the boundary from Italy to Switzerland over the Pennine Alps there might be trouble.

I wrote, therefore, to my old friend, Guido Rivetti, one of Italy's foremost mountaineers, whom I had first met at the

Charmoz-Grépon Col when Alice Damesme and I were making our manless traverse of the Grépon, to ask if he could get us special permission to cross the frontier as well as send us advice on the best route. Should we, for instance, start from Alagna? His answer to my letter came back almost at once. The Alagna route might be subject to avalanche danger at this time of year. He advised starting from Gressoney-la-Trinité, spending the night at the Capanna Gnifetti, and from there crossing the Lysjoch and approaching the Margherita Hut on the Signal-kuppe from the Swiss side. But the most important part of the plans: we must come through Biella and visit him on the way. In addition, he felt confident he could get us permission to cross the frontier and would set about it at once.

The drive from Pontresina to Biella that May day stands out as one of the most beautiful I have ever enjoyed. It was winter when we started over the Maloja Pass where the snow-draped evergreens rose above the white shores of the still-frozen lakes. Adolf particularly enjoyed driving the Buick down the nine-teen hairpin curves below the pass, in what he alleged to be a splendid series of linked telemarks. We had planned not to have Adolf driving when we reached the frontier, but it was always difficult to get him out of the driver's seat and, since whenever asked, he 'thought' the frontier was still far away, it turned out that he was still piloting the car when we pulled up at the barrier. But we needn't have worried. The frontier guards had seen him jump when he won the Swiss ski championship and no courtesy was too great for our party.

Although it had been winter in the morning, as we dropped down into Italy the snow disappeared and the earliest spring flowers began to peek through the brown earth. As we lost elevation the season advanced with a breathless rush and soon we were in the midst of a midsummer riot of flowers. We lunched outdoors at Menaggio, on the shore of Lake Como, on a terrace surrounded by a magnificent and fragrant profusion of roses.

The autostrada from Como to Sesto Calende on Lake Mag-giore, a road with no intersections, no speed limit and none of

135

the animals—donkeys, cows and hens—which make the most baffling obstacles on the ordinary Italian roads, allowed us to travel at a higher speed than our car was accustomed to. Inevitably, I suppose, we overheated the engine and I had to telephone to the Rivettis to say that we might be a little late to dinner.

Never have there been more charming hosts or more hospitable ones than the Rivettis. Everything was done to welcome us and to facilitate our trip. At dinner a maid whispered to Mr Rivetti, who turned to me and asked for my car keys. As I handed them over, I apologized for having left the car in some inconvenient position. But when the time came to go, I found that the chauffeur had put the car in perfect condition, so that we had no further trouble with it. And not only mechanically, but æsthetically. It was as clean and polished, the engine and all, as if it had just come off the assembly line. Mr Rivetti informed us, too, as if it were a simple matter of course, that his cook would prepare the provisions for our trip. But this we did not allow.

It was a disturbing circumstance that, contrary to his expectations, he had not been able to obtain for us permission to cross the frontier. The friend whom he had consulted on this matter, however, had dropped a hint that seemed to him significant, namely, that if the frontier guards did not ask where we were going, we need not volunteer any information. The Rivettis advised our going ahead anyway; they thought things might work out all right. Although this seemed to me like a tenuous assurance, it turned out that Mr Rivetti understood his compatriots better than I did. Things did work out. The frontier guards tried hard, and successfully, to overlook us. That next evening at the little hotel at Gressoney-la-Trinité several of the *bersaglieri* sat around talking with Adolf on every subject under the sun except the most obvious one: where were we going on our ski trip? I feel sure they knew our plans as well as we did and no doubt enjoyed immensely the game of keeping out of sight the next morning when we started out. We never caught even a glimpse of a coq feather any-

136

where as we walked up through the village and into the mountains.

Gressoney was at that season just about at the crocus line, with half the ground covered by melting snowbanks and half by the first flowers. Fifteen minutes above the hotel, however, we could put on our skis and we had them on for a very long and tiring time. For from Gressoney-la-Trinité (5,338 feet) to the Capanna Gnifetti (11,965 feet) is a climb of nearly 7,000 feet, which we carried out in the hottest weather I have ever skied in. On that gorgeous, cloudless day the burning Italian sun beat down, not a breath of air stirred, and the wet snow piled up on our skis. I packed snow inside my hat, which not only insulated my head from the scorching sun but, in melting, ran down my neck in pleasant cool little rivulets. I began to think that there was a good deal to be said for climbing in bad weather after all.

I saw little of Adolf, who was usually far ahead. But once I came upon him sound asleep on a big flat rock. Sneaking quietly by, I should have liked to go on up to the hut and leave him there, but I soon saw him pounding up after me. The scenery was magnificent and all this Italian side of Monte Rosa was then new to me. On the last part of the climb we had glorious views of the Vincent Pyramide ahead and the Lyskamm off to the left.

We reached the Capanna Gnifetti at 3.15 and found it more than half buried in snow. From the back, indeed, the snow-drifts projected over the roof. However, the front door was free and we could get in. We had taken an Italian porter with us, since we had a great deal to carry, food and wood for three days, as well as our regular climbing and skiing equipment. Our ambitious programme, which we were not to carry out, was to go the second day over the Lysjoch to the Dufourspitze (15,217 feet), the highest summit of Monte Rosa, and return for the night to the Capanna Margherita, a hut of the Italian Alpine Club built directly on the summit of the Signalkuppe (14,964 feet). A single room, the kitchen, of the large hut was left unlocked in the winter. The third day we would climb the Lyskamm and go down to the Bétemps Hut on the Swiss side.

137

The next morning we were up at four and rejoicing in what appeared to be, through the window, another perfect day. But on starting out we encountered one of the most violent and bitter winds I have ever experienced. It did not take us long to turn and hurry back to the hut. Every hour or two we put our heads tentatively out of the door and quickly drew them in again. We raged, of course, at this wasting of a clear day. But the wind was so overwhelming that we finally realized we should have to give up our climb and spend the day at the hut. We had plenty of food, but oh, how we suffered from the cold! Although I had on all the clothes possible—and that was a good many—and blankets wrapped around me besides, I was numb with cold, and my whole outlook on life became bleak. The porter just sat there and shivered violently. There was no wood available for purchase in this hut, as there usually is in Swiss huts, and the wood we had carried up had been calculated very closely—just enough to cook the necessary meals, and not a splinter left over for heating. Now, Adolf is an enterprising chap, and he was cold too. When I detected his eye wandering around speculatively over the furnishings of the hut, I understood.

'If you'd like to burn up a chair or something, I should be willing to pay for it,' I suggested.

I didn't have to say this twice. Adolf sprang up and, followed around by the scandalized porter, who was begging him not to commit this depredation, made a purposeful survey of the combustible material. The porch railing seemed to be the wood that would give us the most heat for the least damage. When Adolf's decision had been made the porter offered, on condition that we would promise not to tell he had been with us, to divulge where the hut-keeper kept his private supply of wood. Following the porter's directions, Adolf prized out a few nails and came upon a good lot of logs. To atone for this burglary, I asked the porter for the name of the hut-keeper (Giovanni Anselmo Nacer, Alagna, Valsesia), and a few days later sent him an explanatory letter and a money order. I sent him a bit more than wood probably sold for down in the valley, on the chance that he (and not a mule) might have carried it up there on his back. (And then it is a nice question, ethically, whether one shouldn't pay somewhat more for things one steals than for those one merely buys.) I received in return a very cordial letter of thanks from the hut-keeper. Adolf nailed the place up again just as it was before and I shall not reveal even here where it was!

How everybody cheered up as soon as there was a fire going! By noon we had had four hot dishes, had dried our socks in the oven, and I had washed my hands in warm water, as pleasant a pastime as I know when there is nothing else to do. About two Adolf and I unfolded the blankets again and settled down for a nap. Hardly had we got to sleep when the porter woke us up to say that the wind had died down and wasn't it a pity it was too late? To start up Monte Rosa at 3.05 in the afternoon is not the usual custom, but that is what we did. All too soon we found that the porter's assertion that the wind had died down was one of the grossest of exaggerations; we had a frightful wind all the way. And then, too, the snow surface had been scoured by the wind to such an extent that there was nothing left but hard ice, which not only offered the sealskins no grip, but cut the webbing straps that held them on; two of my straps were worn all the way through. Still, whenever I tried walking without skis (which worried Adolf—I was going to fall into a crevasse, surely) I would come upon a patch of powder snow where I had to put the skis on again. I must have had my skis off and on half a dozen times that first two hours up to the Lysjoch. But our first view over the other side, a glorious sight if ever there was one, was ample recompense for all our struggles to get there. The Dent Blanche rose up magnificent above the intervening glaciers and, spread out to its right, stood those other Zermatt giants, the Gabelhorn, Rothorn, and Weisshorn. We drank in all this beauty—for a moment, until we had to turn aside to breathe; the wind was coming from that direction.

We were now, at 5 p.m., a little less than halfway, in time, to our new destination, the Margherita Hut on the Signalkuppe.

It was then that Adolf said we could not go any farther; the porter did not have adequate clothing and was suffering too much from the cold. Of course, I agreed that we should return at once to the Capanna Gnifetti. But since the porter wouldn't hear of this, insisting that he could make the Signalkuppe all right, Adolf took off some of his own clothes, which he made the porter put on, and we proceeded. Once over the other side of the Lysjoch the wind was, in fact, a little less violent for a while, as we skirted along under the Ludwigshöhe and the Parrotspitze. But as we got higher it resumed its full force, and never shall I forget that last hour up to the Margherita Hut.

'Follow in our tracks,' Adolf said to me. 'We'll go ahead. I'd like to get things ready in the hut before dark. We'll have hot tea waiting for you. . . . Come along, Arturo.'

But the porter stood still, aghast.

'You can't leave a lady alone in a place like this!' he gasped. This was the second time today that Adolf had scandalized him, but this time was worse. Why not? inquired Adolf. There was no danger here. No crevasses and no steep drops. She would come along all right.

It was only when I, laughing, assured the porter that I didn't mind, that he consented to go off with Adolf. And really I didn't mind. I liked the idea of hot tea waiting up there. It made it seem possible to put forth my last ounce of strength to advance another step or two, whenever I could get enough breath to do it with. The wind was the trouble. The high elevation, too, of course, but the violent wind seemed to blow away what little oxygen there was! Of course, I could not breathe when I faced the wind. Neither could I breathe with my back turned towards it, since the wind swept by with such force that it seemed to create a vacuum in front of my face and I felt suffocated at once. Only by turning my head to the side, just the right amount, could I get any air at all.

At the foot of the last little steep pitch below the hut I left my skis where I found four others stuck in the snow and followed up a line of steps cut in the ice, crouching close to the

140

slope as I went to avoid, quite literally, being blown off. I
don't mind admitting that it took a good deal of will-power for
me to make that hut. Resolutely I kept my thoughts fixed on
the shelter I should find there, the warmth and the good hot
tea.

But the reality, when I got inside the hut, was quite different. No tea, no fire even, nothing but bitter, acrid smoke.

At some earlier time the outer door of the hut had been
completely torn off and a hole smashed in the inner door. Snow
had then blown in to a depth of about three feet all over the
room except on the left side, where it filled completely the space
to the roof. This, we discovered later, was where the bunks
were, with the blankets piled on them. In the far right-hand
corner of the room a stovepipe rose up out of the drifts, providing a good clue as to where to start digging first. Adolf and
the porter, who had been there some time, were valiantly working away in this dense and suffocating smoke. With ice-axes
and a frying-pan they had dug down to the firebox but their
best efforts could not get a fire to burn.

It was 7.30 at night, too late to go back down, no matter
what; we had to spend the night right there. For the next
hour and a half I would stay in the hut, choking and gasping,
with the tears coursing down my cheeks, as long as I could
stand it. Then I would stumble outside, gulp down a breath
or two of fresh air, feel the wind, and hurry back in again. At
length Adolf, having discovered that the stovepipe was filled
solid with ice and that there the trouble lay, climbed up on the
roof, took the pipe down inside the hut and then apart, chopped
the ice out of the individual sections, and reassembled the
whole thing. The hut is built on the very summit of the
Signalkuppe, and while the side we had come up is relatively
gentle, the other side is not, being one of the most magnificent
precipices in Europe. It made me more than a little uneasy to
see Adolf, unroped, working up on that sloping, icy roof. I'm
not always so squeamish about heights, but one slip there
might well have landed him many thousands of feet below.

Although there was, indubitably, a serious amount of real

141

physical discomfort, how could I keep my mind on it in a *mise en scène* of such stupendous beauty? The magnificence of the sunset was beyond words. The valleys below, the Zermatt valley, the Zmutt, and countless others beyond, were filled with a soft, cottony sea of clouds, with only mountains rising above. Miles on miles of mountains we could see, in a complete circle, and everything, valley clouds and snowy mountain peaks, was lighted with the most gorgeous and glowing sunset colours. There is something about height itself that elates me and here we were high—higher than the summit of the Matterhorn to the west, higher than anything else in Europe except the other summits of Monte Rosa right at hand and Mont Blanc more than fifty miles away, which rose up distinct and imposing in the clear transparent air. In spite of cold, wind and smoke, I was gloriously happy to be there!

At 9.30 we had our hot tea. Then we had a fine, nourishing soup which Adolf whipped up out of snow, bouillon cubes, sticks of Maggi powdered soup, beaten-up eggs, and lots of butter, everything in the rucksacks, it seemed to me, except the ski wax. After that I was all ready for a good night's sleep and did in fact doze off with my feet up on the stove. Adolf woke me; he had dug some of the blankets out of the snow where they had been lying for nobody knows how many months. My bed was to be on the table drawn up next to the stove, while he and the porter would sleep on the floor in a sort of lake region between the stove and the wall. The porter in any case had to sit up with his back against the wall. After the stovepipe incident he had pretty well collapsed. His heart was bothering him a great deal and he could not get his breath, could not lie down, could not drink the tea or eat the soup. Of course, he could not sleep.

From then on, everything was done by the cheerful young Adolf. As far as I could see, he was bustling around all night long. For one thing, he kept the fire going. We could find no axe in the hut, but all the wood, the stolen wood that we had brought along from the Capanna Gnifetti, was in two great chunks. With a jack-knife Adolf carved a wedge of wood,

142

made a small crack with an ice-axe at the point in the chunk where he wanted it to split, and then, with the side of the ice-axe, pounded in the wedge. In this way he split the wood into fine enough pieces to keep a minute fire going all night. But it takes a long while to do it that way! And even with this continuous fire, it was only very close to the stove that the snow melted at all; around the periphery of the room the snowbanks were still crisp and hard even when we left the next day. And in a way that was a convenience. Usually in these high mountain huts you have to go outdoors for the snow you need to melt into water; here the cook could reach out and get all the snow he wanted without taking a step away from the stove.

Those blankets! Stiff and rigid at first, they had seemed dry enough, like the slabs of solid ice they were. It was only as the night wore on and my body heat had softened them up a bit that I realized how much water they held.

Although the situation may sound grim, a lot of jokes were flying around the hut that night. Except for our natural concern over the porter, Adolf and I were having a gay good time.

At four in the morning Adolf made tea again and this time the porter was able to drink some, highly sugared. This made a big improvement in his condition. He was now able to contribute his share to the conversation, but on one subject only: the dire results of spending the night at such a fearful altitude. There had to be, he told us for one thing, three hut-keepers for the Margherita Hut when it was kept open for mountain climbers in the summer season, instead of one as usual. These men took turns staying there a few days at a time, since one man could not long endure at such an altitude. (It seems to me that Himalayan climbers have pretty thoroughly disproved this theory of the porter's. After all, we were only about 15,000 feet high.) One of the hut-keepers recently, the porter went on, had sat down at the table to write a postcard, the same table where I was lying, and died. They found him a day or two later. After this cheerful 'four o'clock tea' the porter at last dozed off for the first time in twenty-four hours. I could hear his breathing, very loud and exactly twice as fast as mine. I got a little sleep too—in my experience the only hindrance to sleeping at 15,000 feet is companions who make too much noise—but only for half an hour. Adolf woke me then to see the sunrise, like the sunset of the night before one of the finest experiences of my life. I even went outdoors in the nippy air to see more of it. There was not a cloud or a bit of mist anywhere in the extraordinarily lucid air over the (literally) thousands of square miles we could see: all Switzerland and parts of France, Germany and Austria. And beyond the Alps, to the south, lay the Italian Lakes and the plains of Italy as clear-cut as if they had been at our feet. The light was different from that of the night before, more fresh and golden, with tones of salmon-pink and apricot.

After that I could have gone to sleep again easily enough, but Adolf, who had slept practically not at all, was up for good and wanted to talk plans. To the north of us, along the ridge forming the frontier between Switzerland and Italy, rose those other summits of the big Monte Rosa massif, the Zumstein-spitze, the Grenzgipfel and the Nordend; on a subsidiary ridge running west from the Grenzgipfel into Switzerland rose the Dufourspitze, the highest, which is also the most lofty point in Switzerland. To the south of us the next large mountain was the Lyskamm. Which would I rather climb, inquired Adolf, the Dufourspitze or the Lyskamm? Or we might perhaps, he went on, go over to the Dufourspitze that morning, come back to the Margherita Hut for lunch, and in the afternoon do the Lyskamm and then ski down to the Bétemps Hut in Switzerland. But it would be long. We should have to carry our skis part of the way. And I, moreover, would have to carry mine, since the porter was not well enough to come with us. Should we try it? Although this programme naturally tempted me, I believe I was wiser to decide that one mountain would be enough, and of the two I preferred the Dufourspitze. We would do the Lyskamm another time (and so we did, in 1953).

At 6.45 we started, leaving the porter, who seemed to be

ABOVE: The Capanna Gnifetti, on the Italian side of Monte Rosa, and
BELOW: the Margherita Hut on the summit of the Signalkuppe.

Four summits of Monte Rosa; ABOVE, LEFT: the Zumsteinspitze, ABOVE, RIGHT: the Grenzgipfel and Dufourspitze, with our route of ascent marked, OPPOSITE, LEFT: near the top of Dufourspitze, OPPOSITE, RIGHT: the Nord-end.

ABOVE: Adolf beside a crevasse on the Boden Glacier on our descent of Monte Rosa. LEFT: The Grenz Glacier on the Zermatt side of Monte Rosa, down which our route of descent lay.

much improved in health, at the hut. Arturo, seriously concerned, did all he could to dissuade us: it wasn't possible, he said, to traverse that ridge to the Dufourspitze at this time of year; except in midsummer, the Signalkuppe was considered the summit of Monte Rosa; moreover, we could not possibly do that trip at any season of the year without crampons. This mention of crampons reminded us of the scene in the Boval Hut, and we exchanged glances. We still had not carried crampons. They were somewhat heavier in those days than they are now and, added to everything else we had to carry, it seemed just too much weight.

It was a perfect trip, every minute of it. The weather was marvellous, sunny and cold but not unendurably cold, and the fairish wind was not strong enough to bother us much. At least, it did not seem remarkable after the wind of the day before. We skied to the summit of the Zumsteinspitze, left our skis standing up in the snow there, and proceeded on foot along the narrow ridge, which was equipped with some striking cornices, over to the Grenzgipfel and the Dufourspitze. There aren't adjectives enough to describe the scenery, particularly the view down the stupendous Italian side of this great wall. The Marinelli Couloir, in particular, was a most sinister-looking ice-sheathed gash, how many thousands of feet long I do not know. There was, I admit, a good deal of dry powder snow with ice underneath, on the rocks, where we might indeed have found crampons useful. But they were far from essential. Our ski boots had a few nails in them and we could always cut steps when necessary. We spent a long time on the summit, part of it studying the Grenz Glacier that we were planning to descend, and part just revelling in the surroundings.

At 10.15 we were back below the hut, where the astonished and admiring porter was waiting for us. He was a really nice lad, and had done a fine piece of work under great difficulties with never a word of complaint. It was not his fault that the conditions had knocked him out a bit. He insisted that he was now quite all right and could safely ski down to Italy alone from the Lysjoch, where we parted. We arranged that he should telegraph us when he arrived home (which he subsequently did) and, sitting in the sun, we watched him as long as he was visible, a little black speck far below.

'I think he has passed the crevasses now,' said Adolf. Then we turned to our own descent into Switzerland, the most magnificent ski run I have ever taken. The weather was perfect; the snow was perfect. And from the summit to Zermatt was a drop of 10,000 feet. Near the top, although the snow was hard, the surface held the skis well enough. Lower down it changed into real spring snow with just the thinnest top layer melted, and it was all very, very fast. How exhilarating it was to sail back and forth across the Grenz Glacier! Quite low, where the crevasses became more numerous and the snowbridges perhaps less reliable, we roped.

'It is not really necessary,' said Adolf, 'but if anything should happen and they found us not roped, what would people say?'

At the Bétemps Hut we stopped for a long and leisurely lunch. In April Adolf had left some provisions here, marked with his name, and we had thought that, if they were still here, we might spend the night and go out the next day over the Adler Pass to Saas Fee. But the food was gone. We didn't care much; it would be a fine run down to Zermatt too.

We went down the Gorner and Boden Glaciers as Adolf had done with Avis and John in April. But a month, from April to May, does a great deal to soften up the snow-cover on a glacier as low as the Boden. As we skied by, snowbridges fell in and crevasses opened up. I would hear rumbling noises and look back to see caverns where our ski tracks had been a moment before. Naturally we were roped here and it was cheering to find that it takes a little time for snow to fall in after it has been disturbed; if you are skiing at a reasonable rate, you can get by first. The only essential is: no falling.

But our descent through the icefall was really an extraordinary experience. We were in gales of laughter at the rock-climbing acrobatics we had to go through, sometimes on skis and sometimes carrying them in our arms, to work our way down through this one. What astonished me more than once

146

(as Adolf held the rope from above) was that weak-looking and hole-pierced snow, in a snowbridge sagging down into its crevasse, will actually hold skis if it doesn't have to hold them for long. There was one fairly large crevasse where the snowbridge had fallen in about six to eight feet, the downhill edge lying against the ice wall of the crevasse some ten feet below the surface of the glacier. I picked a course through here pretty gingerly, with blobs of snow falling away from under my skis, revealing great dark holes. Although of course I knew that if all the snow fell away from under the skis, Adolf was ready to hold me securely on the rope, I didn't particularly relish the prospect. I finally reached the ice wall on the farther side where, standing on the most insubstantial scraps of snow adhering to the ice, I had to get my skis off and the ice-axe out of my rucksack, and then, with skis and sticks in my arms, cut a half-dozen steps up to the level of the glacier again.

We could not ski quite into the village of Zermatt. In the suburbs we had to remove our skis and walk down the paths, surrounded by beautiful flowers in such a hurry to spring up that they were even pushing through the thin edges of the retreating snowbanks. We met an old peasant with a beautiful white beard who naturally, on meeting two strangers coming into town like this, wanted to know where we had come from. When Adolf told him, he shook his finger in Adolf's face and pronounced solemnly, 'Du bist ein böser Knabe!' I suppose he was thinking of that frontier.

The only hotel open in Zermatt at this time was the Buffet de la Gare, which had a few bedrooms upstairs, and we could go over to the Hotel Victoria opposite for baths. There were five other guests, botanists from England, who had come out for the early spring flowers, and who very cordially moved over and made room for Adolf and me too around the stove. They had all been taking walks, to the Gorges, and some had even been up to Findelen. Had we been walking, too? Yes, we replied, we had come in from Italy over Monte Rosa. We neither of us knew then—and I, for one, didn't happen to find

147

out for some years—that this particular traverse had not been done on skis before.

But after this trip my passport was never right. Whenever you crossed the Italian border you got a stamp, 'Entrata' or 'Uscita', on the page bearing the Italian visa. Each time I went into Italy or out again, after that, I wondered if some astute immigration officer would discover that these stamps did not match; that it seemed that I had been into Italy twice and out once, into Switzerland once and out twice, and so on. Although nobody in fact ever noticed it, I was just as happy when that passport expired and I could start over again with a new one.

VII

Manless Climbing

I. THE GRÉPON

Very early I realized that the person who invariably climbs behind a good leader, guide or amateur, may never really learn mountaineering at all and in any case enjoys only a part of all the varied delights and rewards of climbing. He has, of course, the glorious mountain scenery, the exhilaration of physical acrobatics, the pleasure that comes from the exercise of skill, and these acrobatics often require skill to a considerable degree. But he is, after all, only following.

The one who goes up first on the rope has even more fun, as he solves the immediate problems of technique, tactics and strategy as they occur. And if he is, as he usually is, also the leader, the one who carries the responsibility for the expedition, he tastes the supreme joys. For mountaineering is a sport which has a considerable intellectual component. It takes judgment to supply the ideas, to make wise and proper decisions on the route, the weather, the possibility of danger from stone-fall, avalanche, concealed crevasse, etc., and above all, to know what one's own capabilities permit. This exercise of proper judgment is of more consequence than in most sports, for mountaineering (like lion-hunting or white-water canoeing!) is a game with a real and sometimes drastic penalty for failure. You don't have merely to pretend that it is important to play the game well.

I saw no reason why women, *ipso facto*, should be incapable of leading a good climb. They had, as a matter of fact, already done so, on some few scattered occasions. But why not make it

149

a regular thing, on the usual climbs of the day? Henry de Ségogne went to some pains to explain to me why a woman could never lead a climb. There is a lot more to leading, said Henry, than first meets the eye, a lot that must be learned, and that is best learned by watching competent leaders attentively and coming to understand their decisions. Women, however, never bother to do this. Since they know that they will never be allowed to lead anyway, they just come walking along behind, looking at the scenery. Therefore, even if they were given an opportunity to lead, they would be completely unprepared. I didn't find this argument too convincing, but I did realize that if women were really to lead, that is, to take the entire responsibility for the climb, there couldn't be any man at all in the party. For back in the 1920's women were perhaps a bit more sheltered than they are today. And in any emergency, particularly in an outdoor sport like mountaineering, what man wouldn't spring to the front and take over? I decided to try some climbs not only guideless but manless.

The first step along this path was to learn to lead the rope, with a competent man behind. Early in 1927 in the Dolomites I had done a little leading where the going was pretty easy, although it did worry dear old Antonio almost intolerably. With Angelo I could lead all I liked, just so long as we were out of sight of his father, but the places I went with Angelo were almost invariably too difficult for me to go up without the security of a rope from above. For it does make a difference! You need a much greater margin of safety when you are leading; with a rope from above that would hold you if things got too tough for your ability, you can launch out on pitches much nearer your limit.* Later in the summer of 1927 I laid plans to lead the Grépon at Chamonix and my guide Alfred Couttet agreed to come along as second man. I took this decision late in the season and the weather was never favourable for the

* Either a rope from above, or with your rope running through a nearby piton in the modern manner, which often amounts fundamentally to the same thing. The essential point is that there should be some arrangement that will prevent your being killed if you fall off.

150

attempt. The next year, however, I did lead the Grépon, taking with me the porter Georges Cachat.

The Grépon now, in these days of improved technique and equipment and thereby higher standards of difficulty, does not count for so much as it used to. Even in those days many longer and much harder climbs had been done. But it was at that time among the most renowned of the Chamonix Aiguilles, having for many past years enjoyed the reputation of being one of the finest rock-climbs in the Alps, and it was still a climb that not all the licensed Chamonix guides could lead. On September 8, 1928, Georges Cachat and I traversed the Grépon with me in the lead. Everything went well. Although not attempting to hurry, we were on the summit a little after 10 and back at the Montenvers at 1.15—good average time for a competent party. That was on a Saturday. Early Sunday morning, asleep in my bed at the Hotel des Alpes in Chamonix, I was awakened by a congratulatory cablegram from my mother back home in Dedham, Massachusetts. Black Magic! I could think of no other way she could have learned about this. It developed however that Black Magic had been helped out by the machinations of the Associated Press.

But I still wanted to do the Grépon really manless.

The next season, having found out that leading was simpler than it had looked from a distance, I turned to real manless climbing. In spite of Dean Peabody's later observation that it must have been hard to find a woman who was 'strong physically and weak mentally', I had many women friends who were excellent climbers and I was able to persuade some of them to go with me.

My first manless climb was an ascent of the Aiguille du Peigne with Winifred Marples on August 14, 1929. The Peigne, shorter and easier than the Grépon, still presents the same type of climbing up its bold, precipitous walls of good, firm Chamonix granite. We spent the night before our climb at the little chalet of Plan de l'Aiguille, just under the Peigne. That evening we walked out a little to look over the route we should have to take the next morning, while it was still dark, up across the grassy

151

alplands and rocky moraines, towards the peak. That's something you never worry about when you go with a guide, but before each manless climb I always scouted the start of the route. It would be entirely possible, and embarrassing, I think, to get lost leaving the hut.

The ascent of the Peigne went off well, and three days later, August 17, Alice Damesme and I made the first manless traverse of the Grépon. Starting from the Montenvers at 2.35 a.m., in three hours we had reached the Rognon des Nantillons, a rocky promontory emerging from the lower end of the Glacier des Nantillons. This was the standard breakfast spot and here we joined several other caravans bound for the various peaks above. Naturally, on an occasion like this, everyone chats a bit about their various projects and when, under questioning, it developed that Alice and I planned to do the Grépon it caused some commotion.

'Vous deux seules?' was the incredulous exclamation.

They were too courteous to laugh at us outright, but we did intercept quite a lot of sideways glances and barely-concealed smiles. Alice and I pretended not to notice. Breakfast over, the other parties all held back and allowed us to lead off up the glacier and over the bergschrund to the rocks below the Charmoz-Grépon Col, that depression between the Charmoz to the north and the Grépon to the south. The present-day route varies in some minor points, but we followed of course the route of 1929. The weather was none too good, with a lot of clouds and mist. Still, the only party actually coming down was Bradford Washburn's movie crew, who had decided that there would be no sun for pictures that day.

The bergschrund really did give us quite a lot of trouble but we couldn't waste much time on it with that large and rapidly-growing audience below. Finally we crossed under a big boulder and then squirmed up a steep narrow crack between the boulder and the ice, clawing away with our axes for holds on the outside of the ice wall. Above the bergschrund we started up easy, half-familiar rocks but soon we felt sure we were going much too far to the left. There was mist all around us and we

ABOVE: A general view of the Grépon. BELOW: With Alice Damesme, at left, on a terrace of the Grépon after the first manless ascent. *Photo by Guido Alberto Rivetti.*

Robert climbing the Mummery Crack.
Photos by John Holden.

could see very little. The routes to the Charmoz and the Grépon diverged about here and we might well be on our way to the Charmoz. We wouldn't have asked directions of any of those men for the world! We were playing a game and we must abide by the rules: no help from men! With a few rapid, surreptitious whispers we took our decision: we would go right ahead with feigned assurance, and if we later found ourselves on the Charmoz we would traverse both peaks and pretend that was what we had meant to do all along. (I believe we might have done it, too!) But later we found a way to edge over to the right and get near the proper couloir. It was not the usual route. As we approached the col, still on the north bank of the couloir, the rocks were steep, icy and loose. When the porter Alfred Burnet, who was already at the col, first saw us through the mist, he excitedly shouted that he would throw us down a rope. We declined with thanks this superfluous rescue.

As we got still nearer the col along came Armand Charlet with Guido Alberto Rivetti of Biella, Italy, whom we met there for the first time. They had come over the Charmoz, bound for the Grépon, and we took it for granted, since they had reached the col first, that they would go right along up the Grépon ahead of us. We were a little disappointed since we had hoped to be the first to climb the Mummery Crack. Perhaps Armand realized this, and it reinforced his decision.

'We will have lunch here, Monsieur,' said he, casually, as he sat down.

Guido Rivetti looked astounded, as well he might. It was no time for lunch, and hardly a suitable place for it, either. And such a suggestion to come from that speed demon Armand! But he caught on at once: something was about to happen here that Armand wanted to watch.

The summit ridge of the Grépon, as almost every mountain climber knows, resembles a crenelated wall, approximately horizontal, with five or six great spires or pinnacles. The traverse of the Grépon consists in reaching this ridge at its north end and climbing over and around the pinnacles to the south, where one descends to the Col des Nantillons. On the west side the sheer granite wall drops in one sweep 1,500 feet to the upper reaches of the Glacier des Nantillons; on the east, nearly 5,000 feet to the Mer de Glace. To attain the ridge in the first place, from the Charmoz-Grépon Col, it is necessary to tackle what was one of the most famous climbing problems of the day, the Mummery Crack. The wall of the Grépon rising above the col is unbroken except for a narrow crack between the main wall of granite and a half-detached slab that lies against it, the Mummery Crack. It does not lead directly from the col, but starts somewhat off to the side, above the precipice to the west. This narrow crack is climbed by a caterpillar motion. You jam in the right hand and the right foot, and raise them alternately, first supporting your weight on your foot and working your hand higher, then holding everything on your jammed fist and again wedging the foot a little above. The left hand feels over the outside of the slab clinging, as Mummery says of another of his climbs, 'to slight discolorations in the rock'. There is not much for the left foot to do. All this takes place pretty far up in the air. Not only is the crack itself sixty feet high, but there is nothing below its base to break the view for another thousand feet. The second man, assuring the rope from a little notch just above the col at the side, would not be of much use if you once started bounding down the cliffs below the crack. Climbers have fallen out of the Mummery Crack but no leader has ever fallen from near the top of it and lived! The ascent of this crack is easier if you stay well outside and insert your hand and foot just a short distance. But the exposure is so great that there is an unconscious urge to jam yourself inside the crack as far as possible. This leads to tense and rigid muscles and is the shortest route to getting stuck and having a serious struggle. The key to an easy ascent of the Mummery Crack is complete relaxation.

Alice and I changed our boots for light climbing shoes. There was no question of who should lead: I had already had that pleasure; it was Alice's turn. When I was firmly installed at the little notch above the col where the second man does what he can to belay the rope for the leader, Alice started off in a matter-of-fact way although there was around us an atmosphere of some tenseness and excitement. Nowadays climbers, starting from the col, reach the midpoint of the crack by a traverse on small holds and a couple of pitons, but then it was the custom, at least for the leader, to climb the whole crack from the bottom. To reach this base of the crack it was necessary to descend 45–50 feet from the notch. The rocks 'in the couloir here were icy and loose, and Alice dislodged quite a sizeable one. Considering that several parties were already congregated at the col, we were surprised to hear a vehement outcry from two more still in the couloir below, as they heard this rock bounding down towards them. They successfully took shelter.

'Are you up the Mummery Crack?' shouted Maurice Damesme, Alice's husband, who was traversing the Charmoz that day with Winifred Marples and René Picard, and who could not see us for the mist.

'Almost,' cheerfully replied Alice, who had not yet reached its base.

At the bottom of the crack Alice left her rucksack and started up. The take-off is a difficult pitch, not vertical but overhanging for about the first eight to ten feet, so that Alice was leaning backwards as she tried to pull herself up the smooth rock. She did not get it instantaneously, but soon she did, and was climbing upward smoothly and confidently. It was, as might have been expected, the performance of a real expert.

'Dîtes donc!' shouted the boys down below in the couloir. 'Is it safe to come out now?'

Alice stopped short just where she was and called down to them the most ardent apologies.

'Toutes mes excuses. . . .'

This indeed testified to a poise and sangfroid quite out of the ordinary!

The boys poked their heads out from behind their rock and I was immensely amused to watch the expressions on their faces when they saw where Alice was, and that there was no one above her. In reply to her apologies they stumblingly assured her that it was indeed a pleasure and an honour to have rocks knocked on you by a lady who . . . Still, they couldn't quite believe it.

About this time it occurred to me that even though the day was cloudy I should like to have a picture; my camera, however, was some six feet away. Alice offered to wait until I got it. Never mind, Armand was bringing it to me. As I accepted the camera from him I realized that this was our first deviation from the manless principle!

Midway up the crack an outward-sloping shelf affords a welcome rest. From there on, although the crack is somewhat wider and the angle eases off a little from the vertical, still this second thirty feet continues to be laborious and fatiguing, particularly for the climber who has climbed the entire sixty feet. When Alice reached the top, the watching crowd broke into enthusiastic and well-deserved cheers.

Then in my turn I went down the couloir to the base of the crack, and for the first time realized that our two rucksacks should have been pulled up from the notch on the side, and not all the way from the bottom. It was no easy job for Alice to haul these things up sixty feet with our nailed boots and other heavy gear inside.

When I had led the Mummery Crack the preceding year it had seemed to me surprisingly easy and I was astonished this time to find it had once again become much more laborious. There is indubitably a stimulation to going up first, it seems to me; the excitement and elation bring on a real increase in strength and skill.

The usual custom for a guided party then was to have the tourist swing across on the rope to the middle platform, but today Armand refused to allow Guido Rivetti to do this.

'Today, Monsieur,' he suggested, 'I don't think that today, since two ladies have climbed the crack from the bottom, it would be appropriate for a man to take an easier route. Would it not be better if you started where they did?'

'But naturally. Of course,' Guido Rivetti replied, shaking

On the Grépon. ABOVE: The Rateau
de Chèvre, and RIGHT: the Boîte aux
Lettres.

Roping down on the Grépon. ABOVE: Dean Peabody, on the Grande Gendarme, and RIGHT: Robert, from the summit. *Photos by John Holden.*

with laughter as he made his way down the couloir to the take-off. Some climbers could easily have been inconvenienced by this, but since Guido Rivetti was one of Italy's foremost alpinists and had made many difficult climbs guideless, he was more entertained than discommoded.

From the top of the crack Alice and I called to Maurice to reassure him and started on, with me ahead for the moment, up through the Trou du Canon and out on to the Mer de Glace face. After a little traverse there is a short chimney with an overhanging block closing in the top, a tricky pitch, although of course not long. I remembered how uneasy Georges had been the year before when I had gone up here. A few snowflakes had drifted down as I was climbing the Mummery Crack and now we were caught in a brief but severe blizzard of snow, with a high wind and extreme cold. We stopped in a sheltered place to put on our sweaters and mittens. We should really have changed to our nailed boots again too, but for the moment it seemed just too cold to do so, and we kept on as we were.

Then came the other famous pitches on the Grépon, the Boîte aux Lettres, that narrow crack where you wriggle through side-ways with the crack going on down indefinitely below you, the Rateau de Chèvre, and the Grand Gendarme. To get off this Grand Gendarme to the notch on the farther side, a descent of fifty sheer unclimbable feet, you rope off—but not in the usual way, straight down as the rope hangs, which would land you not at the notch at all but somewhere out on the Mer de Glace face. Instead, laying the mid-point of the rope over a little projection, you then slide down the sharp vertical edge of the summit block à cheval, holding one strand of the rope out on the left wall and one on the right. The start is sensational, backing off into space with a drop below of more than a thousand feet. I have seen big, strong men (but, to be honest, men inexperienced in climbing) hesitate before getting up their courage to do this even though they were held firmly on a second rope by a guide above. Alice and I were not held on any second rope. Being too lazy to carry two ropes, we were climbing on my

157

150-foot alpine line. When we needed it for roping down, as here, we took it off our waists.

The actual summit of the Grépon is a large flat rock. The Rivetti-Charlet party had passed us on the traverse but here we four met again and had lunch together, watched (since the snow flurry had stopped) through the telescope in Chamonix by my mother and Christiane, Alice's little girl. (Christiane today will not permit her children to do any mountain climbing with Grandma and Grandpa, but will allow a little skiing!) It was a gay lunch, enlivened by an impassioned oration, no less, by Guido Rivetti on the humiliation suffered by a man, and a man who had considered himself a good climber, at being escorted over the Grépon by a guide on a day such as this.

To leave the summit of the Grépon you rope off on the Mer de Glace side, where the drop to the glacier below is a vertical mile. Armand had already placed his *corde de rappel*, which he invited us to use. Just casting to the winds all our scruples about taking aid from men, we accepted. As Alice was roping down and I was belaying her, I saw Armand's hand shoot out a time or two to grasp her rope. He thought in time and did not touch it, but his desire to do so was almost irresistible. From the Col des Nantillons we went down the glacier in the usual way to the Rognon, where we met Maurice, Winifred and Réné.

'The Grépon has disappeared,' said Etienne Bruhl, sadly, that evening in Chamonix. 'Of course,' he admitted, 'there are still some rocks standing there, but as a climb it no longer exists. Now that it has been done by two women alone, no self-respecting man can undertake it. A pity, too, because it used to be a very good climb.'

A. F. Mummery, that superlative climber who made the first ascent of the Grépon in 1881, wrote:* 'It has frequently been noticed that all mountains appear doomed to pass through the three stages: an inaccessible peak—the most difficult ascent in the Alps—an easy day for a lady.' He went on to say: 'I must confess that the Grépon has not yet reached this final stage,

* *My Climbs in the Alps and Caucasus*, p. 160.

and the heading . . . must be regarded as prophetic rather than as a statement of actual fact.'

II. THE MATTERHORN

The next season my first climb was a manless one: the Torre Grande of the Cinque Torri at Cortina d'Ampezzo, on June 25, with Marjorie Hurd, one of my Bemis Crew comrades. By the route we took it is not a difficult climb. Marjorie, I think, has rather successfully summed up our sport in general: in climbing, says she, practically never are you really comfortable—always you are either too hot, too cold, hungry, thirsty, exhausted or just plain scared to death; however, it all comes under the head of pleasure!

Later that same season I met Alice Damesme, with a group of our G.H.M. friends, at Courmayeur. Our aspiration, after a few climbs at Courmayeur, was to go over to Zermatt and climb the Matterhorn; however, as happens all too often, things did not work out favourably. The next year we returned to this idea with renewed determination. The Matterhorn, although not nearly so difficult as the Grépon, is *the* mountain, the type. This famous peak is big and striking, with a formidable history and reputation. And it is a reputation on which nothing, apparently, can cast a spot of tarnish. The Matterhorn has been climbed by a man with a wooden leg, by two women alone, by a kitten. Yet it still continues, in the popular mind, to stand for the symbol of alpine mountaineering.

In 1931 Alice Damesme, Jessie Whitehead of Cambridge (Massachusetts or England, either one), and I were to meet in Zermatt to climb the Matterhorn. In July, to get in training, I did a few climbs in the Oberland with Micheline Morin. To date most of our manless climbing had been done on rocks; we here tried a little snow and ice. Our climbs up the Jungfrau and up the Mönch by the southwest ridge, with descent by the ordinary route, while not uneventful, still presented no great difficulties. We had other Oberland climbs on our list, but our programme was cut short by unfavourable weather. On August 2, as agreed, Alice, Jessie and I gathered in Zermatt, but since

Alice was bothered by a bad knee she preferred to wait a few days before setting out for the Matterhorn. The weather, too, was in no way suitable for the Matterhorn, and, to anticipate a little, never during the first three weeks of August did it become good enough for us to accomplish the climb.

'If you can learn when to turn back,' said Geoffrey Winthrop Young, who was in Zermatt at the time, 'you are safe to undertake any climb.'

'Turning back is what we didn't learn nothing else but,' reported Jessie, in the elegant vernacular.

While waiting for Alice's knee and the weather to improve, Jessie and I climbed the Alphubel (13,803 feet) by the Rotengrat, where neither of us had been before. This was a longish climb of 6,500 feet above the little chalet of Täschalp, where we spent the preceding night. We reached the summit in good order over a route of mixed snow and rock. It was the descent by the ordinary route down the southeast ridge to the Alphubeljoch and from there across the crevassed Wandgletscher, that provided the complications. The clouds had been low all day, but now we were surrounded by a thick mist with not a track or a trace to be seen anywhere—just whiteness. The problem was to get down the Wandgletscher and stay on top, on the surface of the glacier, and not get buried in some crevasse. Only constant attention on our part, I think, accomplished this. The distance across the glacier was a mile or perhaps a bit less. In clear weather, I suppose, we should have walked across in a few minutes, easily picking a good route. As it was, with visibility cut to a few feet, we set our course by guide-book, map and compass, with Jessie, behind, carrying the compass and keeping the direction of the rope approximately correct. The glacier was covered with a thick layer of rotten, disintegrating snow, which concealed many crevasses without effectually bridging them. We walked with almost the full length of the rope between us as a precaution against our both breaking through into the same crevasse at once. I did not dare take a single step forward without first testing the footing underneath with my ice-axe.

160

Micheline Morin in a high wind on the southwest ridge of the Mönch. The Jungfrau is in the background.

ABOVE: Descending a snow ridge on the Mönch on our manless climb. *Photo by Micheline Morin.*

Sir Arnold Lunn congratulating Micheline and me on our manless climbs.

'I am trying to figure out the basis for your decisions,' remarked Jessie. 'You plunge your axe into the snow; it goes in easily up to the hilt, and you step forward with confidence. You plunge it in again; it goes in easily up to the hilt, and you draw back in alarm.'

The two situations did seem much alike, even to me. All this deep snow, suffused with water, was soft and yielding; but if the resistance seemed to grow slightly firmer as the axe went down, I assumed glacier underneath. If the texture was less firm, or seemed like plain air, I knew there was a crevasse and tried somewhere else. We found a lot of crevasses, some open and some snow-covered. Some of these we could cross, while others we had to walk around. How uneasy I was when the walking around brought us both into a line parallel with the general direction of the crevasses! An alternative route, we knew, ran down a rock rib in the middle of the glacier and eventually we did make out such a rib off to the right, and eventually also we reached it, although we had a difficult time weaving a route through the crevasses. Once on the rocks, however, we found a small pile of broken glass, indicating the breakfast place, and knew we were on the right way. Never before had broken glass looked so good to us!

It was 8 p.m. before we were back at the Täschalp, where we ordered and consumed an enormous dinner. We might again have spent the night there, but deciding that our climb was really not of sufficient importance to justify two nights out, we lighted our little candle lantern once more and walked down to Zermatt, arriving there at 11, after twenty hours of good strenuous exercise.

We passed the rest of the season trying to get up the Matterhorn. Jessie felt that our attempts provided the comic relief in an otherwise deplorable season in Zermatt and that the guides, in the long winter evenings ahead, could amuse themselves by thinking of those girls who had tried so hard. On August 6 we three started for the Matterhorn Hut, 5,500 feet above Zermatt, on mules hired for us by my mother. The mules would save our strength for the 4,000-foot climb the next day. In the hut everybody was chattering at once in German, French, Italian and English. Not nearly enough linguistic confusion, thought Jessie, so in Latin she addressed some remarks to the room in general. Sure enough, two Italian boys took her up at once, and they had a most animated discussion which at first appeared impressive enough until my ear picked up a few phrases that I thought I had heard before, such as: 'Gallia est omnis divisa in partes tres.' So that's what they were talking about!

The Italian boys noticed that the Italian Alpine Club badge on my coat was not of the most recent model, with the Fascist symbol on it, and one of them insisted on exchanging it for his own. They then inquired if perhaps Alice and I were the girls who had done the Grépon manless, and when it turned out that we were, the second boy presented Alice with his badge. She had no right to wear this, Alice demurred a bit, but the boys courteously insisted that there was no question of 'right', it was an honour to the Italian Alpine Club for her to do so! Poor Jessie was left out with a polite, but brief, 'We regret, Mademoiselle, that we haven't another one for you.' To us, Jessie alleged that she was furious, and that Alice's flashing black eyes had a lot more to do with the matter than her having climbed the Grépon.

That afternoon, since none of us had been on this ridge of the Matterhorn before and the early part of the ascent would have to be done in the dark, we scouted out the route, climbing up the rocks for perhaps half an hour. For the pre-dawn rock-climbing I intended to use a flashlight, even though it is an awkward thing to hold in your mouth. The usual custom was to climb with a candle lantern, but that has its drawbacks too, since you often need both hands for the pitches on the Matterhorn and while you can carry a candle lantern in your teeth, it is then likely to bob back and forth, burning alternately your nose and chin. A flashlight is cooler, although in the mouth it does interfere with conversation. We noticed one pitch in particular, where the route made an abrupt turn up some steep rocks to the right, away from a rather obvious line, where it seemed to me that the way could easily be missed in the dark.

After supper we retired early to bed. We were to be called at 2.30 a.m. The hut was crowded as usual and Jessie later took pleasure in telling her more conventional friends in the valley that she had slept next to a young man who kicked her all night long. In these Swiss huts there is usually at least one blanket apiece, but I shall never forget my first night in a French hut, the old Couvercle, where the hut-keeper, doling out the blankets, said to me, 'Here is a blanket, Mademoiselle. Share it with the gentleman next to you'.

We were not called at 2.30. When, some time later, Jessie woke up and discovered this, she was disturbed enough to crawl out of her blanket and walk over her sleeping companions to the window, to find out why.

'It's snowing,' she reported.

The next thing I knew she was shaking me.

'The weather is fine. Of course, seven o'clock is pretty late, but Bernard Biner is starting up now with Yvonne Jérôme-Lévy, and why can't we?'

Naturally we could, and twenty-five minutes later, having pulled on our boots and had breakfast, we did. There was snow on the rocks, but not enough to hold us up seriously, and the weather for the moment looked passable. At 9.15 we caught up to Biner and Yvonne, and at 10 we reached the Solvay Hut, that small refuge shelter a little more than halfway up the Matterhorn ridge. The weather was none too good, so here we waited for an hour and a half, sitting in the snow and chatting gaily. I took a picture of Bernard surrounded by Yvonne, Jessie and Alice which he liked immensely, since it gave the impression that he was taking three girls up the Matterhorn, a considerable achievement for a single guide!

The weather got worse and worse but we didn't start back until it actually began to snow. Then down we climbed to the hut, and walked back to Zermatt. The next day it cleared a little and in the afternoon we again rode mules up to the Matterhorn Hut. Again the following morning we were not called. At daylight we opened our eyes to a Christmas-morning scene. To wake on Christmas morning and see the window-panes covered with little drifts of fine, dry snow seems pleasant and suitable, but to see the same thing on August 9, when you want to climb the Matterhorn, is not nearly so attractive. This time, on the way down to Zermatt, we went by Staffelalp for variety, and while glissading the scree slopes Alice injured her knee again and could do no more climbing that year. Since this was a real snowstorm, laying down an accumulation of snow which would prevent any climbing for several days, Jessie and I left for the Oberland. Things might be different there. But the only difference was that the snow we saw was falling on the Oberland instead of on the Valais. On the evening of August 12 my brother Lincoln, who had remained at Zermatt, sent us a telegram: the barometer was slowly rising and a clearing north wind was blowing. Back to Zermatt we hurried the next day, and spent that night again at the Matterhorn Hut.

The hut-keeper, Kronig, was by this time a great friend of ours and sincerely in sympathy with our manless aspirations. He understood that we would like to start out first. Not only does it make a bad impression for a guideless party to follow close on the heels of one with a good guide, but we genuinely preferred to find the route on our own. So great were the crowds, however—we weren't the only people who had been waiting for weeks for a chance to get up the Matterhorn—that our only chance of climbing first was to have a good head start. When it turned out fair the next morning, Kronig's method of arranging things for us, if indirect, lacked nothing in effectiveness. It is the hut-keeper who is in charge of the stove in the morning and who provides the climbing parties with the hot water for their tea. This morning, with everybody waiting around impatiently to be off, Kronig first served a pot of tea to Jessie and me. No one, of course, took exception to this, since we were the only party of women. Then, inexplicably, it developed that there was no more hot water. The other parties had to wait, with what good grace they could muster, while the hut-keeper stirred up the fire, chopping a little wood to do so, and finally heated water for the rest of them! This gave Jessie

164

and me a good fifteen minutes' start and we got away at 3.10. We had put on our rope in the hut, for in five minutes the rock-climbing would begin.

This time it took us longer to reach the Solvay Hut, since the rocks were still covered with a great deal of snow and ice. The weather was turning bad again. From long experience, well did I know the signs. Yet, hoping that it might clear up, we waited an hour at the Solvay Hut. Although it definitely did nothing towards clearing up, we finally decided that the storm might perhaps hold off long enough for us to make a quick dash to the summit, now not so very far away. So on we started.

We climbed for perhaps an hour longer and reached the Shoulder, that snow-covered projection just before the final rise to the summit. Here we had no choice; we had to admit that the weather was very bad. Great black clouds were rolling up out of Italy before us, and if we looked the other way we could not avoid seeing a snowstorm raging on the Weisshorn behind. (Below, in Zermatt, Bernard Biner was trying to explain soothingly to my mother at the telescope that this was not a real storm she was looking at, but merely a 'local disturbance'.) Now, obviously, we must turn down. An exposed ridge at 14,000 feet is no place to be in a thunderstorm. To stay on the crest of the ridge is to run a very real risk of being struck by lightning; to drop down to the side, on the wall below the ridge, would be to get in the path of falling rocks. But, most incomprehensibly, not one of the other parties had turned back. Surely they must see the bad weather approaching! There were twenty-four people strung out along the ridge, each of the parties, of course, led by a man, guide or amateur. Since they obviously all thought it proper to continue, who were we to set our judgment above theirs?

But in spite of this, we turned back. And promptly, three-quarters of the others did the same, too. They wheeled about in unison, as if on parade. Our error dawned upon us. We had misinterpreted the continued upward movement of the other parties. They had kept on, not necessarily because they judged

165

the conditions suitable, but because, being men, they could not possibly admit defeat until the two girls did! Only one or two parties, I think, kept on towards the top. As one of these, led by a guide, came up to us, the guide put his arm around me and urged me to rope on with his party; he would be happy to take us to the top. (His tourist looked surprised.) It was very kind of him but, thanking him, we declined. The danger from lightning is the same with a guide in front as without one, and in any case we didn't want to do it that way. I do not know who he was, nor do I know whether his party reached the summit.

The climb down was really tiresome this time. We had a long way to go and the wind, cloud and driving snow chilled us through and through. Our hands, particularly, were most uncomfortable from handling the stiff, wet and twisting rope. And in addition we were discouraged. Jessie had only a week left before sailing home, and this storm could very well mean the end of the season's climbing.

But as usual we left our equipment in the Matterhorn Hut when we went down to Zermatt. Five days we waited there, and then at signs of clearing we rode up again to the hut for the fourth time. Jessie said there was not a mule in Zermatt that didn't recognize her. Kronig had reserved the best mattresses for us, as we had directed him to do on the first good day, by placing our crampons in the middle of them, points up. The next morning it was snowing again. This time we admitted that the season was over and took all our things down to Zermatt with us. But first we arranged with Kronig to spend the entire summer of 1932 *en pension* at his hut, paying our board by the month, until we should climb the mountain. Kronig considered this rare humour.

Back in Zermatt, too, the world was cold, wet and cheerless, and had been for weeks. Mother, Lincoln and a friend of his, as well as I, longed for something different. Wasn't there any place in the world that in August would be warm and dry? The only possibility, we felt, would be North Africa. As we sailed across the choppy Mediterranean in one of those small boats we realized that this was the day Jessie was leaving

166

England for home on the *Homeric*. We would like to send her a *bon voyage* radiogram, but the only message we could think of was, 'Sick as hell and hoping you're the same'. I have always been sorry that we felt too languid actually to send this; we should have got back, I feel sure, an appropriate reply.

In 1932, unfortunately, Jessie did not get over to the Alps. Alice and I would have to climb the Matterhorn without her. The weather that season started out just as it had ended the season before. July was wretched. It was well into August, I think, before the Matterhorn was climbed at all, or almost any of the other big peaks in the Valais. Alice and I waited around Chamonix for days at the end of July, hoping to do a training climb or two before setting out for the Matterhorn. Finally the rain and the snow drove us down south to the Dauphiné, where conditions weɪe a bit better, as they often are.

With seven members of the G.H.M., I spent the night of August 5 at the Refuge Tuckett above Ailefroide. The rest were heading for the Agneaux, but Alice and I decided to climb the nearby Pic Jean Gauthier directly by the west face, which we were told had not been done. This would be a 'first manless first', and Alice and I had all the fun of working out a good route; not until I later succeeded in obtaining a guide-book of the region did we discover that we had been, not on Jean Gauthier, but on the Pic des Pavéoux all the time, and that its west face had been climbed in 1892.

Then, since there had been two days of sunshine, Alice and I drove around to traverse the Meije. But the Meije was a sorry sight, plastered white, and on inquiry we learned that it had not yet been climbed that season. We made a lightning change in plans and set out instead for the Tour Carrée de Roche Méane, much lower than the Meije and consequently likely to be in better condition. At the hut, the Refuge Adèle Planchard, that night we found three boys, two French and one Swiss, who planned to traverse the Tour Carrée and the Jumeaux the next day. Well, of course, we didn't want them on our mountain at all. Hoping to divert them, at least for the early morning hours, to the Jumeaux, I inquired if they might not find the traverse more interesting in the reverse direction. They saw through this, grasping my real meaning at once, and like the gentlemen they were, gallantly offered to abandon the mountain entirely to us and go and climb elsewhere! (And subsequently they did so.) Throughout, we have had the most pleasant co-operation from men climbers, guides and amateurs alike, who have sometimes gone out of their way to an extraordinary extent to facilitate our manless climbing.

The Tour Carrée is a pleasant enough rock-climb, of high repute but of no really exceptional difficulty. The rock seemed solid enough at first glance but, as one of the boys put it, it holds '*jusqu'au dernier moment*'—it holds up to the last moment before it breaks away! On the way down to the road we met a party of four more nice young French boys who said they too would indeed like to do the Tour Carrée, but that they could not, because for that one must have a *premier de cordée qui ne craint pas la vertige*.

Alice and I arrived in Zermatt at noon on August 12, and slept that night at the Matterhorn Hut. (It was suggested at the time that I write a book on my 1,001 nights at the Matterhorn Hut; here it is at last.) The next day we climbed the Matterhorn. It was as easy as that. Starting out, we got stuck behind another guideless party of three young men. I should have liked to pass, but short of asking them outright to let us by, there was no convenient way. I hesitated to ask, for while we were faster than they, we were not much faster. I would wait patiently for a minute or two; that blind turn would be along shortly, and they might miss it. Sure enough, they did. Unobtrusively I took the right route. Soon the others seemed to hesitate; they had no place to go. Only then did I suggest to them helpfully, shouting down from above, that perhaps they should have turned to the right a bit back. Although there was a great deal of snow and ice on the rocks, particularly above the Shoulder, and crowds of people showering snow down on one another, we found no insurmountable difficulties. We reached the summit at 8.30. It was a beautiful day, warm and sunny, but with a few little clouds that presaged the snow that

Jessie Whitehead (in foreground) during an early manless attempt on the Matterhorn.

The Italian summit of the Matterhorn.

OVERLEAF: Alice Damesme returning to the Swiss summit of the Matterhorn from the Italian summit.

was to come before we reached the bottom again. Always lazy about carrying heavy packs, Alice and I had brought only the sketchiest of lunches. However, there were lots of people on top that day, including several inexperienced climbers for whom the unaccustomed altitude had brought on just enough mountain sickness to eliminate their appetites—but not their generosity. Their guides and we ate well! We walked over to the Italian summit, having in the back of our minds a notion that we might go down the Italian ridge if conditions were good. But definitely they were not. The Italian ridge was deeply snowed under; no one had been over it that year.

The descent to Zermatt demanded a lot more care than had the ascent, for in the two hours that we had spent on top the sun had considerably softened the snow. A lot of it was sliding off, leaving bare ice underneath, and much more of it was all ready to do so. We put on our crampons and wore them down to the Solvay Hut, treating this part of the mountain as an ice-climb instead of a rock-climb. During the last hour down the rocks it was snowing gently, just enough to make us feel at home there. Never until 1952 did I go down that part of the mountain except in a snowstorm.

I was expected to go with Alice back to Chamonix, where our G.H.M. friends had prepared an elaborate reception at the railway station with enormous bunches of flowers, a 'band' and 'orations', in honour of the first women to climb the Matterhorn alone. But instead I went over to the Eastern Alps to join Florence and Dean Peabody and Robert Underhill for some guideless—not manless—climbing. After that, for nineteen years, my constant companion on every climb was Robert Underhill. Manless climbing is fun for a while, but this other arrangement is better!

VIII

Dent Blanche by the Viereselgrat

fter some climbs in Austria and Italy, we arrived back in
Zermatt again early in September. The Peabodys set off
to do the Matterhorn but Bob and I looked around for
something else. The Viereselgrat (Ridge of the Four Jackasses),
that magnificent east ridge of the Dent Blanche, was in excellent condition, our friend Bernard Biner, the Zermatt guide,
told us. He was taking a man up there himself the next day,
and invited us to come along too. With thanks we declined to
follow on his heels but did decide to undertake this fine climb,
leaving a respectable distance between our two parties. I
could lead the rocks, offered Bob, if I would let him lead the
snow. The rocks, friable and mixed with ice, turned out, when
we reached them, to have no great appeal but we passed them
soon anyway and started on the more important section of the
ridge, that famous upper part that is often, and perhaps always,
draped with stupendous cornices, like the huge waves of the
hurricane-driven sea, caught and frozen into ice. To the right
or to the left, in a capricious manner, and sometimes on both
sides at once, their crests overhung.

Even though Biner and his tourist had left the hut earlier
and, by the time we caught sight of them, were an hour or two,
and later several hours, ahead of us, still their steps and those
of one or two previous parties along this ridge were a great help
to us. But conditions can change almost from hour to hour on
a sunny day and Bob, always cautious, led like a master, constantly on the alert, checking and testing the snow, feeling out
the changing directions of the cornices in a laudable endeavour

On a traverse of the Ortler in the Eastern
Alps with Dean and Florence Peabody.
ABOVE: Ascent by the Hinterergrat, and
LEFT: a crevasse on the descent.

With the Peabodys on the Cima Piccola di Lavaredo (Kleine Zinne): two ways of passing an awkward spot on the famous traverse.

to be sure we were making our way up snow that was still based on solid rock and not suspended over air. And snow that was based on the rock firmly. For Bob had had experience with snow that was not firm a few years earlier when he and my brother Lincoln were attempting the first ascent of the Emperor Falls Ridge on Mt Robson in the Canadian Rockies. On that occasion, as they advanced up the narrow ridge the snow had become so lacking in cohesion that no reliable steps could be fashioned, while great masses of it would break away and avalanche down the precipitous sides. Each man in turn tried without success to find some safe way of getting ahead. While Bob, loath to turn back, was again making a futile effort, Lincoln, after observing him for a while, said quietly, 'Bob, if you really want to go on, I am of course willing to go with you. But may I remark that if our object in life is to make first ascents, I think in the long run we shall make more of them if we give up trying to make this one.' Which thereupon they promptly did!

That day on the Viereselgrat I think Bob was constantly looking to see if the snow had without warning turned into the Emperor Falls variety. But to our great satisfaction it remained firm and excellent throughout. From below I belayed the rope around my ice-axe driven in deep, which gave us some feeling of security. Yet I for one was pleased that we never had to test these belays.

Frequently, after warning Bob to stop a minute, as I was not holding the rope, I took pictures—Bob and I agree that they were undoubtedly the most beautiful pictures I ever took! —of the lovely graceful curves of the ice fringe, curling around a patch of blue sky, and to give scale a small figure off to the side making his way upwards. I had put in a new film at the end of the rock section and its twelve pictures were finished just as we arrived on the summit. But we got there a little late (3 p.m.), as guideless climbers often do, and after we had eaten decided to start down at once, without taking time to change films again. The best opportunities for pictures were undoubtedly over for the day anyway, and we wanted to get off the glacier before dark. It would get dark early this September evening.

On our descent of the ordinary route along the south ridge, as I was struggling down a narrow little chimney my camera case rubbed against a projecting rock, which loosened the catch and tipped the case up. The camera fell out, and I watched it break into countless pieces as it crashed down the precipitous western wall. The long curling ribbon of film was drifting down too, fast for such a light object. I think I felt almost worse about the pictures than I did about the camera, bad as that was! In any case it was the film that I watched, ruined now of course, for the few seconds it was in sight.

I was resuming my descent when there came an appalled shout from Robert above, 'Miriam. That was your *camera*!'

'Yes, I know.'

Another moment of stunned silence on Robert's part. Then, 'Well—why don't you *cry*?'

To which I replied, 'Certainly I'll cry, just as soon as I get down this chimney. Right now I'm too busy.'

The ridge of the ordinary route is not difficult, we made good time and were, as we had hoped, off the glacier before dark (7.45). But just barely. Now that we had rocks underfoot instead of the lighter ice we could see almost nothing. Bob remarked that here was where we turned to the left and that we should soon join the path. 'Oh, no,' I protested quickly, 'to the right.' We hadn't much time, but Bob explained patiently the lie of the land, the direction of the moraines, the ridges and the streams, and it all added up to why we should go to the left. I could only agree with him that what he said sounded most logical and entirely convincing, intellectually, but still I just had a feeling, no reason but an instinct, pulling me to the right. It was a moment of crucial decision! If we turned the wrong way now we'd spend a cold night, shivering and hungry, out on the rocks, instead of in the shelter of the Schönbühl Hut, with blankets, and warm food before we went to bed. How attractive that hut seemed to us, as we each thought that we might not reach it! Bob made the

172

Looking down on the lower part of the Viereselgrat, below the corniced section of the Dent Blanche.

Rock climbing exercises on the Clochetons de Planpra at Chamonix. ABOVE: Robert on a Tyrolean traverse photographed by me, and RIGHT: myself photographed by Florence Peabody.

decision: 'You're usually good at those things. We'll go your way.'

Naturally there would be no point in my telling this story if it hadn't turned out that I was right, and naturally I am omitting all mention of the numerous occasions when I was wrong and Bob right. But this time we turned as I wanted to and were soon running down the path.

The night before we had been almost the only people at the Schönbühl Hut, but this night we found it teeming with great crowds, all men, all French Swiss. 'What in the world is going on here?' we asked the hut-keeper. 'It is a celebration,' he answered in English. Some men, he went on, had recently been killed on the Zmutt Ridge of the Matterhorn; members of their section of the Swiss Alpine Club had come up with a priest to have a requiem mass for the repose of their souls. 'Celebration,' I thought to myself; that word has another meaning than the one I first assumed. But as the evening wore on I began to wonder if perhaps my first interpretation had not been the right one after all. The hut-keeper, expecting us back from the Dent Blanche, had insisted on reserving for us places in the bunk-room, but the others jammed in as they could. The priest and a few of the men slept downstairs, but most of them were lying with us in the big dormitory above, singing. Singing, hour after hour, while we who had left the hut that morning at 2.30 might have preferred, understandably, to sleep. Robert was seething. The Swiss Alpine Club had rules, he reminded me, about hours for quiet in their huts. He was going downstairs to speak to the hut-keeper. I restrained him. What was the use? The hut was theirs. The hut-keeper was in their employ. Only two people—we two—wanted to sleep, and we were so enormously outnumbered. In my efforts to soothe Robert, it made things simpler, on the whole, that he was objecting merely to the volume of the songs and not to their content, to which he paid no attention. For as the night wore on, the songs got more and more raucous, finally becoming such as are not always sung in the presence of a lady. Possibly the men assumed that we did not understand French. But I

173

did understand French, and those songs as well. I had heard them all before. And, indeed, I think it quite unlikely that the Swiss know any songs of this type that are not familiar to my climbing companions of many years, the French members of the G.H.M.!

And then much of the time my thoughts were running along other lines. What a splendid climb we had had! Except for losing the camera, everything had gone well. I liked climbing with Bob. We made a good, harmonious, efficient team. That incident of his taking my turning when we got off the glacier was out of the ordinary, as men go! Only a man of considerable ability himself would so generously recognize ability in someone else, if one could dignify by that word my animal-like sense of location and direction. All in all, I mused, a man like this would be the sort to marry!

That autumn I wrote for *Appalachia,* the journal of the Appalachian Mountain Club, an article on my manless climbs, under the title, 'Without Men'. Several of our friends were much entertained by the coincidence that on the same day when *Appalachia* was delivered to them in the morning mail, containing 'Without Men', they then picked up the evening newspaper and learned of my engagement to Bob. Adolf Rubi and many others wrote me asking who was going to lead. Alice Damesme rallied me as follows: 'Vous voilà enfin, vous aussi, en puissance de mari!' 'Peak Scaling Couple to Wed', announced another Boston paper the following morning. And a letter from Bernard Biner reported that he 'surely would not have let you go alone' on the Viereselgrat had he realized how things stood between us. He hoped that mother blessings would not prevent our returning to the mountains.

Robert, when friends inquired how he happened to get himself into this predicament, had his own answer. Recently, he explained, he had done two good climbs with each of which he would not have been unwilling to have his name associated, the first traverse of the Aiguilles du Diable and a guideless ascent of the Viereselgrat. What had happened? One of the local French newspapers carried a long story about the climb

174

over the Diable ridge accomplished by Miss Miriam O'Brien, Armand Charlet and Georges Cachat, identifying them all at length, with praise for their achievement. At the very end came one single line: 'A Mr. L. M. Underwood was also along.'

And the Viereselgrat? The *Alpine Journal*, revered publication on matters alpine, published a brief paragraph under the heading 'Ladies' Mountaineering',* on Miss O'Brien's manless ascents of the Tour Carée de Roche Méane and the Matterhorn with Madame Alice Damesme, and her guideless ascent of the Viereselgrat. They mentioned no companion on this latter climb; for all the readers of the *Alpine Journal* could find out, Miss O'Brien might have been quite alone.

'Now,' concluded Bob, 'what are you going to do about a girl who constantly steals the act on you in that fashion?' He submitted that he had chosen much the best way he could think of to remedy the situation.

* *Alpine Journal,* XLIV, p. 343.

IX

Idaho

'Rugged country. Awful rugged country. Miles and miles of sharp, jagged pinnacles of firm granite,' an artist friend of Bob's in the Tetons had asserted when he described, some twenty-five years ago, the Sawtooth Range of Idaho, which previously we had never heard of. Since firm granite is not at all common in our United States mountains, this seemed to us something that we should look into, and we spent many hours searching in appropriate mountaineering publications for some mention of these Sawtooth Mountains. With no success at all. And for a good reason, since we discovered, when visiting them in the summers of 1934 and 1935, that although fishermen and big-game hunters had fished the lakes and climbed the cliffs of this charming region, we were the first mountaineers to aim for the peaks.

It didn't matter that the peaks were small (10,000 to 11,000 feet) and the general level of the country high, so that our climbs were short. Or that on the whole they were easy. They still offered short stretches of entertaining rock-climbing at their summits. And to make up for the lack of sustained difficulty of high degree, we found compensating joys in camping in idyllic sites where no one had camped before, in making a dozen or so first ascents, in being the first climbers to explore this beautiful region, where practically none of the summits had ever been trodden by man.

A pack-train we should need in order to get into the range, but, although we learned that there was a dude ranch not too far away, and wrote to them, their prices seemed to us prohibitive. So when we started out West in June of 1934 we still had no idea where we were going to find horses. On our way through Hailey, Idaho, we stopped at the office of the Forest Supervisor, Mr Miller S. Benedict, and laid our problem before him. If he were going in there himself, said he, he'd ask Dave Williams to take him. A finer piece of advice we never received.

Dave, without much in the way of formal education—as a matter of fact, he went to school for only a few months, he told us—was nevertheless a man of great enterprise and accomplishment. Making his way out West when hardly more than a boy, one of his first jobs had been to carry the mail twice a week over Galena Summit, 8,752 feet in elevation, between the railhead to the south and the upper Salmon River valley to the north. Understandably, during a large part of the year this pass was not open to wheeled traffic and in winter the conditions of wind, cold and depth of snow became rigorous indeed. (Later we received a letter from Dave's wife one January reporting a temperature at their ranch of 50 degrees below zero, Fahrenheit.) As the autumn advanced young Dave would carry the mail on horseback, then by dog team, and finally on his own back as he struggled along on a pair of primitive skis. Now and then, of course, blizzards prevented his getting through at all, and on one of these occasions the postal authorities in Washington protested at the irregularity of the service. 'At that,' Dave told us, 'I sat right down and wrote 'em a letter. I said, "If you've got any man in Washington who can carry the mail over Galena Summit every Tuesday and Friday, you send him right out here quick. We'd sure like to see him." I never heard another word out of 'em.' Dave was older now and a prosperous rancher in the valley, running beef cattle and horses, but he still had this most engaging sense of humour and a natural wisdom that made his company a treat. He was to be a dear friend of ours as long as he lived.

Williams' Ranch lies thirteen miles south of Stanley, Idaho, and just about opposite the best of the Sawtooths, which rise to the west of the incipient Salmon River. Dave agreed with enthusiasm that we could start the following afternoon. In the morning he'd have to round up and shoe us some horses, of which he owned large numbers; he wasn't sure exactly how many, for he had not yet caught them all that spring. In the West, only the horses that have work to do through the winter are allowed to live in the stable and be fed. The others are turned loose to shift for themselves like wild horses.

At four o'clock the following afternoon, after one of Carrie Williams' big Sunday dinners, our little party of three saddle-horses and two pack-horses finally started off, winding down across the flats of the Salmon River, with fourteen miles to go. Dave rode ahead on his mount, Chowder, leading Frances, the more tractable of the two pack-horses. Diamond, the other, and a most ornery beast, was left to run loose and it was up to Bob to see that she came along. This wasn't so easy, for Diamond always knew better than the other horses, or than Dave himself, the route that should be taken, or indeed whether we should go at all. 'She leads like a cat by its tail,' observed Dave, in explanation of why she was not tied behind Frances in the usual manner of a pack-train. Bob soon developed the habit of filling his pocket with small rocks to hurl at Diamond when the occasion required. I was riding a pretty little horse with better-than-usual gaits that Dave had named Indian because he had bought him for five dollars from an Indian. 'He's gentle, on the whole,' Dave had remarked, 'except when he's bucking.' To cut the bucking down to a minimum Dave advised me not to allow my coat, or any bush or other horse, to brush him in the rear. I found all this far from reassuring, especially since horses never inspire me with much confidence.

The sixth horse in our outfit was Frances' colt, who was too young to be left at home without Mother. He spent much of his time on the trail in dashing directly in front of the other horses, and in camp in bucking practice, usually in the midst of whatever was going on. I felt sure that when he grew up to be a big horse, he, too, would be a splendid bucker.

We worked up into the Sawtooth Range, the horses wading

178

around big boulders to cross Hell Roarin' Creek on the way, to lovely little Imogene Lake (8,500 feet). The country was wooded—mostly pines—but underbrush was scarce, and everywhere between the peaks were acres and acres of *roches moutonnées* and quantities of little blue lakes. The rock, we rejoiced to see, really was granite.

We reached Imogene Lake as dusk was fading and cooked our supper by the light of the campfire. Then Bob and I spread our sleeping-bags under the great pines, with no tent between us and the stars, while Dave took the horses up to little Lake Vella above for their night pasturage. A horse's preferred night schedule is the following: graze for several hours, sleep a bit, and with the first faint anticipation of dawn, start home. It is this last part of the programme that the packer is out to thwart. You shouldn't tie the horse up; he must be allowed to wander around in order to find sufficient food. Hobbles—those leather bracelets connected by a few inches of chain and buckled around his front ankles like handcuffs—are, of course, an old story to a horse and he has learned to leap along rapidly and far with these on his feet. Dave told us that one morning he tracked his hobbled horses for twenty miles before finally catching up with them just as they were turning in the side road to Williams' Ranch. 'And I do believe the critters were glad to see me,' he added.

While I doubt that there is any infallible method of keeping the horses with you, you always try to leave them for the night where grazing is exceptionally fine, the grass so much more succulent than the desiccated pastures at the valley ranch that even the most homesick horse will decide it is to his advantage to remain there. More important, you leave the horses in a region where their natural route home will lead them through camp. When the bells you have tied around their necks waken you, you can then take appropriate action.

That evening Dave pointed into the western darkness. 'Tomorrow morning,' he said, 'we'll climb that ridge up there. You folks pick out the mountain you want and in the afternoon I'll take you to it.' Next morning we did just this and chose

Snowyside in the south (later reported in the local paper as 'Suicide') for our first.

Searching for our horses, we worked up along a turbulent little stream, Robert on its right bank and Dave and I on its left. The horses appeared on Robert's side. Dave shouted across the river that Diamond was the only one who would be likely to allow Robert to get up on her. Robert was to mount Diamond and drive the others across the river. No one would have guessed, as Bob swung up on that big, round, slippery horse, unsaddled and unbridled, that he was doing this for the first time. But from then on things went less well. 'Just go after them like you was roundin' up cattle,' Dave instructed.

Bob's primary difficulty lay in steering Diamond, but even when he managed that, and charged up to the other horses, they continued their placid grazing in complete indifference. An expression of increasing amazement grew on Dave's face as he watched the ineptness of this eastern dude. 'It's a funny thing,' he observed to me, 'but I guess there's something to learn about 'most anything.' In the end Dave had to wade the river and do the job himself.

At the southwest end of Toxaway Lake we camped for three nights in a beautiful grove of fragrant firs, and enjoyed two good days of climbing. Dave, an experienced goat hunter— quite like the original Swiss guides—had done a good deal of incidental rock-climbing, often in difficult places, and as he liked the sport as much as we did he usually accompanied us on our expeditions, much to our pleasure. But how he distrusted our alpine ropes! Most of our climbing in the Sawtooths, it is true, we did without ropes, but now and then we deemed it wiser to use them. In particular, on a traverse the following day along the ridge of Snowyside and the peak to the north of it, we arranged several rappels to descend a steep slab of perhaps 200 feet, undercut at the bottom. How uneasy Dave felt! Those thin little ropes did not look as if they could hold *him*. To reassure himself, before starting, he peered over the edge to the valley below and observed that if worse came to worst he could make it in about two jumps.

One cairn we found, the only one that year, on the main summit of Snowyside. But on the top of a bold gendarme nearby lay undisturbed quantities of quartz crystals, proof positive of its virginity. Dave named it Crystal Peak and constructed, as he did on all the new peaks we climbed, a monumental cairn. No little pile of stones, hastily tossed together, would suffice for him.

From the top of Snowyside we first discovered 'Red Finger Peak', quite far to the northwest but so striking in its vertical lines that we set our hearts on it at once. Dave thought it lay on the farther side of the Payette River to the west, and he doubted that there was any trail near it. But he assured us that we would get there somehow, and that to begin with he knew a pass which would take us over into the Payette Valley.

Once down in the valley, however, it turned out that the trail work—what there was of it—had been done by elk, and elk are not specialists on through routes. For hours, with more than a little difficulty, we pushed our way through the underbrush tangles of this lower-lying valley. At a rate of progress for the day of less than a mile an hour we had finally succeeded in getting the pack-train almost to our destination, the point on the river nearest to Red Finger Peak, when a beautiful, freshly-cleared Forest Service trail came in on our left. Apparently it had been running down the valley, parallel to our own dreadful route, for how many miles none of us knew! In a charming little glade on the river bank, a half-mile above Elk Lake, we set up a camp (about 6,600 feet), which was to be our headquarters for four nights.

The following day Bob and Dave climbed Elk Peak just above camp, from which they had a good view of the lie of the land around our chosen Red Finger. This they had finally identified as one of the Rakes. About four miles distant from our camp they estimated it to lie, and not even Dave considered the approach to its base a trip suitable for horses. After putting up two new cairns on Elk Peak and a neighbouring mountain they returned in the early afternoon as I was out 'goat-hunting' with a camera on the cliffs near camp. Good-hearted Dave had

181

felt that my name should be included on the record, left on the main summit in one of Dave's tobacco tins, of those who had made the first ascent, although at the time I was 4,000 feet below. Bob explained that such a procedure was not customary in mountaineering circles, but Dave still thought it unkind to leave me out.

When we started for the Rakes early in the morning we discovered at once that nature had made no provision for our crossing the Payette River. Dave solved the problem quickly and simply by seizing his axe and dropping a large pine tree neatly across the torrent. Once we had worked our way through the thick band of underbrush along the valley bottom we found most enchanting the higher part of the approach, which followed up along Fall Creek through beautiful alpine meadows, broken cliffs and the ever-present *roches moutonnées*. Although it took us three and a half hours to reach the base, the final peak itself did not require so much time as we had anticipated because we could not climb it at all. The huge red granite monolith at the west end of the little group of needles, for which we had originally named the peak 'Red Finger', proved to be without holds. We climbed the other, smaller summits and left a cairn on the highest one that presented a surface flat enough to serve as base.

From the highest point we could reach, however, the final red finger rose some forty feet more, separated from us by a gap twenty feet deep. As we made our way around the base we discussed how we would climb it if we had several hundred feet of rope and a cross-bow for shooting it over the summit. Whether this would really have worked I have my doubts, for the farther side of the pinnacle dropped off for a very long distance without providing any good place to fix the rope, even had we been able to get it securely lodged across the slender, attenuated summit. In any case we were not equipped to try this manœuvre, and without rope-throwing we felt the peak would be unclimbable.

We had originally brought food for a week, although when I am planning food for a mountaineering trip I go along with the

182

In the Sawtooth Mountains of Idaho. ABOVE: Camp on the upper Payette River, and BELOW: bushwhacking on horseback.

LEFT: On the Rakes, photographed by Robert Underhill. BELOW: Dave Williams on Mt. Heyburn.

French in counting a week as eight days. But we had already been out eight days and from over here in the Payette Valley the trip back to Dave's ranch would require two more. So eager were we to have one more climb, however, that we decided to spread our remaining supplies over three days instead of the necessary two, and take in a peak on the divide just south of Sawtooth Lake. When we reached the ranch again, only the dish-towels, a few matches and some soap rattled around in those capacious food boxes that had been so lavishly stuffed on our departure.

Down the valley Dave spied some elk ahead and stopped the pack-train so that I could creep up to them on foot. I got right in the midst of a band of about forty before they discovered me snapping pictures of them. Deer we saw in these hills, too, and higher up and off in the distance, mountain goats. Frequently, stuck on bushes and rocks, we found clumps of their long white hair, which they shed each spring. Dave would extend a handful of this goat hair to me with the sad remark, 'I had hold of him, but he got away.' Farther down the valley we passed Deadman Cabin, a few rotting logs marking the spot where a prospector had lived. 'He winter-killed,' explained Dave.

After climbing Mt Regan, the most striking peak on the divide, we reluctantly left these pleasant mountains and rode out by Stanley Lake Creek. Our first contact with civilization provided us with a rather unflattering welcome to the society of our fellow men. Near Stanley Lake, where a little road wound into the forest, we came upon a parked automobile, an evil-smelling thing after the fresh air of the woods and the mountains. A woman waited not far away, presumably while her husband was fishing. She took one look at us, our costumes and our caravan and, screaming in terror, ran and locked herself in the car. Bob and Dave were a little abashed. After all, it hadn't been much more than eleven days since they had shaved.

The following year, in September, we headed for the Sawtooths again. Since we planned to be away only three weeks, we went out by train. Dave met us, 118 miles south of Stanley, at Shoshone, 'the windiest place on earth', according to him, 'where you can always tell a newcomer because he runs after his hat. An old resident just waits for another hat to come along.'

What would the weather be like? we asked. In the first two weeks of September, Dave replied, there was always a three-day storm. He had never known it to fail. He was planning, however, to take along the big tent and a substantial wood-burning stove which he used for his hunting parties. Hunting parties needed a warm, cosy place, for sometimes they spent less time outdoors tracking game than they did indoors playing poker and drinking. 'I can't understand you, Bob,' Dave once observed, thoughtfully. 'In my experience there's just two reasons for a man to go off into the woods. One is to get away from his wife, and the other is to get drunk. But you bring your wife along with you, and you don't bring no whisky.'

But this was the year when no storm came. There was frost at night, naturally, and sometimes a few snow flurries on our climbs. Dave kept the camps wonderfully warm, building great campfires that made me uneasy for the safety of the National Forest. I'm sure his hunting parties were warm too, even though the hunting season came several weeks later. Technically, at least, it came later. Right now, however, was the time some of the local inhabitants considered the most propitious for laying in their own supply of meat for the winter, before the 'foreign' dudes got to crashing around in the woods, making a lot of noise and scaring off all the game. We met a few friends of Dave's, as a matter of fact, wandering around with their guns, going 'fishing', so they said. Some splendid fish tracks I had seen over yonder, I reported to them, having been informed by Dave as to the sort of 'fish' they were looking for—elk. Elk is in my opinion the most delicious wild meat I have eaten.

This year we wanted a closer view of those prominent, striking summits, Castle Peak and White Cloud Peaks, which we had observed the year before, standing out across the Salmon River to the east. How good it felt, starting from the ranch and heading up into the mountains that warm September day, surrounded once more by that delectable fragrance of sage-brush, mingled with overtone odours of heat, dust and horse, smells that always bring back memories of good trips on the western ranges. In two days, up Fourth of July Creek and over two divides, having climbed one peak on the way, and having had one morning enlivened by the usual horse-caused vicissitudes (on the way down a steep slope a pack-horse bucked off every last item of equipment that was tied to her back), we made our camp on Chamberlain Lake directly beneath the south face of Castle Peak (11,820 feet). Castle Peak had been climbed before, and the report was that there was only one possible route up it. This meant, according to the iconoclastic Bob, that there was at least one easy way.

This south face, lavishly outfitted with a profusion of turrets, spires and buttresses, was imposing. Towards its east end, however, the rock structure suddenly changed and a steep slope of beautiful white limestone succeeded the mass of battlements. At the point where the change occurred there lay a large gully, obviously the 'only possible route' by which the mountain had been climbed, and to the west of this another gully, easy enough save for some rock-scrambling at the top. After making an initial climb and descent of the mountain which employed these two routes, we ascended, on another day, to the west ridge somewhat above its lowest point and then followed this, over and around a long series of gendarmes, to the summit. The climb was of moderate difficulty (perhaps comparable to a traverse of the Jägigrat, at Saas-Grund) and, at least as a first ascent, quite exhilarating. On its course, we noticed several other possible routes.

For the last part of our stay we visited the Sawtooths again, making first ascents of Mt Heyburn, Packrat Peak, and others up Redfish Creek, as well as exploring some of the peaks around the headwaters of Fishhook Creek. There were opportunities here, we felt, for more good climbing. And since then several parties have in fact gone into the Sawtooths and accomplished some first-rate climbs in the modern manner. Our Red Finger was climbed fifteen years later by Fred Beckey and Pete Schoening of the Seattle Mountaineers (attracted to the region by an article Bob had written) by using 'two expansion bolts and one contraction bolt (all $\frac{3}{8}$-inch size)', things which we had never even heard of when we made the first visit. In the autumn of 1949 we were much interested to receive a letter from Fred Beckey telling a fascinating tale of their success. I quote from an article, 'Sixth-Class Climbing in the Sawtooth Range', such items as this: 'several direct-aid pitons in one place at one time to be even reasonably safe . . . Fifteen feet of this, over the space of an hour . . . a solid-sounding bolt . . . drilling had become sheer drudgery by this time, for the drills were so dull as to be almost useless . . .'!* (It was Pete Schoening who later, on the nightmare descent of K2 in the Karakoram in 1953, held the rope that arrested the fall of five men.)

* *American Alpine Journal*, 1950, pp. 415–24.

X

Montana, Mission Range

In the spring of 1946, after seven years of war, we were at last free to plan another climbing trip. Bob and I chose Montana. With other regions in the main chain of the Rockies—Canada, Idaho, Wyoming, Colorado—we were already more or less familiar. But Montana was brand new to both of us. We would look over the climbing possibilities of the state. We realized, of course, that we should not find peaks of the size and difficulty of those we used to climb in the Alps, but Europe in 1946 was hardly ready for holiday-makers. Then, too, exploration is a logical development of mountaineering, and even if the peaks we found were easy, they would no doubt be fun, especially after seven years of no peaks at all.

So absorbed did we become in this new game that for the next five years we drove out to Montana every summer and we have found an immense fascination in this wild and rugged country of great trackless forests. For Montana is three-quarters as large as France, with scarcely more than one per cent of France's population. Since almost all these people live in the cities or on the plains to the east, the mountainous regions of the western third of the state (an area roughly 150 miles wide by 350 miles from north to south) is wild indeed. Moreover, much of it is set apart in national forests and wilderness areas sometimes hundreds of square miles in extent, these latter to be preserved in their original primitive state. Here stand no human habitations except an occasional ranger

187

station or fire look-out tower. Very few trails penetrate. Even some of the trails that had been built earlier to facilitate access in case of fire—and forest fires yearly devastate considerable areas of these magnificent forests—are now being allowed to fall into disuse, partly due to the increased cost of maintenance and partly to the new and more efficient system of fire fighting by 'smoke-jumpers', a civilian form of parachute troops with fire-fighting equipment. These men can be dropped by aeroplane directly at the fire in a matter of minutes after it has been spotted by the patrol plane, a fraction of the time it used to take to get fire-fighters in over the trails by pack-train. How the smoke-jumpers are to get out again through that wilderness after their fire is extinguished, is left to them; they seem to manage well enough.

The peaks of most of the ranges stand approximately 9,000 to 11,500 feet high. Only the Beartooth Range, in the southern part of the state, has summits rising over 12,000 feet; Granite Peak, the highest, being 12,847. Usually on every mountain there is somewhere a fairly easy route of about Hörnli-ridge-on-the-Matterhorn degree, even though, of course, more interesting routes can be worked out. The rock is nowhere of the superlative quality of the Chamonix Aiguilles or the Dolomites (or even of the Tetons in Wyoming, which offer the best climbing in North America outside Alaska). But, with the exception of Glacier Park at the northern end, the rock is good average Zermatt-Oberland rock. Of predominantly snow-and-ice climbs there are none, although there are small remnants of glaciers here and there, and many snow patches.

The most important contributing charm of the Montana mountains is their wildness. Only once in our five years did we meet in the mountains any other climbers outside our own parties. We did meet an occasional sheep-herder, fisherman, or out-of-season hunter in the more accessible regions and now, of course, the prospector with his Geiger counter will undoubtedly show up almost anywhere. But there are plenty of deer, elk, moose, goats, bighorn sheep and bear, brown and grizzly. Too many of these last.

1. DAUGHTER OF THE SUN

The Mission Range, the first we visited, still remains one of our favourites. It lies in the northern part of the state, about sixty miles south of Glacier Park, to the west of the main Continental Divide. The highest summit, McDonald Peak, somewhat over 10,000 feet, was named for the first white settler in that part of the country, Angus McDonald. In 1847 the Hudson's Bay Company sent him, as factor, to take charge of their 'Saleesh House in the Flathead Country', a trading-post established to barter with the Indians for their furs. A sizeable proportion of the Indians in the valley today are named McDonald, and many of them Angus McDonald. While it does seem an odd name for an Indian, we know of one family where the father is Angus McDonald and the two sons are each Angus McDonald as well.

We went into the Mission Range this first time from the east, where the only good horse-trail on either side of the range to penetrate in to the heart of the mountains leads from the Diamond L Bar Ranch on Lindbergh Lake some ten miles to Lagoon Lake. Here we planned to have our base camp, climb a peak or two, and then backpack up west and north to McDonald Peak. Dick Hickey, of the Diamond L Bar, would put Bob and me in with horses to Lagoon Lake.

Our first climb was Daughter-of-the-Sun Mountain, an attractive small peak just south of the east end of Turquoise Lake, a beautiful large lake which lay slightly beyond and below our camp. The first ascent had been made in 1927 from this side. It had been climbed again by Jack Romer, a young man who had done much wandering around the Mission Range and who was at that time staying at the ranch. His ascent by the southeast ridge was no doubt an easier route, but one much more difficult of access. As far as we knew, ours would be the third ascent.

We worked down towards Turquoise Lake at first over slabs and then bushwhacking through 'jungles'—a thick growth of alders and other dense bushes. The outlet of Turquoise Lake which we had to cross was jammed with a mass of driftwood, loosely tangled together, and underneath this log-jam, between great boulders, rushed a considerable torrent of water. I couldn't find any really sound route for crossing. It seemed to me that every log I tentatively stepped on either sank or rolled over. Still, counting on speed to take the place of caution, I skipped over. Certainly my feet were wet when I reached the other side, but one never stays wet long in this dry Montana air.

Beyond, we mounted a scree slope, then worked up easily enough, leaving cairns for our return, through two bands of wooded cliffs to a snow bench, apparently a small glacial cirque, at the base of the final peak. From here a large steep scree gully ran directly up the north face, presumably the route by which the first ascent had been made. But we failed to find it attractive and thought we'd have more fun out on the rock ridge farther to the west.

So, bearing right over moraine and snow to the headwall, we cut steps across a tongue of snow to the foot of the northwest ridge or shoulder, upon which we mounted. The rock-climbing was indeed fun, although at first not of any particular difficulty. The main excitement, as we found in climbing all these small Montana mountains, consisted in working out a route where no one had been before. Will it go? And all the way to the top? You can rarely be sure until you set foot on the summit. Halfway up the main peak of this mountain, above the shoulder, the climbing did in fact become difficult. We were finally stopped by a precipitous step of some twenty feet with nothing in the way of holds on it at all. We moved over to the left to see what the north face looked like up here.

'What sort of route is that, I ask you?' inquired Robert, gazing at the gully, which here near the top was considerably steeper and composed of huge loose blocks most unstably balanced on shifting scree. It looked technically easy but extremely dangerous and as this type of climbing is entirely lacking in appeal for us, we prospected further. A few feet lower down we had noticed the beginning of a little ledge runing around the mountain to the right (west and south), and we climbed back down to have another look at it. It led on and on, with apparently no substantial break as far as we could see, until it disappeared behind a shoulder of the mountain.

'I don't know,' said Robert. 'Two people . . .'

When there are only two people, of course, on a delicate traverse, if one falls he must pendulum the length of the rope before the second man can hold him. And then he may be in a position where it is not easy for the second man to get him up. But the risk of falling off was slight.

'I've been on narrower ledges than that in the Dolomites,' I remarked.

'Who in the world hasn't?' exclaimed Bob, in astonishment.

That seemed to clinch our decision. We set off. The belays were excellent and whenever the ledge broke off, as it did in crossing some of the chimneys, a good big step got us across. With what eagerness and suspense we approached each corner to see if our ledge continued around the other side! Time after time, however, we found it still there. It ran, in fact, quite 180 degrees around the mountain, to the south side, where some broken-up chimneys and gullies led us to the summit. The puzzle had been solved; it had been a good climb.

II. MCDONALD PEAK

Dick Hickey's plan of sending one man with us on our back-packing trip to McDonald Peak having run into some difficulties due to the defection of the man, we finally started with three companions, George Woods, wrangler, Jean Dickson, a high-school French teacher who was spending her summer holidays working at the ranch, and Dick himself. From our campsite at Lagoon Lake over to McDonald was unbroken wilderness, with never a trail except for an occasional game trail, and the game often seemed not to be travelling with our needs in mind. We started back down the horse-trail to Glacier Lake for perhaps three-quarters of a mile, then crossed the ridge to the west and dropped down a very precipitous slope to Island Lake. Although this time we travelled on foot, Dick was keen to find a route by which he could get horses over to McDonald, and was continually speculating on possibilities.

'Bet I could get a horse down this slope,' he would occasionally remark, with what looked to us like exaggerated optimism.

'Not with me on him, you couldn't,' replied Robert, using his hands to steady himself down some steep drop.

Thence we worked west with heavy bushwhacking along Island Lake and an unnamed upper lake. Beautiful, both of them, but hard to make our way around. It was always a problem, when we came to a lake, to decide whether following the bank to the right or the left would lead us to fewer bays, inlets and deep rivers.

'On and on and on!' Dick would sing out every now and then in an effort, I suppose, to encourage us. 'That's the slogan of this Diamond L Bar safari.'

Beyond the upper lake we climbed a grassy hillside brilliant with glorious flowers, wading knee-deep through botanical treasures.

'Good horse-feed,' observed George.

As we approached the narrow pass at the Mission Divide, the slope steepened and the vegetation became more dwarf. I could hardly tear myself away from the calochortus, even to climb a small point to the south, above the pass, where we obtained a striking view of the east face of McDonald. The pass itself was plentifully marked by tracks of mountain goats. Descending steeply once more, we reached Cliff Lake. Its outlet, Post Creek (named for Angus McDonald's trading post, which was situated some miles downstream in the valley), was even here a good swift stream, running well above our knees. There was a log jam on this river too, a few feet downstream, and we looked it over. But it was poised on the brink of a waterfall and without any discussion we all decided to leave it alone.

Dick and George plunged right through the river. No, of course they would not roll up their trousers; only sissies like the Underhills and Jean would waste time that way. As soon as they arrived on the farther side George quickly set down his pack and waded back again through the icy water to carry my pack across for me.

'In Montana,' Jean explained, when I expressed my surprise and gratitude, 'even our roughest characters are like that.'

As we worked south, up the high end of Cliff Lake's alpine valley, the underbrush thinned, the trees became smaller and more scattered, and finally we emerged into delectable alpine meadows, still on July 25 partly snow-covered. Constantly before our eyes, up ahead to the left, gushed the outlet of Lake of the Clouds in its thousand-foot plunge over the cliff, a delicate, slender waterfall, ornamented with great puffs of mist. These meadows at the southeast face of McDonald, all interlaced with streams and carpeted with the most glorious flowers of unbelievable variety, I could hardly bear to leave. If I were a mountain animal, I would live here, and two big bull elk did, magnificent creatures with enormous, towering, seven-point antlers.

'Royal heads!' observed Dick and George with enthusiasm.

While the elk did not allow us to come too close, neither were they unduly afraid of these strange new creatures. Curious, though, they watched us for some time, from safe distances. Two years later I heard of them again, through Jack Romer, who reported that they were still there.

'Deer couldn't winter up here,' explained Dick. 'Too much snow. It's a good place for elk, though. They can stand a lot more snow than deer can. Longer legs . . . higher up off the ground . . . more like a giraffe. Ah, the giraffe,' he went on, warming to the idea, 'there's an animal for deep snow for you. You ought to see a giraffe bounding through deep snow.'

At the end of the valley we climbed west to a higher level and reached a charming little lake even closer to the cliffs of McDonald, just below Icefloe Lake. Here we would camp; higher there might be too much snow. It had been a strenuous day for us all and I don't know any member of the party who wasn't just a bit tired. Throwing off our packs we sank down on a bank covered thick with deep crimson hedysarum, our feet in a carpet of asphodel.

Where to put the tents was a bit of a problem. The only level and snow-free ground was an enchanting little meadow not much higher than the lake, with meandering streams trickling through it everywhere. Bob finally, by walking around barefooted, located a spot perhaps a little drier than most, on the bank of the main stream which poured out from an extensive snowfield. On the other side of the stream, on a slope with rocks and ledges, we would have our kitchen.

'Where do you want the fire, Jean?' asked George.

'Might as well find out,' he explained to me in a tone that was at the same time confidential and sufficiently loud for Jean to hear without difficulty. 'Sure as I build it anywhere without asking, Jean will have to have it moved somewhere else. Awful bossy folks, schoolteachers. Glad I ain't married to no schoolteacher.'

After supper that night, happy and well filled, we sat around in the cheerful warmth of a large campfire and watched the mountain goats on the cliffs bounding our meadow. What system of dynamics, we wondered, allowed them to descend vertical cracks head-downward?

The next morning Bob and I climbed McDonald. Dick and George went with us up our valley to the col at its head to get the view to the west, a striking one indeed, over the Ashley Creek region at our feet and beyond to the Mission Valley spread out, broad, flat, and checkerboarded with fields of different crops. Here Bob and I swung right, north, up the heel of the main south ridge of McDonald. The scree slopes ended in a minor summit, from which a narrow rock ridge, followed by a broad snow one, led a good quarter of a mile without much ascent to the east-west summit ridge; the cairn lay some hundred yards to the west on this, at no noticeably higher elevation. For all its technical ease, however, our climb was not uneventful, for we met a mountaineering hazard new to the books. As we arrived on the minor summit and I happened to glance down to the left, I froze where I was.

194

The east face of McDonald Peak which we climbed by the ridge on the left.

Two Mission Range horse trails. ABOVE:
Coming down from Mount Harding, and
RIGHT:with Dick Hickey leading, into High
Park.

'Look down there!' I gasped.

'Grizzlies, all right,' said Bob, in a whisper. 'Look at those big humps behind their shoulders.'

We were both silent for a moment, watching those two big black bears, yearlings, I guessed, on a snowfield below us, rolling and tumbling over each other like a pair of playful kittens. But oh! so much bigger than kittens! At once I was keenly conscious that there were no bars or barriers of any sort between them and me. No zoo, this. Here the Underhills and the grizzlies stood on an equal footing, each of us free to go wherever we liked all over this mountain and the country around. It was an impressive thought, and I was not sure that I liked it.

'They know we're here,' said Bob, 'and they just don't give a damn.' Indeed, although they turned in our direction now and then, and sniffed the air, they did not consider us important enough to interrupt for long their real business of the morning, which was this uproarious rough-house game. If there had been a fence, any sort of fence, between us, I should have been enthralled by the exhibition. Playing kittens are enchanting, but how much more exhilarating are kittens on this gargantuan scale, with the gaiety, bounce and vigour correspondingly exaggerated. Soon another grizzly, a huge, tawny grandfather bear, strode up the left-side slope to the ridge, with all the ease of a practised mountaineer, indifferent alike to the foolishness of those young things, and to our presence. On second thought, when he reached the crest of the ridge, and cast a glance—and a sniff—in our direction, he decided that he did not wish to associate with us and turned and ambled up the ridge towards the summit, finally diagonalling off to the right.

Bob and I took a few hesitant steps forward along the ridge, and then stopped, more than ever startled by the unpropitious combination of a mother grizzly with two cubs, who broke out from directly below us and ran off to the right across the rocks. The mother, a huge silvertip, was considerably more concerned about our presence than the others had been. Two or three times as I cowered motionless down against the rocks, she would stop short in her course, stand up and sway gently back and forth to get the best smells of us that were wafting towards her. I could read her mind: 'Have I made a mistake? Hadn't I better, after all, go back and eat up those Underhills?' But the cubs were quite the most attractive babies as they rushed along on their little legs, hardly able to keep up with Mummy. Crossing a steepish snow patch, they slipped in their haste, and one of them rolled head over heels down the slope.

'What shall we do?' I asked Bob, considerably shaken.

'All those bears have moved away from us, in one way or another,' he replied, weighing each word. 'At least, those that have moved at all. Even the mother and cubs. They know we're here but they have shown no desire to attack us. I think we'd better go on to the summit.'

'What!' I exclaimed, eyeing a new bear, the seventh, strolling around quite far off to the right.

After all, Bob pointed out, we had come three thousand miles to climb this mountain. To my observation that here we had no trees to climb and that the nearest gun was that one on George Woods, three thousand feet below, he could only agree. We had no weapon but our ice-axes, he added, and there wasn't much fire-power to them.

'All right,' I capitulated. 'But I hope you realize that if any of those bears should close in behind us along this ridge, even inadvertently, it would mightily complicate our getting back to camp.' Bob did realize that, so he said. But we would go fast.

Fast we went, indeed. And noisily! I found it disconcerting to climb along a snow ridge where every foot of the ground was honeycombed with the huge footprints and claw marks of grizzlies, even on the summit ridge. That doesn't happen in the Alps. I have never climbed faster, both up and down.

'What happened? Why didn't you get up?' exclaimed Jean in alarm when we came into camp too early, about 2.30.

I replied that we had got up all right, surrounded by seven grizzly bears. And to George I observed that he had told us this was the time of year when the bears would all be down

196

below in the berry patches. Dick, however, pointed out that if I myself had on a fur coat like theirs I wouldn't stay down in the valleys either, with a snowy summer resort, cool and comfortable like that one, right at hand.

But why were there so many bears here anyway? I wanted to know. Didn't the Indians ever hunt them?

'Didn't use to, no. Scared of them,' said Dick. 'Don't believe an arrow'd bother a grizzly much at that. Of course, now everybody hunts them. There's an open season right here. But you shoot a bear in here, how are you going to get him out? A good hide can weigh a hundred pounds. Do you want to carry a hundred pounds on your back? Through the jungles we came through?'

We went back to Lagoon Lake by a different route. From Iceflow Lake above our camp we climbed to the ridge that separated us on the east from Lake of the Clouds. Here we turned the glasses for a few minutes back towards the summit of McDonald and saw our same bears—the mother with the two cubs, the big tawny one—and several new ones that we did not recognize, going briskly about the business of the day undisturbed by interlopers.

'Just wait until I get my new horse-trail in here,' said Dick. 'There'll be a new rug at the Diamond L Bar.'

'I'd just as soon see them all rugs,' remarked Robert.

The cubs, though, I protested, were sweet, and I should like to have a few of them preserved. But no big ones. Bob felt strongly, however, that one grizzly in a museum somewhere, stuffed, would be enough for him.

Only one other small incident marked the end of this, our first of a dozen or two trips into the Montana mountains. The following afternoon, after Bill and Slim had come up to Lagoon Lake with the pack-string to pack us out, and while they were still throwing the diamond hitches on the pack-horses' loads, four of us, George, Jean, Bob and I, started riding down ahead of the others. We had gone perhaps a mile and were riding along a narrow track cut out of a steep side-hill, at the highest point above Glacier Lake, when George, who was ahead, looked back

197

and shouted out to us in alarm, 'Get your horses off the trail, quick! *Get your horses off the trail quick!*' There was genuine urgency and fear in his voice.

But getting our horses off the trail, either up the four-foot bank on the left or down the precipitous scree slope on the right, looked impracticable. I found an alternative that suited me as well: I got myself off the horse. It was only a step from the saddle across to the bank and there I stood. George had heard the pack-train stampeding. Soon I, too, heard the sound of pounding hooves as seven terrified horses, all tied together in line, came galloping frantically along the trail down towards us, with packs and pack-saddles bumping, breaking, and parts flying off. Leading the charge was Bill's saddle horse, but without Bill, the empty stirrups streaming through the air.

At the very last minute, just before they ploughed into our saddle horses, uneasy and nervous but still standing there, the charging horses swerved to the right down onto the scree slope and galloped by. When they were well past three of us, they galloped up the bank again to the trail and there George Woods, still on his horse, tackled them.

For several minutes a great cloud of dust was all we could see, but the sounds that emerged from it were fearsome indeed as those great beasts thrashed around in terror and turmoil. But they were obviously still there and not continuing down the trail. Since they were in one line, with the halter of one horse tied to the tail of the next one, George had manœuvred himself and his horse into the middle, as some of the pack-horses tried to pass him to the left and some to the right. George, stout fellow, had stopped them.

'I couldn'ta done it if they hadn't been too winded to go on anyway,' he explained modestly. 'That last climb back up to the trail took it out of them.'

III. SINYALEMIN LAKE

Jean's sister Ruth had also been working at the ranch that summer of 1946 and one evening at a picnic I intercepted glances of a certain significance between Ruth and Jack Romer.

Nonsense, nothing to it, said Jean, when I confided my suspicions to her, but Jean had to eat her words, come October, when Ruth and Jack were married. We went to visit them in July of 1947 at their ranch between Ronan and St Ignatius, west of the Missions in the foothills of the range.

Jack had planned a trip for us into Sinyalemin Lake with Jean and Garland Counts, a friend of his. And Ruth? I inquired. 'Shhh!' Jean warned me quickly. Ruth would like to go, she whispered, but Jack thought the trip would be too hard for her. How odd it is that I can hear things like this and not really take them in! This remark might have given me some warning of the sort of trip it was going to be.

We had better start early, said Jack, even though from the end of the road up Mission Creek Canyon where we would leave the pick-up it was only three miles to the lake. (Similarly, it is only one mile from the Matterhorn Hut to the top of the Matterhorn, but one rarely measures it that way.) These three miles to Sinyalemin Lake took us all that day and part of the next.

Our first problem was crossing Mission Creek, a considerable stream too swift and deep to ford. Almost at once we found a tremendous old log lying across it, but rotting away and sagging ominously in the middle. But it had to do, for our efforts to build a bridge brought no success and we could find nothing else. As each one of us, holding on to a handrail we rigged up of our climbing rope, crossed this swaying log as gently and delicately as possible, it groaned and cracked and sank a little lower. No doubt good for many years, the reader is probably saying to himself. But wait: on the descent, when we crossed back again over this same log and the last man, Garland, was almost over, it crumbled apart in the middle and half of it fell into the water. Garland gave a mighty leap and if he had been able to jump just a couple of feet farther he would have landed on dry ground.

Once across the river we felt much closer to our lake, which now lay almost over our heads, in a little depression between two peaks. The main obstacle that separated us from it was three thousand vertical feet of broken cliffs draped with some of the most closely-knit underbrush I have ever worked my way through. There was no trail of any sort. As we zig-zagged back and forth to discover breaks in the rock bands, with great good luck we occasionally found tracks where a bear had just shoved through. A couple of little showers wet the underbrush and Garland's sleeping-bag. But all the time, to our right, the beautiful South Fork of Mission Creek, the outlet from Sinya-lemin Lake, came seething down in an almost continuous water-fall.

About six o'clock we reached the first level place, a little bench at the foot of more cliffs, glowing now in the warm orange light of sunset, which made such a striking contrast with the purple storm clouds drifting above them. I was tired, I reported, and should like to spend the night right here. The others protested not at all. One advantage of being an old lady is that when you are tired, you can say so. A man really shouldn't, and of course no young person can. But I can. And now and then, as this evening, I suspect that my companions are pleased enough to have me do so!

But when we reached the lake the next morning, I felt that being there was really worth the exertion. We had solitude and remoteness and beauty. The lovely slender lake curved along the valley between two parallel mountain ramparts, Sinyalemin Ridge to the north and the St Mary's Peaks to the south. The only breaks in the heights around were the one by which we had entered and where we now had our camp, the outlet of the lake, and Vacation Pass two miles away at the head of the valley. Mountain goats ambled around, or frolicked a bit on the mountainsides above. When I noticed one who was running as if he really meant it, I looked more attentively and discovered a grizzly behind, chasing him. As they went out of sight around the corner, after running across the entire face of Sinyalemin Peak, I was happy to see that the goat was still safely in the lead.

Jack, Jean and Garland climbed Sinyalemin Peak at the near end of the ridge while Bob and I, skirting along the northern

shore of the lake, made our way up the valley towards an unnamed peak perhaps a mile and a half farther along the ridge,
which looked to us as if it might offer more challenge. We did
not travel silently, having no desire to surprise any grizzlies.
A startled bear might act impulsively and unpleasantly, while
one forewarned might slip quietly away. At least that was our
hope.

We planned to try going up a rather steep snow gully in the
rock wall, which would lead us on to the northwest ridge of our
peak, and we had in fact started on this route when I, glancing
up, noticed a large boulder, on the gentler slopes near the top
of the wall, that looked somewhat odd. Its outline was less
distinct than it should have been, more fuzzy. More *furry*?
The glasses showed at once that it was in fact a large grizzly,
placidly turning over the rocks and no doubt lapping off the
accumulations of lady-bugs underneath. A meagre diet, it
would seem to me, for a grizzly, but perhaps it puts him to less
trouble than catching a goat. 'What does this do to your route?'
I asked Bob. We would shout and scare him off, he replied.
But as Garland had mentioned, 'Grizzlies don't scare easy.'
The noise we raised would have sent any black bear scampering
away in terror, but not this one. Since he apparently planned
to stay right there, we decided our best course would be to go
back down, circle around the mountain and ascend by the
southwest ridge.

On the way we met a goat who was tremendously interested
in our climb and who did, in fact, start up the mountain with
us, keeping about fifty feet above our heads. Efficient rock-
climbers goats may be, but certainly they are not neat ones.
The showers of rocks that this one kicked down made him a
most undesirable companion and we were happy when we
finally eluded him. Coming out on to the crest of the ridge we
saw him some fifty feet below, lying at his ease and looking
back down the slope where we had all been, apparently watching for us. He was astounded to see us above him, and all but
rubbed his eyes. After enjoying a pleasant little climb along
the ridge—just the two of us now, no goat—we found no cairn

on the summit and put one there. We had a splendid view of
the country, up north to Mt Harding which we hoped to climb
in a few days, across to High Park Lake, a beautiful deep blue
today, where we planned to be camping soon, and to Gray
Wolf Peak, which would be our first objective from High
Park.

Back at camp we learned that the others had had their
experience with grizzlies too, and a more trying one than ours.
When they had almost reached timberline they had come on a
mother with two cubs who reared up—she stood taller than a
horse, they all agreed on that—and came for them. They ran
for some small pine trees and each climbed one; here they
stayed for an hour or two while the three bears strolled around
underneath. What really embittered the situation for them was
that Jack, who was carrying Jean's camera, had to use both
arms to hang on to his tree, while Jean, sitting comfortably on
a limb with arms free, had no camera. The second missed
opportunity was that Garland had a gun and could have solved
the situation simply and effectively if Jack had not objected
so vehemently. Garland did in fact shoot several times in an
attempt to frighten the bears away, with Jack imploring him
not to aim. 'I have to aim,' protested Garland, 'in order *not*
to hit them.' The bears were quite indifferent to the shots.
Why Jack feels so benevolent towards grizzlies is incomprehensible to me. Still, after all, he has a grizzly rug or two at his
ranch.

IV. MOUNT HARDING

We had left Ruth with the job of finding an Indian who
would take us in to Mt Harding, the most striking peak at the
northern end of the Mission Range. Although no trail was
marked on the map, we felt sure, since this side of the range
was an Indian reservation, that the Indians must have a
hunting trail somewhere that would get us near enough to the
peak. Over at the Indian Agency in Dixon, Ruth had found
Ed McDonald, grandson of the original Angus, and an important man on the Tribal Council. When Ed warned us that the

route he would take us was 'no dude trail' he spoke but the simple truth.

'Which one of you ain't never rode the most?' inquired Ed, when we met at McDonald Lake, a big irrigation reservoir on Post Creek. I was quick to claim that distinction and was allotted the best horse, Brownie. 'Steadiest horse I've got,' explained Ed. 'He carried me out of the mountains once with a broken leg—my leg was broken, that is, not his.' That's the sort of horse that suits me. Ruth offered to ride a newly-purchased 'nervous' mare.

The trail eventually left the main valley of Post Creek with its beautiful great cedars—and mucky swamps—and worked up the sidewall towards a small hanging valley to the north. Here it went up diagonally over some very steep terrain, near the top zig-zagging up ledges above a high cliff, a place where it would not have occurred to us to take horses at all. The footing was bad, with lots of loose stones lying on the ledges; it would be particularly dangerous, said Ed, if the horses were to bunch up. So Ruth, Jean and I were to walk on up ahead, while he led the horses up one by one. He did, in the end, allow Robert to lead one horse, but Ruth and Jean, who were more experienced with horses than was Bob, and who could presumably have done at least as competent a job, were ignored, perhaps because they were women. I'm not sure women count for much from the Indian point of view. The next day it was Bob that Ed asked, and not Ruth and Jean themselves, if he should take the girls over to Elk Lake while we two were climbing Mt Harding.

The next morning, uneventfully, we reached the top of the mountain in some four hours over attractive wild country, with a short bit of rock-climbing at the end. On our return to camp we found Ed packing for our trip valley-wards and telling off sternly, but laconically, some Indian boys who had that morning shot a doe, a nursing mother, and had left the fawn, which they had not been able to find, to die. Although this was Indian land where ordinary game laws do not apply, Ed, an important elder statesman of the tribe, disapproved highly.

We had met these boys the day before, fishing, which is of course an accepted and respectable occupation quite unlike mountain climbing. How they had grinned when Ed, making an effort to keep his own face straight, informed them that we had made the trip in there in order to climb Mt Harding.

While going up over the bad ledges the day before, we had taken some comfort from the fact that we were going home another way, over Eagle Pass farther to the north. But when we found the steep slope leading up to the pass from our side to be deep in snow, we realized that our horses, particularly since they were all unshod, could not go that way. For centuries the Indians, of necessity, never shod their horses and even now, when they could presumably get the supplies, they still cling to the old and simpler ways. 'Shoes make horses slip on rocks,' Ed assured us. We should have to return as we had come.

At the dangerous place, Ed sent Bob on ahead to wait at the bottom, catch each horse as he got there, and tie him up. In spite of the difficulties of operating on a steep side hill, he had done a successful job with the first six and was awaiting the last when he saw me walking down the trail instead. In astonishment—for how could he have missed one?—and some alarm he shouted out that only six had come and where was the seventh? 'The seventh horse is dead,' I had to reply.

You cannot lead a horse down a place like those ledges, because if he falls while you are below him, he pushes you over the cliff first. So Ed had turned each animal loose, one at a time, and himself walked along behind, talking to the horse in a soothing and encouraging manner. The first few horses, although uneasy and frightened, had followed well enough the zig-zags of the trail as it wound down through the more navigable breaks in the ledges. But as more horses collected at the bottom, the remaining animals became more frantic to join them there and would trot and slide down the rocks at an alarming speed. I have heard 'horse-sense' spoken of in a laudatory tone but my personal observation has been that it is occasionally overrated. I have even been told that on a mountain trail 'you are safer on a horse than on your own feet', but of this I remain unconvinced. At least, it cannot be true unless you are a singularly inept pedestrian. This last horse of ours, the new nervous mare, completely lost her head, disregarded the trail altogether, and took a bee-line towards the other horses. Inevitably, she slipped and rolled down the slope. Landing on a switchback of the trail below, for a few seconds she struggled desperately to regain her footing. Ed and I, standing anxiously just above on a projecting rock which overlooked the scene, agreed that one extra pound of pull would have saved her. But no one could give it and she went over the cliff. For 300 feet she fell clear in the air, and then rolled down the rocks below, 200 feet farther, before disappearing into the woods.

Considerably lower down, the trail made a big switchback and returned under the cliff. As we approached, Brownie, my horse, turned his head to the left and pricked up his ears. Something interested him up there among the trees. But mildly —hardly a bear unless it was a very distant bear. Shortly we stopped and Jean and Ruth kept the remaining horses here while Ed, Bob and I hunted for the mare. We had to make sure she was dead and in no need of a final bullet. For one hour and twenty minutes we scrambled through trees and underbrush on a steep scree slope, and I for one have never hunted so hard for something I hoped I wouldn't be the one to find. But it seemed a job that needed to be done and three people can cover the ground faster than two. Now, at nearly six o'clock, with nine miles to go to get home, speed was desirable. During our search Bob was considerably startled to come upon the bleached bones of a horse's skeleton. Ed explained casually that every Indian in the valley had lost a horse at one time or another over that cliff. We picked up Ruth's coat, the halter, and pieces of the bridle and saddle, and finally Ed found the mare herself. Where? Back a bit, almost in sight of the trail, at the spot where my Brownie had pricked up his ears. Ed and Bob reported that there was no doubt about her being dead.

About the financial loss involved in the death of this mare,

Ed was most sportsmanlike. He wouldn't have wanted her anyway, he said. A horse that would lose his head on a mountain trail was of no use to him. He had bought her in a group of other horses, some of which were excellent ones. Being 'horse-poor', he owned thirty-five horses anyway, including a very fine Morgan for a 'Sunday horse', and he wouldn't miss this one.

V. HIGH PARK

A few days later we met Florence and Dean Peabody on the eastern side of the Mission Range at the Diamond L Bar Ranch. We were going in to the High Park region, reputedly one of the loveliest in the range, for a week of climbing. A stay of that length is more comfortable, with bigger tents and better food, if horses can go too, and with them Dick was going to carry our supplies. With great enterprise he had worked out a route and, so he wrote us, 'built a trail' into this region where horses had never been before. Even though the 'trail' turned out to be a few marks of dull blue crayon blending almost invisibly with tree or rock, which not even Dick could find very well, I don't believe it made much difference; the country was rough everywhere. Four hours it took us to travel from the lower end of Gray Wolf Lake to the upper, a distance of two miles. When great jutting cliffs rose precipitously out of the lake, there was nothing for it but to take our three pack-horses up and over. When crossing one steep scree slope I wondered if they would be able to keep their footing. Casually Dick mentioned that on his earlier trip to set up camp one of the pack-horses had, indeed, fallen here and rolled two hundred feet or more down into the lake. The men had got him out, uninjured. As for the contents of his pack, Dick didn't say. Sugar, salt and flour stand wetting badly, and even tins may suffer in a minor way. I have heard a sad tale of campers unpacking a load of tins that had been in the water and finding all the labels a sodden mass at the bottom.

On the pass that marked the watershed between Gray Wolf Lake and High Park Lake, we found extensive snowfields. But

since all these horses were shod, the snow made the going easier
—how much easier we realized more fully when it came time to
take the camp out again, with much of the snow melted, revealing Class I rock-climbing underneath.

About a thousand feet below the pass, in a tiny meadow on
the edge of a stream, with masses of magnificent flowers all
about, a superlative camp awaited us. So delighted were we
with the aspect of the surrounding peaks, as well, that we
decided at once we should like to remain here ten days instead
of the seven we had arranged for. Good-naturedly Dick accepted our suggestion that he could come in again with more food.
This he later did, bringing three guests at the ranch with him,
all of them back-packing T-bone steaks and other supplies.
Dick's rucksack had been packed in an original way, with all
the heavy tins resting on top of the fresh fruit, which was now
converted into jam. Florence devoted an hour or two to washing out that rucksack.

One man, Fred Herrick, who had come in with us, remained
as cook and bear-guard at camp while we climbed. 'We hope
to get Fred here in time to start,' Margaret had said the evening
before we left the ranch. 'He's a grand cook and, besides that,
I know you'll like him a lot. The only reason he isn't here now
is, he's in the jug.' This intrigued us for a moment, but it turned
out that Fred's offence had been shooting game out of season,
which no one except the game warden considers an offence at
all. How else, indeed, when he lives forty or fifty miles from the
nearest store, is a man going to eat?

In the next ten days we wandered far and wide around this
charming region. Many good climbs we had, some of them new,
all of them delightful. Fred gave it as his considered judgment
that 'Bob and Deanie hadn't ought to do such hard climbs.
They're past the prime of life, both of them.' Twenty-three,
says Fred, is the age for mountain climbing. Chivalrously, he
forebore to say whether or not Florence and I, as well, were past
the prime of life.

The first day we went back up to the pass and climbed Gray
Wolf Peak. We hit the ridge to the north near a small sharp

peak that we thought was probably unclimbed (it was) and, feeling that we might not be by here again, we decided to climb it at once. This set us back an hour. We lost a few more hours entertaining ourselves with fine rock-climbing over some of the needles along the ridge that we found later could all have been turned in a few minutes on the snow below. When we finally started up the mountain itself, it was late. A steepish slope of hard snow on the northeast face, requiring considerable cutting by Robert, took us to the bergschrund. When we saw that the rocks above the bergschrund were unalluring and that the bergschrund itself led nearly to the col at the base of the final rock peak, we travelled along inside it for perhaps 200 feet, using a sideways chimney technique in the narrow parts to edge ourselves along. It was a cold, wet and slippery route, but a direct one. The final rock-climb offered several interesting pitches, particularly in its first hundred feet up the steep heel of the southeast ridge. All in all, it was 5.40 in the afternoon before we reached the summit. All mountaineers will know what that meant: we were not down before dark. (There was no daylight saving—summer time—in Montana.) We had, however, discovered a much easier route of descent and, observed intently all the while from below by four goats, we managed to finish the real rock-climbing by dusk. Although we had no lantern, having started that morning in daylight, we worked on until half-past ten. I rather enjoyed this rock-climbing by touch, instead of by sight, as I led down, feeling a way with hands and feet down the few final rock bands and over the big boulders of the moraines. The stars provided light enough to cross the snow of the pass, but when the snow ran out we had to stop. Fortunately, however, here began the first few scrub trees. We would build a fire and wait for the moon to rise. Soon we found the perfect place, a tiny grassy spot between two rock ribs. 'Sit here, Florence, and be a bell buoy,' instructed Bob. 'Sing out every few seconds so we won't get lost while we look for wood.' For of course we couldn't *see* any wood. We found it by running into it or by stumbling over it, as we three spread out and wandered around in the solid darkness. Soon we were lying by a roaring fire, and warm at least on one side. The fire look-outs, we hoped, would all be asleep by 10.30. (But when we heard a patrol plane go over very early the following morning, we hoped it wasn't bringing smoke-jumpers.)

By midnight the moon was up and shining down into our valley. We set out for camp, feeling sure Fred would have hung out a lantern to guide us home. But as we worked down over the ledges, lower and lower, no lantern could we see and no answer could we get to our shouts, all of which made us wonder if we were really on the right route. Eventually, however, we came upon the camp itself, completely dark and silent. As Fred, roused, crawled sleepily out of his bag, and heated up the food, he made his explanation. Said he, 'I had your supper ready at half-past five, like you said. And I kept it warm, keeping the fire going all that time—I had to chop a lot of wood —until eleven. But then when it got to be eleven o'clock and you weren't back, I felt sure there had been an accident and it would be all right for me to go to bed.'

XI

Montana, Swan Range

I. SWAN PEAK, 1948

The Swan Range lies to the east of the Mission Range and roughly parallel with it. Swan Peak, the culminating point of its 100-mile length, stands 9,255 feet high and eight miles in an airline east of the Swan Valley road. One might think therefore that it would be a simple matter to climb Swan Peak; it took us two years to do so. The main problem in climbing a mountain in Montana is usually, How do you get to it? Such was the problem here.

We couldn't get horses in towards Swan Peak at all, said Dick Hickey. But he and one of his wranglers would come with us, and we'd back-pack what we needed. Since the mountain had been climbed from the south by the survey crew, said Dick, that side was probably too easy. We'd approach it from the north over Forest Service trails which, although out of use for some years, we could probably follow well enough.

We pulled out of the yard at the Diamond L Bar Ranch at 7 a.m. on July 26, 1948. As the car was just getting under way Margaret Hickey hurried up with an urgent problem on her mind. 'That man, Dick, that's coming this afternoon?' she asked. 'What'll I do with him?'

'I wouldn't know, honey,' replied Dick, the boss. 'I'm on my vacation now.'

This may have been a reasonable viewpoint at the moment; before he got back, however, less than three days later, he was declaring with heartfelt vehemence that never in all his life had he been so miserable.

That night we camped across the divide, above timberline, in one of the most charming spots I've seen, a little triangular point between two tumbling streams, carpeted thick with flowers, where surely no human being had camped before. At the base of the cliffs beside us a bear had trampled out a bed which enjoyed, along with ours, a glorious view out over the South Fork country, the fabulous Bob Marshall Wilderness, an area of 995,000 acres of National Forest land set apart to be preserved in its original state. All the miles of forest and mountain we looked over contained hardly a human being, but plenty of elk, goats, bighorn sheep and bear.

'I've never seen such a pretty place,' said Bob Flack, in wonder and something like awe. 'I'm going to bring my bride up here. . . . I could do it, even if I had to make two trips myself to lug up the things.'

I don't think the girl was picked out yet, but the honeymoon site definitely was.

We had two small, light-weight tents with us, and we were soon in them. The next morning, early, after a good breakfast, Robert and I set out for Swan Peak. (We weren't to have another real meal for thirty-six hours.) Contouring to the south along the east slopes of the main divide, we crossed a series of secondary ridges and valleys, up and down until, working higher, we reached broad snowfields with rock ribs between, and came to the base of the peak.

The mountain wasn't so easy as it had looked, since the strata sloped against us all the way, like the shingles on a roof. We would work our way up through a band of cliffs by some crack or chimney, then cut steps up a little steep hard snow to the next band of cliffs, and so on; finally we climbed a longer gully, steep and narrow and of very loose rock, to the divide. This last we followed, turning a couple of towers, to the foot of the final peak itself. The rock-climbing from here up, although not long, was unpleasant, as the rock was loose and slippery, with the steep beds of the gullies in places composed of fine scree or almost clay over the smooth rock bottom. Besides, we were in a great hurry, since the fine weather of the

211

morning was turning bad. There was an obvious thunderstorm on the way. At 1 p.m., considerably out of breath, we reached the summit and there, a mile or more away to the southwest, across a deep gap and a long curving, jagged ridge, stood a summit perhaps 800 feet higher, Swan Peak itself. We were on the wrong mountain! It might or might not have been possible, under better conditions, to follow the ridge to the true summit; we hardly cared. All we wanted now was to get down quickly and this peak, as some consolation, had not been climbed before. Our cairn, however, was very sketchy.

But the storm did not break immediately. We were able, by travelling fast, to get down off the peak itself and then, hoping to find an easier route of descent, to follow along the divide quite a bit farther to the north, although we could see little in the clouds and it was hard to stand up against the bitter wind. But we were finally brought up short by a huge drop-off with nothing in sight below except black clouds boiling up. There was nothing to do but struggle back along the ridge to the chimney we had come up, knowing that that at least would provide a possible, if not an attractive, route of descent. How thankful we were for the large cairn that Bob had left at the top of this chimney and that now loomed up in the eddying mists like the life-saving beacon it was. We descended this horrid chimney in torrents of rain and great bursts of thunder simultaneous with lightning, searching frantically for shelter, of which however there was none at all, until we reached the *Randkluft*, the cleft where the top of the snowfield had melted away from the rock. Here we stayed with our fronts against the cold, wet slippery rock and our backs against the cold, wet slippery ice for an hour. It wasn't a very good place. Even though, to avoid stonefalls from above, we chose a spot away from gullies and where there were the fewest stones already lying on the ice, the pelting rain washed down a good many stones just the same. One hit me on the arm but it hadn't come from very far above. We were soaked through and extremely cold.

Although the rain continued, as soon as the lightning flashes

212

seemed to be leaving our immediate vicinity we thought it best to be on our way. Chilled and stiff as we were, we found it awkward enough getting down. With the rain pouring down and the thick clouds swirling by and cutting visibility to a very short distance, we realized that our best chance of finding camp again (and a good deal depended on our finding it, and before night!) would be to start out by following the tracks we had made that morning across the snow patches, as long as these lasted. Although the tracks would be considerably washed out, we thought we should be able to find them. So we could, as it turned out; but so too could somebody else. On reaching the first snow patch we found our tracks overlaid by those of an enormous grizzly. He was following them back towards camp, just as we hoped to, and *his* tracks were fresh, with the marks of his long curved claws all too distinct. When we crossed the various rock ribs, we noted that the bear also took great pains on the farther side to rejoin our tracks again. We'd see the marks on the snow where he had climbed up or slid down to recover our trail, and he was just ahead. We went on in this way following the grizzly, as the grizzly went on following us, until we came to a boulderfield, the débris of a large rock fall, with a lot of the boulders bigger than a bear. One might easily conceal a bear; one might even *be* a bear.

'I don't really want to catch up with this baby,' said Bob, hesitating a moment. 'We can't see well enough in this mist. Let's go somewhere else.' This meant leaving our tracks.

So we circled way around downhill and then, travelling blind, struck out for camp by instinct. We still could see almost nothing, for the wind was howling by, sweeping thick mist with it. The pelting icy rain chilled us thoroughly. No matter how hard we struggled to move fast we could not walk vigorously enough to keep from shivering. Robert had a sharp stone in his boot which left a painful bruise for some days, but the thought of stopping in this cold long enough to remove it was unendurable.

Finally, after crossing several lateral ridges and the streams between them, we came to a stream which I thought must be ours—only, I knew, we were too high.

'Are you sure?' said Bob. 'We've been coming up, of course. But we lost a lot of elevation when we first left the tracks and I didn't think we'd got back yet to the level of camp. It's four o'clock and it'll be dark early tonight. If we go down now when we ought to go up we may not find camp in time.'

I looked around: snow, rocks, scree, flowers, mist, rain, in a small circumference. For Robert's sake I really wanted to find some intelligent reason to advance for thinking we were too high, but my feeling for location is a primitive one and based on no intellectual processes whatever. Like a horse, although I can often find my way back to a place where I have been before, I can't explain how. But this time an idea struck me.

'The flowers,' I said. 'Look at them. They're the same ones our tents are pitched on. But here they're in bud, and in camp the seeds are already forming. The snow went off here more recently. For all we can see, it's about the same exposure, so it must be higher.'

I just hope I'm right, I thought to myself as we made our way down along the cascading stream through some tangles of vegetation and boulders where it would have been arduous to climb back up again.

'What are those two little things below there?' I asked tentatively as the mists parted momentarily, hardly daring to hope, and so soon. If Robert thought so too . . .

'Tents!' said Robert.

Dick and Bob Flack were glad to have us back. At least that's what they said from inside their closed tent; I didn't notice anybody coming out to greet us. Our little tent had been made for one person only but we both crawled in and, crouching on our sleeping-bags, stiff and shivering, with enormous difficulty we shuffled off our wet clothes. Then, since we certainly did not want them on the sleeping-bags and there was no other space for them in the tent, we pushed them outside. They couldn't get any wetter than they already were and they would dry out quickly enough in the first sun tomorrow morning. Storms in Montana rarely last more than a few hours. We then wriggled into our sleeping-bags. It was four hours before I stopped shivering and began to warm up.

About 8.30 in the evening Dick and Bob Flack emerged from their tent. They made some efforts to start a fire and there was talk about nice hot tea, but that was all. Just talk; no tea. When the fire showed some reluctance to get going, the wind, the storm and the cold made the tent look more attractive to them than anything outside. I've seen some bad storms of rain, sleet or snow where Robert was able to get a fire going and make tea, but Robert, this time, was not in the correct costume. Finally I accepted thankfully a cup of cold water that Bob Flack brought us from the stream and ate half a sandwich from the lunch we had taken up the mountain and had had no opportunity to eat. There was more food in our rucksacks but, to eat, it was necessary to take a hand and arm out of the sleeping-bag and nothing in the world was worth that for very long.

I don't know of any snugger feeling than to settle down, dry and comfortable and warm enough by now, in a down sleeping-bag in a tiny tent all closed up, with the storm beating on the roof and the wind howling by outside. You enjoy a keener appreciation of shelter when the roof is thin and fragile. Pretty soon there was a curious muffling of the sounds that made Robert and me chuckle a bit. We knew what that meant: it wasn't rain on the tent any more; it was snow.

The next morning, July 28, we woke to a real winter blizzard. The tent walls were sagging down almost to our sleeping-bags with the weight of the snow resting upon them. Everything outside was white, even the air, where the wind was whistling by with eddies of fine snowflakes. For it was still snowing hard and the temperature was well below freezing. Climbers in the Himalayas, when overtaken by bad weather, simply stay in their sleeping-bags if they can until the storm passes, and Robert and I should have liked to do the same here. We had food enough and we were entirely comfortable. But the other two weren't. They had passed a wretched night, miserable with

215

the cold, and their tent, one of ours, had leaked badly. Our little light tents frequently seem to leak when we lend them to people though they don't when we sleep in them ourselves. Perhaps experience has taught us to treat them more gently.

'We've got to get out of here quick, Robert,' said Dick grimly, his teeth chattering, 'before we freeze to death.'

'Oh, dear,' I murmured to Robert. 'This nice warm sleeping-bag and those clothes outside in the snow.'

'I know,' he answered, 'but I think we've got to go. Those two can't stay here. Put this woollen undershirt of mine on first. I've got another.'

Besides that, I had a little light rainshirt and a dry sweater. Some Providence, or some remnant of common sense, had led me to keep my sweater in the tent during the night and I had stuffed it under the sleeping-bag cover, above the down layer, where heat from my body had dried it nicely. But the rest of our clothes were outside. Although we found them easily enough by digging around in the snow in front of the tent, and shook what snow we could out of them, they had frozen stiff and rigid just as we'd thrown them down. You've no idea, until you try, how hard it is to push your way into clothes in that condition. But they were all we had. Cotton, too. It is the style in the West, in the hot and dry summers, to wear blue jeans for everything.

Dick and Bob Flack had no extra clothing at all. There seems to be a feeling among western outdoors men that it is unmanly to carry sweaters, raincoats, etc. Those things are for dudes. For them, a good heavy flannel shirt will answer every requirement. There was a pathetic little white cotton towel, now, draped over Bob Flack's shoulders.

Packing up was a dreadful business. We could work only a few seconds at a time before our hands became numb and we'd have to stop and slide them inside our clothes to thaw out. How they tingled and ached! I had gloves, not from any foresight— they just happened to show up in my rucksack—but nobody else did.

'I've got a quilted jacket back home that I wear when I cut

ice on the lake at forty below zero,' remarked Dick, with an effort, and one could feel the longing in his voice.

'I've got ski mittens,' said Bob, 'and I'm never going out of the house again, July or August or any time, without a pair.'

'I've got two fur coats,' I added, and I should indeed have liked to have them both with me at that moment.

There was no singing this morning. Dick is usually a great hand for song but although I suggested he favour us with 'When it's Springtime in the Rockies', it was no go. I got no answer at all. I turned to Bob Flack.

'When you bring your bride up here . . .'

Perhaps it would be as well not to quote his reply verbatim, but the upshot of it was that his plans had changed.

Naturally there was no thought of breakfast. Our one idea was to get out and get out fast.

It took us seven hours, from 8 a.m. to 3 p.m., to cover the approximately fifteen miles up over the divide and down to the road, wet through and even our bones, I think, chilled. I, for one, had to clench my teeth and call on a lot of will-power to struggle up over that divide in the face of the blizzard and particularly its wind. But, although the snow on the steep grass slopes made the going slippery for our rubber-soled boots, I got great help from my two ice-axes, Robert, not having any gloves, having declared that he could not carry his.

When we had dropped down the other side perhaps a thousand feet in elevation the snow turned to driving, icy rain. Every bush we pushed our way through added its shower of ice-water to our drenched clothing. Our boots were filled with ice-water all day long. Although our packs were extra heavy due to all the snow and ice we had packed up along with our tents, ropes and other gear, we were too cold to stop for rest.

About two I began to feel faint. It was nothing serious, I knew, just the blood-sugar getting low, and I knew, too, the remedy.

'Has anybody got any candy?' I inquired.

The men just stared at me.

'Do you really mean,' Robert asked finally, 'that you want to stop moving just to get out something to eat?'

Bob Flack had a chocolate bar in the outside pocket of his pack which he offered me. I have never worked harder to eat a chocolate bar than I did that time. Ordinarily a chocolate bar softens up in your mouth, melts a little on the corners here and there as you chew it. But nothing was melting in my mouth that day. Although I chewed and chewed and the pieces did get smaller, they still had the consistency of so much gravel when I finally succeeded in swallowing them, washing them down with ice-water from the stream.

The miles seemed interminable and towards the end, although I could still keep on walking like an automaton, when it became necessary to climb over the tangles of blow-downs I got more and more languid.

'I think I might perhaps have been able to keep on for one more mile,' said Robert in great seriousness when we reached the road, 'but I'm sure I couldn't have made three.'

Dick, who had got down ahead of us and was waiting at the car, spoke up promptly, 'I couldn't have made another hundred yards.'

II. SWAN PEAK, 1949

The following year we made a second attempt on Swan Peak. The best approach, we now felt sure, was from the south, but since the trail up Lion Creek, the obvious route, was not cleared, we tried out first another route that had been schemed out by Stanley Ricketts, a young man of sanguine temperament, who was to run the approach trip for us. Dick Hickey was tied up by some important business at the ranch. That's what he said; in my opinion the truth is that he was too smart to go. Besides Stan, Pete Holopeter would go along, bringing his stock, horses to ride and mules to carry the baggage. And our old friend Fred Herrick, who had been into the Missions with us, would be camp cook. Three men for the three of us—our twelve-year-old Bobby was along too—looked very luxurious, but as things turned out we didn't have an ounce of superfluous manpower.

Three days it required to gain a point from which we could climb the peak. We began to lay bets on who would reach their goal first, the British on Everest or we on Swan Peak. While no one of these three days was a sinecure, the most arduous turned out to be the second when, Stan's original route of access having proved impracticable, we dropped down without a trail into Lion Creek Valley. Twenty-seven hundred feet this drop was, measured by the aneroid. It is safe to say that nobody had ever been down that way before, and I know six people who are not going down again. 'Lewis and Clark never went nowhere like this,' said Fred. While the upper hanging valley was steep enough all the way, when we got out above Lion Creek we found the last thousand feet almost all precipitous cliffs. But we didn't get *there* until a lot later.

The floor of the magnificent primeval forest was tangled thick with the piled-up windfalls of past decades, overgrown with snow-brush, alders, etc. Stan, former Forest Service trail foreman, worked ahead, continually swinging a powerful axe, and picking out the best route anybody could have found, given the terrain he had to work with, but not an awfully good one just the same. Pete led his pack-train with a mighty worried look on his face, the rest of us led our saddle horses. Stan's and Pete's saddle horses walked along with us, loose. I don't need to say that nobody rode.

There was plenty of water, too much we thought now and then, especially when we had two mules at once down in the mud so deep that the boys had to unpack them to get them dug out again. Around 3.30 we were stuck, definitively. Stan and Pete set out, without animals, to see if there was any possible way down and we didn't see them again until 5. Men on foot, unhampered by horses, travel fast and we were alarmed to think that, after all the distance we had come, it could take them so long to get to Lion Creek and back. 'What we ought to do,' suggested Fred, as we waited, 'is build us a good fire. Lots of wet stuff on it. Then the Forest Service would come boiling up here. They'd put ten men to building a trail to get to the fire, and a trail's just what we want.'

Finally the boys returned, reporting that while they had not been to Lion Creek they had come to a place where they could look down over the steep part. They had seen some timber on the slope, which proved that there were no cliffs. This seemed like a *non-sequitur* to me then, and much more so later. So on we started again, dragging the poor tired horses. At one dreadful tangle Stan said he guessed this was the place where he hadn't put any blazes. I knew exactly what he meant: he hadn't been able to figure out a route through here at all.

At the steep part, naturally, our troubles increased. Once Bobby fell and his horse, right above him, could not stop. Casually Bobby rolled off to the side and his horse and the three following mules slid on by. When, pretty soon, I lost my horse, too, I decided that getting the stock down here could fairly be left to the men and that women and children could walk along behind. Bob told me later that while he thought it was perfectly proper for Bobby to do this, he was shocked to see me give up, too. But it wasn't long before he noticed that his own horse, trembling all over, was so tired he wasn't going to be able to stand on his feet much longer. Bob, too, thought he'd rather not be underneath. So, from above, he drove down the six saddle horses, kept them going, and none of them got away, either. Bob has come a long way in the art of wrangling from our first trip with Dave Williams in 1934. Stan, on ahead, was chopping out the route as usual. Pete was leading the three most ornery mules and Fred the other two. As I said before, we didn't have any too many men. Pete, firm, calm, strong, was doing a remarkable job with those three high-strung and terrified animals. It is a pleasure to watch an expert at work. Once they all four got to sliding rapidly down the slope, Pete and one mule passing to one side, and the other two mules to the other side, of a quite sizeable tree. It must have been a remarkably strong rope between mules one and two, for, since Pete and the mules couldn't stop and something had to give, it was the tree that was pulled right over, down to the ground, its roots in the air. The rope slid along the trunk, ripping off branches as it went.

Although the animals naturally fell now and then, only one rolled seriously. This was one of Fred's mules and Fred told me later, putting the matter as if he had had all the time in the world to take his measures, that when he looked up and saw this mule rolling down on him, he studied the slope below carefully, picked out a good log, and went and lay down below it; the mule rolled right over the log and him, too. Onlookers confirmed that this is exactly what happened, but at a faster tempo. Fred had been hired to cook, and when I complimented him on this outside-the-line-of-duty activity, he remarked, 'I suppose I shouldn'ta done it. It ain't really my job to get rolled on by no mules. My job is to look after Bobby.'

The mule that rolled had no broken bones, but he didn't feel well for the rest of the trip. It was the work of only a few minutes now to distribute his load among the saddle horses, except for the saw. When Stan shouted up, 'Would Miriam please carry the saw?' I assented cheerfully enough, although, to be frank, on occasion I rather liked having both hands to lower myself down this slope. A six-foot cross-cut saw carried over the shoulder—with teeth away from the neck, suggested Stan—has a remarkable resiliency. At every step of mine it would bound up into the air, practically lifting me off my feet. It added an element of surprise to every movement I made. At this early stage the saw still had a wooden handle on each end and I wasn't clever enough to keep the rear one from catching on almost everything.

Although the slope was astonishingly steep and there were cliffs all around us, Stan was, apparently by magic, slowly finding a way down between them. It was, however, getting on towards dusk. Bob and I exchanged a few whispers: we ourselves could of course survive the night anywhere here, but what disposition could be made of the horses and mules? Bobby entertained himself by keeping a keen watch out for a place level enough for a single sleeping-bag. He never found one. And then, providentially, we came upon a long rock-slide and below that one, another. We went straight down them. The slides were steep, the rocks football-size and unstable, and the weary stock frightened and reluctant. But at least there was no chopping to be done here and we lost altitude fast.

At last the slope eased off; we were getting down into the dense cedar forest in the valley. It was after ten now and really dark. When we reached the trail we camped in the first wide place, even though we should have to carry water quite a distance. Our preparations for sleep were sketchy; just a little cold food—whatever Fred found first—and then our sleeping-bags.

Late the following afternoon, after we had reached the head-waters of Lion Creek, just under the Swan Divide, Bob, Stan and I walked up the side-hill far enough to get a fine view of Swan Peak. We were here quite a bit farther away from it than we had been at the end of the first day, and a lot lower down. But we had a practicable route of approach.

We planned our strategy for the next day, watched six goats strolling around on some cliffs opposite, picking out their sleeping places for the night, and one goat right above us, and Bob and I went home to supper. Stan went a bit farther up and when he came in to camp, 'Get ready for a stampede, folks,' he said cheerfully. 'There's a big grizzly about a quarter of a mile above the horses and working down towards them.' This time, thank heaven, it was a false alarm.

The following morning we started on what turned out to be one of the finest days Bob and I have ever enjoyed, and Stan, who came along, agreed with us. Usually the men who go on these trips will have nothing to do with the climbing itself. Where the horses stop, they stop. We've found only a few, natural-born mountaineers, who love it, and Stan was one of those.

In the first place, once we were up above timberline and wandering along near the Swan Divide, the country was surpassingly lovely, with the most enchanting little lakes, streams, waterfalls, cliffs and alpine meadows, which very few people indeed had seen. And such masses of magnificent flowers everywhere! In the rock-slides grew luxuriant carpets of *Dentaria rupicola*, that plant that had been collected only a time

222

or two, and only on McDonald Peak in the Missions. It is everywhere in the Swan Range (one of the few regions in the United States that has not been much explored botanically). To think that the first time I found it, also on McDonald Peak, it took me sixteen months and five universities to get it identified! But we had too little time for botany that day. The animals too were a pleasure—the half-dozen elk in the little glade just below us, a goat or two taking his ease in the shade of a cliff—all of them surprised, of course, to see us, but not extraordinarily alarmed.

Swan Peak presented no technical mountaineering difficulties. On the approach we followed along the divide, unnecessarily roundabout but providing open and easy travelling, and just the sort of walk I enjoy most. We roped down twice on the descent of some small towers that had to be traversed. Stan was charmed with this manœuvre, new to him, although on the first rope-off, one of sixty feet, he declared vehemently when he reached the bottom that his pants were on fire. On the subsequent rope-off it was Stan who wished to tie the sling, place the rope and retrieve it. The only mistake he made, he said, was in not going back up (hand over hand on the rope, I assume) to rope down again, it was such fun.

We strolled up the final peak and had a good look around. The ridge from our north peak did not look alluring. Farther off to the north rose Great Northern Mountain which we had climbed on my birthday in 1948. Farther still were all the peaks of Glacier Park. Across the Swan River valley to the west stood our friends the Missions from Harding to McDonald to Gray Wolf. South stood the other peaks of the Swan Range and to the west the South Fork country which we were to penetrate in 1950.

We had come up by the southeast ridge (the divide) and since we all liked rock-climbing we decided to go down the much more precipitous south ridge, composed of a series of five or six large drops marking the bands of limestone that made up the mountain. All but the last one we made all right, usually by climbing along the crest of the ridge itself or by weaving from side to side through 'pack-rat holes' which Bob and Stan, being bigger than I, didn't find so amusing. But the last big grey precipice was too smooth to climb directly and too long to rope, and we had to turn it on the horrid west face of scree-covered ledges.

The dinner that Fred had ready for us that evening deserves to be recorded: tomato soup, chicken, gravy, mashed potatoes, asparagus, apple sauce, apricot pie, jello, cocoa, tea, coffee. Followed by hot roasted marshmallows prepared by Pete and Bobby. There had been two fires maintained in camp all that day, one for Fred's cooking and one for Bobby to play with!

XII

Montana, Beartooth Range

The highest mountains in Montana lie in the southern part of the state, in the Beartooth Range; consequently this was one of our objectives on our first trip to Montana in 1946. Granite Peak, 12,847 feet, being the state high-point, had naturally received more attention from climbers than most Montana mountains; it had been climbed as early as 1923 by three men from the Forest Service, and three or four times since then. But back home we could not seem to get any detailed information on a good way to approach Granite. Norman Clyde, for instance, the outstanding California mountaineer who had made the second ascent, wrote Bob that some route other than the one he had followed would almost surely be preferable. We decided that this first year we would settle for Mt Wood, 12,661 feet, the second highest and, once on the ground, lay our plans for a trip to Granite later.

When Bob had written Eddie Ikerman, owner of the Beartooth Ranch at Nye, Montana, about taking us with horses to within striking distance of Mt Wood, he had replied, 'May I have the privilege of climbing Mt Wood with you?' This was indeed astonishing. For in Montana man's normal means of locomotion is the horse, and one who travels on foot is a bit queer. In our five years out there, only two or three Montana men have ever showed any willingness to climb. Most shared the views of Milt, one of Eddie's sons-in-law, who told us, 'I'm not a fussy man. I like almost everything. But there's just

two things in the world I can't stand, and both of 'em's mountain climbing.' But Eddie, although without experience in
alpine technique, loved climbing and had, in fact, made the
first ascent of Mt Wood. Ours would be the second.

On our trip to Wood we camped the first night in a slight
depression on the Stillwater Plateau, a charming spot in a little
grove by a spring, with the horses grazing contentedly just
beyond in rich, extensive meadows thickly dotted with clumps
of arctic gentians (*Gentiana frigida*). The horses carefully
munched around the gentians, leaving them untouched; apparently their flavour is inferior to their appearance—and a good
thing, too, from my point of view.

From there we set up a fly camp on the south end of the
Stillwater Plateau, at the foot of the last small rise separating
us from Mt Wood. Along the side of the tent to the west Eddie
and Bob constructed a fine windbreak of large rocks, chinked
and banked with sod, but nothing they could do, at that elevation of 11,000 feet and with that wind, could make the place
really cosy. There was no shelter even for the stove, which
refused to burn, so high was the wind. For it we built another
rock-and-sod windbreak, circular this time and about a foot in
diameter. Robert, the cook, reached into this kitchen over the
top. We missed the big, roaring campfire to which we had
become accustomed in our Montana camps; it would have felt
good that evening. One of the main inconveniences of camping
above timberline is that there is no wood.

Nobody wanted to be outside after sunset; by eight o'clock
we were all in our sleeping-bags. It was a cold night, and one
lacking somewhat in comfort. Bob has complained since then
that I, reinforced by Eddie, rolled down on him, crushing him
against the windbreak and forcing him to sleep on a sharp rock
ridge. But actually it was I who was in the hollow and Bob
and Eddie, one on each side, rolled down on me. At times I was
so constricted that I breathed only with difficulty, but the
arrangement did keep me nicely warm. In any case, we all had
to sleep close together since the tent had been designed for two
people, and I think small ones. To make it accommodate three

226

we lowered the peak and spread out the sides. It became a question in my mind whether it was still a tent or just a bedspread.

By six the next morning the sun rose and so, at once, did Eddie, although I think he may have found that this was a mistake. 'I wonder when the folks up here have summer?' he mused, his teeth chattering, as he started the preparations for breakfast. 'I guess it's one of those places where it's winter ten months of the year, and the other two months it's way late in the fall.'

At seven o'clock we were off, wearing all the clothes we had. We quickly crossed the intervening summit, only about 500 feet above us, and came down to the saddle at the base of the north-west ridge of Mt Wood. Here Eddie on his first ascent, seeing this rather jagged rock ridge in front of him, had dropped down some 2,000 feet to the west, circled around the base of the mountain and gone up, finally, by a steep gully on the south-west face, a route which we followed on the descent. But now, on the way up, this looked roundabout to us. After all, we liked rock-climbing, we would see if we could make a way directly up the ridge.

About halfway across the saddle, on reaching the first of a series of slender gendarmes, we roped up. There were going to be some delicate traverses as we turned these pinnacles on one side or the other. I was leading here and as I made the first such traverse, across some small snow-and-ice coated footholds on the north, I wondered about Eddie, coming third on the rope. Shouldn't we perhaps have put him in the middle? After all, it was his first experience with roped climbing, and beginners are sometimes squeamish on a place like that. To my surprise, he stepped along casually, apparently with the greatest relish.

We learned the answer: during the two World Wars Eddie had got a job as a structural steel worker. On one occasion he worked on a bridge 160 feet above the Missouri River, in a winter sleet storm, with blocks of ice swirling along in the river below. Any sissy, says Eddie, can work on a skyscraper, where

227

you have stationary ground underneath; it takes more of a man to work over water. No, Eddie didn't mind the exposure on Mt Wood!

We had fun with the pinnacles, turning the first few mostly on the north, later ones on the south. When we reached the main mass of the mountain and the northwest ridge became more indeterminate, we worked up diagonally towards the south, crossing successive ribs and gullies. We climbed quickly. There is great suspense, after you have planned a route to the crest of a ridge, until you reach the point where you can see if the route continues around on the other side. I don't know anything that is much more fun. The uncertainty and the series of minor triumphs when the pitches go make this one of the most entertaining pastimes in life. And so much more uncertain, of course, and consequently more entertaining, if no one has been that way before. And here, too, the climbing looked more fearsome from a distance than it actually turned out to be when we came to grips with it. Apart from loose rock we met no great difficulties—but it often looked as if we were going to, and that is pleasant.

'I don't think it's true, what folks say around here,' observed Eddie, after we had been climbing for several hours, 'that a horse can go anywhere a man can.'

We finally crossed the main southwest gully near its head and joined the ridge connecting Mt Hague with Mt Wood. This we followed, turning one large gendarme and passing over two small ones, to the summit, which we reached at noon. We had a glorious view over all the Beartooths and other ranges farther off, including our old friend the Grand Teton, rising most impressively more than 100 miles to the south.

For a hair-raising account of a trip I have never heard anything to equal the report of this climb that Eddie gave back at the ranch, sitting at the head of the long dining-table with the rows of guests on either side. 'It was real Big League stuff,' said he. Infallibly, step by step, we had chosen the one route by which we could have got up. So impressive did it all sound that only an occasional detail suggested to Bob and me that

228

this was really the same climb we had been on too! It was settled that next year we would climb Granite Peak together.

II. CATHEDRAL POINT

One more climb we did that summer, Cathedral Point, a granite pinnacle 8,880 feet high, which rises abruptly some 3,200 feet above its base by the Stillwater River. Unclimbable, one would say after a brief glance. But Bob had given it more than that. On our way to the Lake Plateau, while riding up the Stillwater valley on gentle old Pedro, he had had this peak before his eyes for about an hour. Leaning back against the cantle, with the reins, I am sorry to say, tied together and draped over the pommel, Bob had studied the peak with the binoculars, particularly the lines of vegetation here and there, sure proof of a break in a rock wall. The obvious route ran up a steep couloir to the right of the summit, broken in two places by large chockstones that would have to be turned by the lines of vegetation on the face. He came to the conclusion that we could link up those lines well enough to make a trial worth while.

The route up the couloir worked out very much as Bob had planned it, except that, instead of two chockstones, we found four. We turned them all successfully, however, and arrived, triumphant, at the top of the couloir—to find that we weren't even on the right mountain! But it wasn't far away, separated from us by a large open gully which broke off in cliffs before reaching the main valley. We could get down into the gully by following a narrow goat-track across the face of the peak we were on, but to cross the gully, through a thick tangle of alders, turned out to be a strenuous undertaking. Once clear of these, we followed another tributary couloir, much narrower and increasingly steep, up the peak itself. (On the descent we roped down the upper part.) The route at the very top took the neat form of a modern clover-leaf highway intersection. The steep little gully debouched under a natural bridge of rock, which we had seen from the valley below. The highest peak stood to the left, but the route up looked uninviting. We found it easy

229

enough, however, to climb up to the right, cross over the top of the bridge and so reach the summit. We were building our cairn at two o'clock. And we put it, not exactly on the highest point, but out towards the east, where it would be visible from the Stillwater valley! There had been only a step or two of delicate rock-climbing, but six hours of strenuous work, and many intriguing problems solved.

Two years later, driving by fairly near the ranch but without time for a visit, I rang up. Milt, the only member of the family at home, told me with glee that two young men had recently set out to make the second ascent of Cathedral Point and had got within 500 feet of the top. What really turned them back was bad weather, but Milt had affected not to believe this and had had a good deal of fun at their expense. 'I told them,' he reported, 'that old-timers is a lot smarter than kids any day.'

III. GRANITE PEAK

The following summer, 1947, brought a disappointment to us all; Eddie couldn't go with us to Granite Peak. He did, however, arrange for a substitute outfit for our party of four—Florence and Dean Peabody were coming with us too. Raymond Guthrie would be wrangler and Bud Pike, cook.

Granite Peak lies just off the south end of the Rosebud Plateau. The nearest horse-trail at that time, an excellent Forest Service trail, ran from Mystic Lake in the West Rosebud valley up over the north end of the plateau and down to the East Rosebud valley. Our plan was to follow this trail to the height of land, and then work our way southwest along the plateau in the direction we supposed Granite Peak must lie, as far as horses could go. We had equipment with us for a fly camp farther along if it should be necessary.

As we made our way along this high, open, rocky plateau a band of a dozen buck deer trotted around watching us. They made a pretty sight as they stood, at one moment, side by side on one of the small peaks rising slightly above us, themselves and their antlers outlined against the sky. Later we had a good view of two mountain sheep, with their great curving horns.

Certainly it was rough going for the horses, but after all, horses haven't always had the smooth paths of city parks to walk upon. As wild animals they must have had to put up with rocks and irregularities. Montana horses handle simple rock-climbing very competently.

After things had gone well with us for a few miles, we began to run into trouble. The ground became more and more marshy, apparently suffused with water flowing down from large melting snowbanks above us on the left. Although all of it looked like any ordinary ground, every now and then with no warning a horse sank down as if into quicksand. We had never seen anything quite like this before in the mountains. When my horse fell in, I quickly pulled my feet out of the stirrups and jumped. Dean observed facetiously that 'Miriam was thirty feet away before her horse hit bottom.' Then Bob and I, thinking that we might detect the dangerous places better if we tried them out ourselves first, took to walking and leading our horses.

'Miriam, he stepped on my foot,' said Bob, in a flat, weak small voice that indicated to my ear real trouble. But it turned out that although Bob's foot was badly bruised nothing, apparently, was broken. The ground underneath had been so soft and yielding that the foot had merely been pushed down into it instead of being crushed.

The next moment Dean's horse was down on his side with Dean pinned underneath. The horse scrambled up fairly soon but Dean just lay there, not moving, and looking the whitest I've seen a person look. The thing that had saved him, again, was this same softness. He had just been pushed down into the bottomless mud, rocks and ice-water, and no harm was done.

Then three pack-horses went down at once into the worst morass of all, and all our attention was turned to them. Ray hurried to separate them from one another, cutting the ropes when he found they had tightened. The last two horses he got out one by one, after a serious struggle both on his part and that of the horses, but with the first, Blackbird, it was another matter. The men removed his load; they shovelled; they tied

231

ropes to the top of his pack-saddle and set other horses, on firmer ground, to pulling while Blackbird himself struggled; they tried everything they could think of. Blackbird just sank slowly in, deeper and deeper.

'Drain the water,' I offered, 'and then you can dig him out.' It was the water that was making the trouble. With every shovelful of silt and rocks the men removed, the water brought down more to pack around the horse even more firmly. Everyone ignored this suggestion of mine except my courteous husband, who pointed out, patiently, that it would not be possible to drain the water. I didn't insist. It looked all too evident to me that what Bob said was true. And what he wanted me to do now, Bob went on, was scout around on foot, travelling light and fast, to find two things: first, Granite Peak, and second, a good campsite for the night, sheltered from the wind and with wood. We had seen no wood on this high plateau. Although it was now only one o'clock, sometime we should have to begin thinking of where we could camp.

Although I generally like to have a finger in anything that's going on, such as getting this horse out, I didn't really hesitate to leave this time. After all, there were four men here, more men than shovels, two of them professionals in the care of horses and one an engineer (Dean, who was a professor at the Massachusetts Institute of Technology). They should be able to handle this situation without me.

At half-past four I was back, having covered a considerable distance and with 50 per cent success in my missions. I had found Granite Peak and knew the best route of approach. But there was definitely no campsite, sheltered and with wood, ahead of us. We were far above timberline, the sides of the plateau were precipitous, and the easiest route to reach wood, which we should of course not take, would be back the way we had come. But there was now no longer any question of where we should camp; it would have to be right where we were, without shelter, without wood, with almost no horse feed. Of the three essentials for a campsite, wood, water, and horse feed, we had only water—but that in abundance.

Our pack horses caught in the quicksand on the Rosebud Plateau.
ABOVE: Just after the accident, and BELOW: the rescue operation.

ABOVE: A cold breakfast on the Rosebud Plateau. Dean Peabody (left), with Florence dining in bed, photographed by a wrangler.

Robert and Dean clearing our campsite on Tempest Mountain. Granite Peak is in the background.

The situation here had deteriorated. Both Robert and Florence took me aside privately and whispered that there wasn't a chance of getting the horse out. Ray would have to shoot him and they wished he would do it right away and get it over with. Blackbird was in deeper, with only his head and neck and a bit of his back visible above the great pool of water. The workers had drifted away, for lack of anything to do. Only Ray was still there, a shovel in his hand, and a very depressed and discouraged look on his face. The horses belonged to him and no doubt represented a considerable investment, but more important than that, I feel sure, was the fact that he loved his horses and would work to the limit of his strength for any one of them.

There was that little bank below the horses that they were still not using; no harm now in trying out my theory. So from a point well above, with my ice-axe I sketched out two curving ditches, like a giant wish-bone, enclosing the horse. We dug these ditches deep, prizing out boulders, scraping out gravel and mud. Gradually, as they got deeper, the streams of water flowing down them helped. But still the banks would fall in now and then and new channels, ones I did not want, would open up of their own accord. When I thought the wish-bone ditches were sufficiently well established for me to take care of their maintenance alone, I told Ray to clear out a ditch below the horse from the pool to the bank. It drained. In a minute or two the whole pool had gone, and it did not fill up again. Nothing was there but mud and silt, rocks and gravel.

Ray now set to work to dig out the horse's body, then his legs. And as he did so, I kept the ditches in working order, racing back and forth as need arose, in mud over the tops of my boots. For the hour and a half that the whole operation required we worked hard. Afterwards I found out that Ray had had a splitting headache, perhaps from the altitude. 'But I would have done the same for any horse,' he told me, simply.

There was one dreadful moment, when three legs were out, and only the front left one still stuck. Blackbird tried to stand up. But he was weak and tottery and he fell over towards the

233

left. I saw the leg curve as the horse fell. As he lay there on his side, with three legs sticking out straight and one bent backwards, Ray shovelled as he hadn't shovelled before, and in a minute the leg snapped out, straight again, and not broken.

Gently, then, Ray coaxed Blackbird to his feet and gradually he and the other men got the horse out of the danger zone. But after a dozen weak, shaky steps Blackbird simply fell over on his side again, his head down and his eyes closed.

'Is he going to die?' I asked, alarmed, since by this time I felt a tremendous personal concern over his well-being.

'I don't know,' replied Ray. 'He looks like an awful sick horse to me.'

But Florence had taught first-aid during the war and she now took over. She covered Blackbird with the canvases that had wrapped the packs, tucked him in well, wiped the mud off his face, and for almost an hour just sat there by his head, occasionally talking to him encouragingly. Once she gathered a particularly fine bunch of grass and offered it to him, but he could not eat.

'I wish I could give him a hot drink,' complained Florence. But she couldn't. The same old problem we had met before: above timberline, no wood.

The rest of us would have liked a hot drink too. It was cold up here at 11,000 feet, between Tempest and Froze-to-Death Mountains (such fine, suggestive names!), and the wind was strong. Clouds covered the sun and we had been having little squalls of hail and a few snowflakes. When we had left West Rosebud in the morning the day had been warm and sunny and we had put our thick clothes in the packs. I had nothing on but light cotton clothing, much of it wet, and my boots had been filled with ice-water for many hours. A warm nourishing soup would have been pleasant but the dinner we had, ice-water with tinned corned-beef hash, bread, butter, jam and biscuits, all well chilled, was unbelievably delicious. We had had no food at all, hot or cold, for twelve hours. And how luxurious were those down sleeping-bags, soft and warm! As I dozed off there was only one little cloud of worry in my head: should we find Blackbird lying dead in the morning?

With the first faint beginnings of dawn, when I heard Ray, who was eager to get out of this place fast, up collecting his horses, I unfastened our tent and looked out. Blackbird, Ray told me, was up on all four legs, nibbling around at whatever he could find. He had survived in fine condition his five hours' soak in ice-water!

The morning turned out to be sunny but very cold, with a high wind howling by. Our breakfast was more chilled food with ice-water, which I ate walking about to keep as warm as possible, hugging my sleeping-bag around my shoulders as an extra wrap. That morning, of course, the horses would have to go down to where they could find adequate food and Florence, having perhaps more sense than the rest of us, decided to go down with them. Dean, Bob and I would take a fly camp and push on, on foot, to Granite Peak.

About 10.30 we three walkers arrived on the edge of the plateau opposite Granite. There would have been time enough to climb the mountain then and there but by now the weather was turning bad and for the rest of the day we experienced a series of short, but violent storms. There was really no good site for the tents, but by moving around some of the large rocks on this shoulder of Tempest Mountain we prepared a space for them that was approximately level. Although we spent the dry intervals prizing out rocks to make a more 'comfortable' base for our sleeping-bags, Dean reported the next morning that more rocks had come up from underneath during the night. Also we built a sheltering wall which warmed us while we were building it but, since we had no sod for chinking, not noticeably afterwards.

Since there was no water where we were, we had to 'go out' for meals. Perhaps a half-mile back down the slope, below a snowbank, we found the same sort of unattractive small puddle of water, slush and snow, with dust-scum on top, that one can find along the sides of the streets of any New England town during the January thaw. For dinner that night we had a fine

235

hot soup, our first warm food in thirty-six hours. Does this sound odd? There were those of us who had known that our alcohol burner was with us all along and could have been used before, had we not short-sightedly brought along a minimum supply of alcohol which we preferred to reserve for our highest camp.

Our alcohol was so limited indeed and we had put in such a small amount on this first filling that our burner went out just as we started to heat up our dessert cocoa. Since at the same moment another drenching downpour broke out, we piled rocks on our cooking equipment to hold it down in the wind and raced for the tents.

It was a wild night. Brad Washburn says the advantage of an igloo is that it does not flap, and I can understand now just how great an advantage that is. Such an unearthly racket those tents made all night long! Bob and Dean, so they reported, never closed an eye, feeling sure that the tents were going to be ripped to shreds and blown away, and they wanted to be awake when this happened. Why, I wondered, was that something they wished to witness? As for me, I really slept quite well. Two people, in my opinion, can do all the worrying necessary over this sort of catastrophe; it doesn't require three. In any case, I might as well get some sleep first.

The morning was just as bad. Obviously, since it was no day for mountain climbing and we did not have much extra food, we must go down. But why not leave our equipment here and come back again in better weather? Bob and I still wanted to climb Granite Peak. We two could come back later with Bobby (then ten years old), Eddie Ikerman and a wrangler who would stay with Bobby and the horses at a good camp at the last wood. People have asked me if we were not afraid someone would take the supplies we cached here. Frankly, no. It was not a place where many people passed!

A fortnight later at Eddie's ranch we spent a most entertaining Sunday afternoon watching Eddie and several others loading six reluctant and high-spirited horses into a truck. No Wild West show was ever more hilariously funny. We needed seven horses but by the time six were in, Eddie remembered how much he himself liked walking; he would not bother to take a horse. Bob, too; he would share the walking with Eddie. This worked on the way up, but on the way down Bob found Eddie, walking ahead, a hard man to catch when it was time to change.

Monday noon we established a fine horse camp just under the plateau at about 10,000 feet, in a grove of trees with a little stream and lots of good grass. High-altitude grass, says Eddie, although it may not look like much, is considerably more nourishing than the grass of the lowlands, and the horses relish it more. We carried a small amount of oats, too, for a little extra snack. The system: each horse in turn eats his allotment of oats from the dish-pan. When all the horses have finished, the dish-pan is available for washing the dishes. Not all packers bother to carry oats, but one practical value of this extra feeding is that it provides an easy means for catching the horses on those mornings when they are feeling wild—and are there any others?

After a copious lunch—the easiest place to carry food is inside—Bobby and Dale rounded up the horses once more and took us along the plateau, stopping, however, short of the quicksand. There were many deer around and a bobcat raced across the boulder-fields ahead of us. Dale gave Bobby a horse to lead too, when they rode back while Bob, Eddie and I set out on foot. From here to the mountain was still a long way, perhaps five or six miles of rough going, but we reached our kitchen by sunset. The snowbank had almost melted away and our puddle was gone, with even its site uncertain. Only by the gleam of one aluminium pan shining through the rocks did we find our cooking things. And shortly we found another little puddle of slush. How enthusiastic Eddie was over the elaborate menu we enjoyed for dinner. 'Biscuits with the soup at this elevation!' he marvelled.

The next morning we dropped down off the plateau over large unstable rocks, a tiresome job, some 700 feet to the col between Tempest Mountain and Granite Peak and then walked up the obvious northeast ridge, here little more than a scree slope, to

237

a snow col. Here we roped and enjoyed two hours of rock-climbing to the summit. Bob thought that since no woman had climbed Granite before it would be appropriate to have the woman lead this time. I can admit now that we went out of our way now and then to enjoy a good pitch, avoiding the easier gullies and chimneys on the face to the left, of looser rock, and staying close to the crest of the ridge where the rock was splendid firm granite.

On the summit, between bites of lunch, gazing off into the beautiful distance, we added up and found that the combined ages of the three of us came to 172 years.

On the descent, while making a somewhat difficult traverse just under the summit, Eddie suddenly thought of Milt. 'It's lucky we haven't got him with us now,' he observed. 'We couldn't get him up and we couldn't get him down. We'd just have to shoot him!'

XIII

Return to the Alps

He would rather keep his memories of beautiful, peaceful days in Europe before the war, said Robert, than see the ruin and sadness of the new reality. He did not want to go there again. And in this summer of 1951 he did not want to go anywhere. Absorbed in a demanding piece of work, all he asked for the summer was to be left in solitude and quiet. But Bobby at fourteen had developed an unusual interest in things cultural—we suspected that his school at Exeter was at the bottom of this—and, said Robert, should be taken to Europe by me to see cathedrals, art galleries, and scenes of so much in history—if there were any time, that is, left over from mountain climbing. Brian, at twelve, his perceptive father went on, was a little young for culture. If he, a scientist of one-track mind, were taken to Westminster Abbey, all that would interest him there would be how the place was wired up electrically. As for me, my longing to see the Alps once more after all these years had become intense.

In the autumn, when Bobby and I returned home and showed our pictures and told our tales, Robert changed his mind. He too, wanted to see those mountains again. For the two following seasons, therefore, we all four drove around the Alps, climbing here and there, and most of the time we took Adolf with us. For Robert and I agreed that, even though for the last twenty years all the climbing we had done had been guideless, with our inexperienced boys in the party, Adolf added a substantial and welcome element of safety. Besides, Adolf was an old friend and we just liked to have him around anyway. To him I explained that even though we should probably not do too much in the way of climbing, it always looked better to travel with a good guide. People would think, at least, that we were engaged upon big climbs. This idea I had taken over from him. 'Take your crampons as far as the Jungfraujoch,' he had told us; 'I do not think that we shall use them, but it always looks better to travel with crampons. People will think . . .'

Besides climbing with any number of us, from one to four, on our main projects, Adolf took over the interim entertainment of the more energetic boys. In any spare moment the three of them would be out rock-climbing on the cliffs behind the hotel, or ice-climbing on the glacier, cramponing up séracs and having step-cutting races up some wall of ice, where the man who cut his steps too sketchily might find himself back at the bottom. If the parents occasionally enjoyed a pleasant day of leisure the 'three boys' would be setting off for the Riffelhorn or the Trais Fluors.

Zermatt, of course, we had to see again. (I shall want to go to Zermatt even when I can no longer walk at all. For it is one of those mountain villages, mostly in the Alps, where I feel: This is where I belong.) When the train rounded the last curve into the town, the Matterhorn was out, gigantic in the evening dusk. The last time I had seen it was nineteen years before, when Alice Damesme and I had come down from our manless ascent. A long time ago, that climb was, but I remembered it and so, it seemed, did a few of the older Zermatt guides. 'Aren't you Miriam?' they asked in surprise. For 'Alice' and 'Miriam' we had apparently become.

We all climbed the Matterhorn, Robert and I in 1952, the boys the following year. It was the fourth time for Robert, the third for me, and the last for both of us. For while we were happy to climb it once more, to establish a certain link with those earlier years of ours, we found less attractive the great crowds of people that nowadays flock to this fashionable peak, waiting for a turn at the fixed ropes and wondering, when they meet in the ice-steps near the summit, how they are going to pass each other. Sixty-three people went up the mountain the day we did, in spite of indifferent weather and almost no views; it was not unusual for one hundred to do so on a good day. The loose stones had been swept clear from the beaten route— a good thing, that—and many of the handholds polished. But the Matterhorn rises still imposing and as if undisturbed by these crowds of trippers swarming up its easy route.

Bobby and Adolf started up the Matterhorn as soon as we arrived in Zermatt in 1953 and caught the finest day of the season, warm and cloudless, with magnificent views. A few days later Brian (then fourteen) and Adolf went up, and on the descent from the summit, where there was considerably more ice than usual, they tied on two of our friends. I think Adolf rather liked this appearance of taking three people on the Matterhorn—although one of the added climbers was in fact coming down behind all the rest—for there had been some murmurings among the Zermatt guides when he had taken two, Bob and me. (The Zermatt guides apparently have an understanding: on the Matterhorn, one guide takes one tourist.) Adolf maintained that as long as Bob and I had each led the Matterhorn guideless, he thought we'd make out all three together.

Since clouds had prevented my taking many pictures on our own Matterhorn climb—and there had been no Kodachromes back in 1932—Adolf suggested, when about to start up with Brian, that I lend him my camera and tell him how to operate it. Better still, that I lend him two cameras, for it would be quite impossible for him to learn to change a film. Sitting in the Seiler tea garden he practised bringing the two images together for the distance setting, and as for the rest, I made my instructions brief and simple. He came back with some excellent results and very proud that he hadn't taken more than two pictures with the lens cap on.

Poor Adolf worked constantly every day, Sundays included, with some part of our family and when we finally offered him a day of rest he replied that he would rest in November and where should we go tomorrow? Castor and Pollux, I suggested, for in all these years I hadn't done them. We eventually extended the trip to include the Lyskamm as well, which we had omitted on our 1930 ski trip. Bobby too would come along and add to his list of four-thousanders. Since the Zwillings Glacier by which we should descend was badly broken up, Adolf thought it wiser to take along a second guide in case someone fell into a crevasse. As it turned out, someone did, and who was it? The second guide. The crevasse, however, being a very small one, the guide caught the opposite side with his feet almost at once and worked his way out before Adolf and I got there. But Adolf had to lower him down into it again to retrieve his ice-axe, which had clattered to the bottom.

After a night at Testa Grigia, when the sun rose the following morning we were already high on the hard, crisp snow of the Breithorn Plateau. I enjoyed once more that glorious sight of miles upon miles of rosy peaks. I like to be high. Why is it that climbers feel uplifted in spirit as well as in body when they have climbed to heights? The same elevation gained by aeroplane, for instance, affords views certainly as beautiful, but carries no trace of that feeling of joy and exaltation. Perhaps the aeroplane, being detached from the earth, provides no immediate foreground to give scale to the stupendous peaks, or perhaps you cannot experience the 'feel' of a big peak unless you are in actual physical contact with it. Or perhaps there is a relationship between the satisfaction gained and the effort expended. To some extent the last, I am sure.

All that day we were climbing up and down at well over 12,000 feet as we skirted along on the Italian side of the Breithorn (which I had climbed in 1921) to the Zwillings Pass between Castor and Pollux. From here we ascended both Pollux, by its easy southeast ridge, mostly of rock, and Castor by its northwest face on hard snow, crossing some ominous avalanche tracks. Nearly at the top we sat down for a little pause. 'Why did you stop, Adolf?' complained the second guide, in Swiss German. 'They were climbing well enough.' 'I know,' replied Adolf, also in dialect, 'but after a moment's rest, they will go even better . . . isn't that so?' he added, turning to me.

Beyond Castor we followed the frontier ridge, with Switzerland to the left, Italy to the right, over several small snow summits, one of them—but we didn't know which—the Felikhorn. The other guide and Bobby, on ahead, properly followed the accepted route all the way to the Felikjoch before turning down to the Sella Hut; Adolf and I took a short-cut directly down the snow-ice wall, shooting the bergschrund in a sitting glissade as our party had done after the Diables climb, on the descent from Mont Blanc du Tacul. 'I like my climbing a little quieter than that,' observed Bobby's guide, while Bobby asserts that the peak we omitted by these manœuvres was in fact the important Felikhorn!

Although it was only one o'clock when we reached the Sella Hut, crowds had already arrived, but only a fraction of the still greater ones that were to pour in that afternoon and evening. In the end we must have been close to the ninety-four people which is, they say, the maximum that has ever spent the night in that rather small hut, consisting of dining-room, sleeping-room with tiers of narrow bunks, and attic. Adolf climbed down from an inspection trip to the attic and observed to the hut-keeper reasonably that there did not seem to be room for him up there. 'Room! Room!' expostulated the hut-keeper. 'There's always room. Everybody just move up closer.' Bobby and I, I think, were about the last comers to be assigned a bunk apiece. Two bunks for three people was the next thing I heard, hardly a practical arrangement for that third person. The two windows in our sleeping-room were shut tight both day and night and the odour that grew progressively more intense made us glad enough to leave the room a bit after three the next morning, when Adolf tiptoed in to call us. Half awake, I took my rucksack, which I had got all ready the evening before, and my boots, and stumbled out into the dining-room. One side of the room had been cleared by piling up the tables, and on the floor along this side, heads to the wall and feet to the room, lay a row of sleeping people, each one rolled in a blanket and all lying as straight and close together as if they had been corpses ranged there. Corpses, indeed, they looked. And no wonder so many had died, I thought, the air in here being what it was.

And breakfast? I looked over to the one remaining table, where we had eaten supper the evening before on the bare, weathered wood. This morning it was covered with a magnificent white linen and lace tablecloth. Far more candles than an economical hut-keeper usually sets out were burning in beautiful silver candelabra. Rarely have I been so startled. No one unfamiliar with the rude simplicity of a high-mountain hut can realize the incongruity of a scene such as this. Then I noticed the two priests. They were saying mass. Had someone really died? No, said Adolf, this mass was for the priests themselves; they were going mountain climbing. And to my eager question, where?—for I assumed that only some death-defying *tour de force* would require preparations like this—Adolf told me the name of some quite ordinary climb. Breakfast, moreover, was ready to be served, Adolf went on, and all these other people standing around, mostly Italians and seemingly in no mood for worship, were likewise eager to eat and get started. But the table . . .

While it had taken us barely a half-hour to descend from the frontier ridge to the hut, running and sliding in the soft snow, it took much longer to climb back up again. Around to the east we went, following the beaten Monte Rosa track, until we were south of the main peak of the Lyskamm. From here a ridge runs up which Adolf and I climbed as we had so often in the past, with me in front on the rocks, and he leading the snow and ice section just under the beautifully corniced summit ridge.

From the top what a glorious view we had of a whole circle of peaks! To the west we looked down upon the Matterhorn, below us by 200 feet, but with even greater interest we looked to the east where the whole route that we had made in 1930 on our ski traverse from Gressoney to Zermatt lay spread out before us.

The ridges of the Lyskamm which we followed back to the Felikjoch are often a most difficult and demanding ice-climb, involving hours of step-cutting. This year, however, the unusual

ABOVE: The summit ridge of the Lyskamm with the Matterhorn in the background. OVERLEAF: Monte Rosa, the Lyskamm, Castor, Pollux and the Breithorn seen across Zermatt Valley from the terrace of the Rothorn Hut.

LEFT: Adolf Rubi on Zwillings Glacier. RIGHT:
On Ago di Sciora photographed by Adolf.

amount of snow that had fallen in the early summer still remained, compacted and firm. Not a step did we cut, but merely walked along on our crampons, following the slender crest of the ridge, where a slide down into either Italy or Switzerland would have lasted for so many thousands of feet.

From the Felikjoch we went down the broken-up Zwillings Glacier. It was a constant surprise to me, looking ahead at the maze of crevasses, to find that we did actually get down quite easily. But after we had passed the Monte Rosa Hut and arrived at the farther side of the Gorner Glacier, at the foot of that path that rises some four or five hundred feet up to Rotenboden, somebody discovered that we had only a few minutes in which to catch the next train. It really took more than a little effort on my part, after those three wonderful days of climbing, but the train and I pulled in to the station simultaneously—the train gliding easily behind its electric locomotive, I puffing in the old-fashioned way.

On our first trip to Europe in 1951 we had not planned to include the Dolomites. They were too far off our route and one can t take in everything (so they say). But when cold and snow drove us from Zermatt to the Bergell and pursued us even there, it suddenly occurred to me that we might do what I had wanted all along. We were sitting on the summit of Monte Rosso, crouched close together against the bitter wind and holding inside our clothes our aching hands, which had been fumbling for holds through the fine, new snow. 'Tomorrow night we could be in the Dolomites,' I observed. 'For a woman,' replied Adolf, 'you make up your mind very quickly.' Why not? Even though we had only four days before we must start for home, there was little point in just waiting around here as long as we had Adolf's car available. It wasn't far. At least, I amended honestly, it wasn't far compared with driving across North America. And even though we were travelling at the height of the season with no reservations, we always found a place to sleep. I wasn't nearly so fussy about rooms, said Adolf, as Mrs Rubi. If only both of them could see some of the places

245

where I've slept in earlier years, in the American West! And the restaurants, too.

In Cortina, as soon as we arrived, I asked the hotel manager to get me Angelo Dimai on the telephone. In a moment Angelo was over at the hotel. It was very good indeed to see him again. When we came to the question of whether he would go with us up the ordinary route on Punta Fiames, 'Signora Miriam,' he replied, 'I haven't done any guiding for sixteen years, and I haven't climbed for three years. Let me get you a good young guide.' Certainly not. I would have nothing to do with good young guides; I preferred an old, bad one.

'The young guides are laughing at me,' reported Angelo ruefully the following morning, as we started out. He had told someone he was going to do the Variante on Punta Fiames. Now they all knew it and considered it extremely funny that a climber of Angelo's stature should sink to this.

The Variante I had never done, but had chosen it for Bobby's first serious rock-climb because I assumed it to be easier than the Via Dimai. And, indeed, Angelo and I did much of the first part unroped—and unroped, essentially, I continued to feel all through this climb, for Angelo had told me the rope he was using might well be the same one I had climbed on twenty years earlier! After a while, when we had left the Via Dimai at the foot of the big chimney and traversed out around the corner to the left, we ran into several pitches which I found really hard. This I should have taken as distressing proof of a diminishing power to climb rocks if Adolf, too, hadn't noticed the suddenly increased difficulty. 'When I led the Spigolo and Mrs Rubi did this Variante,' he confided to me, 'I thought I was doing a real climb and she nothing. But now I think she did just as big a climb as I did. . . . If this is only third degree, I'm going to stop climbing right now. . . . What did you mean,' he shouted up to Angelo, 'by telling me this was a third-degree climb?' Oh, much of it was, Angelo assured us cheerfully—especially the lower part.

Finally Angelo decided to traverse back considerably to the right. He was moving rather slowly, for him, over what looked

Rock climbing exercises at Susten Pass. ABOVE: Ascent, and
BELOW: descent of a gendarme, by young Bob.

from below like a pretty smooth wall—but delicacy, fortunately, was something I felt I could still manage. 'Adolf,' advised Angelo, pausing for a moment to look ahead, 'on this traverse you must start with the left foot, otherwise . . . But it is really not difficult.' Adolf thanked him but at the same time he was quietly tying one end of his rope to the loop around my waist. 'You take this up,' he said. 'I don't know what I'm getting into here.' A good measure, this turned out to be, because once our nylon rope was up there Bobby could come third instead of fourth, with Adolf following just below him to coach and cheer. But Bobby climbed well, considering that this was his first experience with real exposure. 'Pretty straight up, isn't it, Bobby?' suggested Adolf. Cheerfully he replied that that was all right. He didn't mind the straight up. What bothered him was the straight down!

Never for a moment had he been off the route, Angelo assured us earnestly after the climb was over, when I brought up this possibility. I didn't say what I thought. I was remembering that he had done that route only once before, twenty or thirty years ago. And the man who had made, with Giuseppe and Comici, the first ascent of the north wall of the Cima Grande, how could he distinguish between those lower degrees below sixth? They would all look alike to him, not worthy of notice.

We let Angelo get us those good young guides he so much wanted to the next time we came to Cortina. For we did come again, all four of us, in each of the two following years. Dolomite climbing, with its balance and delicacy, was still enormous fun and the boys liked it as much as we did. Brian in particular, light and compact, was right in his element and took to this climbing just as I had done thirty years earlier. And even I found that, though strength in the arms may wane, a sense of balance and some technique stay with you longer; and above all, experience and a knowledge of mountains and their ways.

When I wrote the news of Cortina to my old friend of the early Dolomite days, now ill and crippled in Budapest, Baroness Rolanda Eötvös, whose father had pioneered so many Dolomite

247

Brian on a long rope-down in the Engelhörner.

routes, I received a touching reply (in English). '. . . your letter brought back to me and made me feel so much of those beautiful days I had in the mountains. Not causing melancholy but the joy that such wonderful experiences were given to me in life. Nothing, nothing can compare with the delight of climbing! . . . I remember what an enormous event it was for my sister and me when . . . Papa with guides took us up Cima Piccola for the first time. . . . During the siege of this town in 1944 a cannon projectile crushed into my room. Quite lucky I got away with the loss of only one eye. But the other is damaged too. . . . Please tell Bobby that the physicist Eötvös on the stamp is my own adored mountain-climbing father. . . . I do hope we shall go on remembering each other still many years, and you well and happy. . . .' Alas! she died the following winter.

The delight of climbing! It has been with me all my life. As a child, spending summer holidays at my grandmother's house in northern New Hampshire, I noticed as I wandered around the countryside with my little cousin that my feet just naturally took me uphill. They still do. For when you have spent in the hills most of the time you have for recreation and pleasure, they come to mean much more than just the fun of acrobatics. The most urgent desire, after an illness or an absence, is to climb a mountain again. And in occasional times of strain just to walk in the hills brings a strengthening of the spirit, a renewed courage and buoyancy.

XIV

The Four-Thousand-Footers
in Winter

It did seem to us, my husband and me, Charter Members of the Four-thousand-footer Club, that climbing the New Hampshire four-thousand-footers in winter would present a challenge suitably more sporting than ambling up the well-trodden trails in summer. In winter there is no footpath visible under the snow and, particularly in open hardwoods, finding the route may be a puzzle. In winter you can take only the briefest of rests, no more of those sybaritic siestas, stretched out on the warm, soft ground. Days are shorter. The rucksack is heavier with all those extra clothes, not to mention the crampons clanking away and the ice-axe. Then there's the business of finding water, which is much more of a problem than in summer, with the rills trickling around here and there. It may sound strange but dehydration is a more serious concern in winter. Every breath you exhale carries away a lot of good moisture which the inhaled air, cold and so dry, cannot replace. Add to this the fact that the water in your canteen, as well as the sandwiches in your pack, are all too likely to be frozen rock-hard. Unless, that is, you have been careful to carry them under your outer garments, close to your body, where they often become tangled up with your camera and films, which do not like to get too cold either. Most of all, the real work of breaking trail in deep or heavy snow, or kicking steps up steep slopes, is often considerable.

All these may sound like splendid arguments for staying home, but not to us. We were old winter climbers from way back, thanks to the good old Bemis Crew, many of whom were veterans of the Alps. In a later year we found that more than half the members had climbed the Matterhorn. They knew how to handle snowshoes, snowshoe creepers, crampons, ice-axes, compasses and maps. In that first year of my acquaintance with them, we ranged over the Presidentials and Carters unaware, as we reached the summits of four-thousand-foot peaks, that more than thirty years later these ascents would give us points in a game, the game of Climbing the Four-thousanders in Winter.

This game was an offshoot, of course, of that very popular game of the Appalachian Mountain Club, Climbing the Four-thousanders, which was set in motion, and such vigorous and enthusiastic motion, in 1958. Our game—"ours" because we were the first to play it—followed right along. As the initiators we set the rules, which concerned the definition of "winter." "Snow on the ground" and other namby-pamby criteria definitely did not count. "Winter" was to be measured exclusively by the calendar. In 1960, for instance, winter began at 3:27 P.M. on Wednesday, December 21, too late to get up to Crag Camp by daylight.

Before setting out on this game Robert and I had each climbed, in winter, about half the Four-thousanders. We had not, however, always done the same ones. Those not done by both of us we put on our list, along with the occasional peak about which we might have a shadow of doubt as to whether we had reached the exact summit. (The Four-thousand-footer Club had checked on exact summits. Trails did not always cross them.) The one-day climbs, or those which would pass as one-dayers in summer, were naturally the easiest, although we did not, by any means, always get up them in one day. Weather, snow conditions and manpower were the limiting factors. We did very well with manpower, having lots of friends. Of course, when the breaking is heavy, the more manpower the more miles.

Often, in the short winter days, there was time to go only part way, and before we could get going again heavy snow would have come down once more. Even in that case we still would

The Bemis Crew on Old Speck. ABOVE: Approaching the summit, and BELOW: with everyone at the summit.

Patty Severance celebrates her twelfth birthday by joining us on a winter ascent of Middle Carter.

have gained something, for though you cannot see the tracks you made yesterday your feet can feel the firm underpinning. Quite decisive is the plunge into deep powder when you step off the old tracks. When Robert and I were climbing alone we would break what we could, after which it would snow, after which we would again break out the part we had done earlier, and perhaps a mile or so more, and so on. Surprisingly, sometimes we got to the top, just the two of us.

I. OSCEOLA

Strict as our rules were on the definition of "winter" they said nothing against taking advantage of a lucky break, and our chance came on the first day of winter in December, 1959. Snow had fallen earlier in the season, but in the valleys it had now pretty much melted away. Well aware of the great advantage of attacking Osceola while the Tripoli Road was still open, Merle Whitcomb, Robert and I hurried down there. The ground we had been looking at, near North Woodstock, was bare, and we felt that even though snowshoes might be needed for a short distance at the top, it was a bother to carry them. Anyway, we did not mind a little wading through snow, although as it turned out, we got all we cared for. It never occurred to us to take crampons. It never occurred to us, either, that the trail would be so icy that we would have to bushwhack along its edges. As we approached the height-of-land on the road, we came upon untracked snow, some six inches deep, which had apparently softened, become more compact and then refrozen. With the jeep in four-wheel drive, low range, we laboriously and ever so slowly crunched along up. Occasionally we had to back off and get a running start to drive through a heavy place.

On the summit of Osceola we looked at our watches with consternation, even though it would be only a mile to Osceola East. It turned out, however, not to be one of those rapidly-covered miles, what with hard ice on the steep slopes and deep snow everywhere else. I remember a particularly uninviting north sidehill slope on the approach to the summit where, stamping vigorously through the crust in order to stay on the slope at all, we were rewarded with a plunge into snow above our knees.

As we started down from the main peak on our return the snow under our feet glowed red from the sunset, and across the red snow the dark parallel shadows of the tall trees reached way down into the valley. Through the woods near the bottom, as we felt our way along by hand, we met many more large boulders in the trail than we had remembered. But we were buoyed up by Merle's cheerful thought: "Every day now," she observed, "the days are getting longer and longer."

II. ISOLATION

For the weekend of January 16, 1960, Bob Collin was leading a one-night camping trip up Mt. Isolation by way of Rocky Branch Shelter No. 2. From the shelter to the Montalban Ridge above, with its Davis Path, was a bushwhack, but one which Robert and I had done in summer and found fairly innocuous. We were, of course, going on the trip too. On the preceding Tuesday afternoon Robert and I broke out the trail towards the shelter for a short distance and on Thursday, after a new snowfall, Robert, Merle and I broke it out again up to the height-of-land, where we cached our tents and some other gear. On Saturday, although we drove down to see the others off, my two comrades preferred to chicken out. Their trifling excuse was merely the vicious weather. In the fall of 1967, I checked up on that weather, and found the following in the official records: "January 16, 1960, 19° maximum, −12° minimum, wind WNW, 79 m.p.h. average, 123 peak." This was on the summit of Mt. Washington, and our friends were not too far away from there when they got up on the Montalban Ridge. A wind of 123 miles per hour, even just a gust, has considerable cooling power. The records from Pinkham Notch, in the valley only a few miles away, include the notation: "High winds, snow flurries."

The party later reported more than the usual difficulties on their trip, and I quote: "Intense cold, winds of gale force. Collapse of only one tent (this was Chris Goetze's; he continued to use the tent as a bedspread). Frost-bitten cheeks were evident. One climber was picked up and literally blown to the summit." Merle's diary adds the report: "Dave Sanderson broke his snowshoe into three pieces."

On Monday, however, after our friends had gone home with their frozen cheeks, the weather turned magnificent. I even have a photograph of Merle and Robert, sitting on the bench in front of the Rocky Branch Shelter, holding their teacups with bare hands. Still, it wasn't warm enough to take off their down jackets.

Beside us roared the river. Thin edges of ice bordered the open patches of swift water. As we strolled around in the sunshine we admired for some time the lacy patterns which these ice edges assumed. When the afternoon was well along, Merle and I decided to go up the mountain right away. Robert would put up the two tents and get dinner ready, and then we would all three climb Isolation again the following morning. The views from the summit in the limpid evening air were breathtaking, even though they were composed more of shadow than of sunlight. We were back at the shelter in good time, for it is entirely possible to run downhill on snowshoes, and a fortunate thing that is.

That night, snuggled in our down sleeping–bags, Robert and I awoke to find a snowstorm of considerable determination raging outside. Climbing Isolation was of course out of the question, said Robert. At the first inkling of daylight he would like to start for home. Since we always feel that we should look after our little friend Merle, so much younger than we, we woke her up. "Merle," we called, "it's snowing." "It's been snowing for two hours," she called back.

Soon we heard inexplicable sounds from Merle's tent. What could she be doing in the middle of a cold, black night? Rolling up her sleeping–bag, that's what she was doing. Speechless,

253

Robert and I crawled a little deeper down into ours. Merle was all slept out, she explained, and with her flashlight she was going to start breaking trail up the mountain. Robert must get up Isolation, even though yesterday's tracks would not show under the new snow. And that was that! Of course a storm is never so bad as it looks from a place of shelter and warmth. And it is never so bad, anyway, when you are dressed for it. When we reached the summit we gave a quick glance around, in the driving snow, and rushed back to the shelter, all three of us ready now to start home traveling light and fast. We left the heavier pieces of our equipment neatly piled (Merle must have done that) in the northeast corner of the shelter, since we lived nearby and would come back again soon. It was most unlikely that anyone else would go in there in the meantime.

As it happened, we did not come back soon and when we did it was to follow the tracks of other people. We pondered, of course, the likelihood of our finding anything still there in that corner. When everything turned up apparently untouched, I expressed my gratitude to those unknown men of integrity by doing a very thorough cleaning job around the shelter.

III. ZEALAND

Now, sad to say, it looks as if the day of the man of integrity is passing and the day of the vandal coming in. Or, as I should prefer to believe, men of integrity are still with us, but becoming outnumbered by the vandals. Popular targets for vandalism seem to be A.M.C. huts, a circumstance which has brought about the end of those old days of friendly hospitality in winter, when the kitchen or crew's quarters were often left unlocked for refuge. But back in 1959, when I asked George Hamilton, at that time manager of the A.M.C. huts, if we might spend the night at Zealand, he told us cheerily just to open the back door and walk in.

It took us two hours to open that door. First we had to find it. Stretching back from the ridgepole of Zealand Hut to the rocky bank on the north lay an expanse of hard, windpacked snow completely filling in what, in summer, is a gap eight or nine feet wide at its bottom and narrowest part. As for the door, we had to guess where it might be, under all this snow. Choosing what looked like a reasonable location, we dug. Ice-axes make rather poor shovels, and snowshoes are not much better. But finally, using a small saucepan, we could get some work done. As soon as we had dug a hole down to the eaves of the roof and could peer underneath we could make out the door, off to the side, some distance away from where we had been digging. This suggested, naturally, a new start. To get the door open we should have to dig to the bottom of the door and a little more. We needed a shaft a good eight or nine feet deep from our starting point at the snow above the eaves. The excavation was carried out with system and efficiency. I stood in the shaft, Merle outdoors on top of the snow, Robert about halfway between, where he could pass things to either lady. There was not room enough in the narrow shaft for saucepan, ice-axe, and me all at once. So our system worked as follows: with the ice-axe I broke up some of the underfoot snow—or, lower down, ice—as much as could be accommodated around my legs; to clear the way I handed the axe up to Robert, who passed it on to Merle; Merle passed the saucepan down to Robert, who forwarded it to me. And so on, over and over, for the major part of the two hours. Certainly my comrades offered to change places, but the rhythm was working well. And besides, I couldn't see how I was ever going to get up out of that thin, slippery shaft. There came a time when I could see through the top edge of the glass window in the door and there, staring me in the face, hung a shovel, totally unreachable. Finally, all the ice around the door which could be reached by the axe, or by a jackknife blade, had been chopped or pried away, and still the door would not budge. I squirmed around to face it squarely, put my feet against the bottom, and pushed. With a great rending noise, the glass window in the door cracked all the way across, while the door itself remained frozen tight.

255

I was dejected. Robert was able to drag me up out of the depths, then descended himself and put his great boots against the door. According to all the laws of common sense these should have caused even larger cracks. But no, the door opened as easily as you please. (Note to vandals: Later we reported this to George and paid him for the repairs. And let's see you do the same!) Robert could then reach the shovel and gouge out a line of steps up the shaft, steep and not very close together, but tremendously welcome. Immediately Merle, using the same saucepan, began carrying down into the hut the snow and ice which we had worked for two hours to get out of there. She was going to make tea, a laudable activity after all. Bill and Iris Baird dropped in for tea, having left Lancaster after Bill's work and walked up to Zealand to keep us company overnight.

Not long after we were in bed, when all was dark, we heard curious metallic clankings. Merle, it appeared, was lighting the fire to start breakfast; she was hungry. We pointed out that it was not quite 11 P.M. and suggested that she make herself a good lunch and then go back to sleep.

To report that the next morning we reached the summit of Zealand Mountain without incident may sound like an anticlimax. But when we left the hut and started home we discovered that the Zealand rabbits had got into the act, too. To pull our equipment into Zealand initially, we had used a light fiberglass toboggan which I had bought in a toy department. We had left this at the foot of the steep little pitch leading to the hut and carried the loads up the short distance on our backs. The rabbits, however, had found the toboggan rope just delicious and had chewed it into small pieces.

IV. GALEHEAD

The next time we visited an A.M.C. hut, Galehead, George Hamilton came along with Robert and me on a reconnaissance. We wanted to take up some supplies as well as find out if we could get into the hut. Alas, all too easily! Some earlier visitor had left the back door ajar and snow had filled the kitchen. How George worked, and Robert, too, with shovels and brooms, to get that snow outdoors! Some remained, however, and this, with all the hard ice layer on the floor, never melted during the whole time when we were in the hut. The snow came in handy, however, to pack against the cracks around the door and keep out a lot of furious wind which day after day was attacking the hut.

Two days after our reconnaissance Robert and I, with Merle and Louise Baldwin this time, went in again on the main trip. On starting out I was astonished to hear that little Merle weighed 157 pounds and Louise even a bit more. But so they did, including their loads.

The Forest Service usually knew about our plans, because we made a point of telling them. Many of the rangers were friends anyway, and they liked to know what was going on. After all, if they find a car standing on the edge of the wilderness day after day in winter, they may indeed wonder if all is well. "The man I don't like the most going into my woods," said one of the rangers, "is X., because he never communicates." Once, when we had not told anyone beforehand, we put a sign in the window of the jeep, on the inside looking out, with a brief mention of our plans and the date when we expected to come out. This naturally was convenient for burglars as well, but back in the good old days. . . .

Hutch (District Ranger C. W. Hutchinson) told me that he could see the roof of Galehead Hut from his window down in Bethlehem, nine air miles away. If we got into trouble, or even if we "just wanted something, build a fire and we'll be right up." Then Hutch went off to Detroit. But he left two younger rangers with the job of watching Galehead. Did they see it, with or without signal fire, even once? No. The day we moved to Galehead was the day before the start of some winter weather. Twenty-one inches of snow came down on Mt. Washington, and Galehead was near enough to have about the same. Actually it seemed to us like a great deal more! The following day some additional snow appeared; the day after that, only a small amount, but there were clouds enough to keep everything covered.

For countless hours we sat around in our cramped quarters, now and then venturing out to find and cut up a few more dead trees for the stove. Fortunately we discovered a group of these at a little distance from the hut. The ladies were quite proud when they succeeded in cutting down six trees in a couple of hours. We then timed Robert, who finished off twelve trees in fifteen minutes! So the ladies specialized in dragging the trees to the hut and cutting them up into stove lengths. We had no sawhorse, but discovered a way to hold the tree braced between two uprights of the hut. Two of us held while the third sawed.

Also, in the oven of the stove we parked some opened cans of food. It was the only way to keep the contents soft enough to get a spoon into them from time to time. We had no definite meal hours, anyone ate what and when he liked. But now, at last, Merle's predilection for getting up early really paid off. She felt just as she had down below; all slept-out long before the rest of us. No one but the unflinching Merle would have pulled herself out of a warm sleeping–bag, in that icy hut, to get the fire started. Merle did it every morning. And one morning she brought us all hot orange juice in bed. She explained that she had got herself winterized.

All this time our thoughts were projected ahead to our plans for those post-storm days and they all started with South Twin. If we could keep the trail broken out for those first 1,126 feet of elevation, which certainly does not sound like much of a job, it would be a help on the start of our walk. Though the deep snow was working against us, as was the wind as we got higher, at least we kept track of where the trail lay.

Late one afternoon Merle and I, who happened to be outdoors, noticed a glimmer of clearing. Off we dashed to make a final check of our job. As I cowered behind the summit cairn of South Twin, most ornately decorated with enormous frost-

258

Mt. Guyot from the Twinway.

ABOVE: To the summit of South Twin from Galehead Hut, and BELOW: the Presidential Range
over a sea of mist from South Twin.

feathers, I looked down on a new, fresh, immaculate world. But a chilly one.

The following morning all of us were off well before sunrise. Every twig of every bush and tree was coated thick with snow and frostfeathers. And standing around were a few of those fantastic gnomes, small trees completely covered with snow, in sparkling white like everything else. As we again neared the summit of South Twin, climbing over the hard, moulded and wind-packed ripples, ridges and small dykes, we had to rely strongly on the crampons attached beneath our snowshoes.

One glance over to the east of the Twin Range and I realized that not everyone would consider this the glorious day that we were finding it. The summits of the Presidential Range stood out strongly but down in the intervening valley regions were thick masses of clouds. On these clouds, far off to the northeast, floated a firetower on a tiny island of snow. Cherry Mountain.

I cherish the memory of that day's walk from Galehead to South Twin to Guyot, to West Bond, to Bond, and then back to Galehead. The sunshine on the snow, the sparkling air, the chance to stretch our legs after sitting still so long gave me a fine feeling of exhilaration. And I liked knowing that for so many miles nobody had stepped on that new layer of snow except a large wildcat, who paced us for most of the way between South Twin and Guyot.

When we reached Guyot and looked over to the south towards that broad col below Bond, I was astonished to see many fewer trees than usual, and much smaller ones. Where had the trees gone? Buried, most of them, and some merely shortened, by the snow. The general effect was of a snowfield, not a forest as in summer. And everywhere the snow was furrowed and grooved with parallel lines which looked like glacial striations, only much deeper and more irregular. For a while the going was easier, since we did not sink far into the windslab, except of course now and then, and that deeply.

But there was never anything very easy about getting to West Bond in those days before a trail existed. As we went up towards Bond, and particularly as we turned off for the bush-whack to West Bond, we found traces of Bob Collin's party, who had come up the day before from the Zealand side. In this area the extremely thick vegetation, vertical and horizontal, had protected the snow from the wind. It was still light and fluffy and very deep. One of the hazards of winter climbing is stepping near a buried coniferous tree. When snow falls on or-dinary ground it either packs down or not, in any case more or less evenly. But when it falls on evergreens it has great diffi-culty in getting in underneath the branches, with the result that near the trunk of the tree there is just empty space. If you cannot see the tops of the trees, and if you happen to step near one, you are headed for trouble. Even snowshoes will not save you. It's a helpless feeling to drop suddenly into snow not any more solid than a cloud, and thrash about with noth-ing to grip. I know, for it happens often. I remember one time, when I fell in, that Al Robertson called, "I'm coming, Miriam, I'll be there in just a minute." So he was, but he came too close and fell into a hole of his own. Another man came to rescue us both, with the same result. And so there we were, three in a row, all down in holes. I don't wonder that we looked funny to the two remaining men, who finally got us out. Then there was the time when Ken Turner, on falling into a hole, stretched his arms up above his head. All we could see was just the tips of two pairs of mittens waving for help. And a faint voice from faraway said, "Get me out of here, it's cold." Of course, you understand, pictures always come first in cases like these.

But to come back to West Bond, Merle's diary said that "the whole area was pockmarked with holes where Collin's party had fallen through. But Miriam said to lie down on our stomachs and crawl. We did just that and it worked fine except for the huge blocks of snow which crashed down on our heads from every overhead branch which we disturbed."

The winter view from West Bond was extraordinarily fine, with the white summit of Mt. Washington in the distance looking like Cho Oyu (only I didn't know it then).

ABOVE: The summit of Mt. Bond, and BELOW: looking eastward from West Bond.

The Twin Range from the summit of the Franconia Owl's Head, with South Twin at the extreme left, Mt. Guyot just to the left of center, Bond-cliff at the far right, West Bond and Bond between the last two. The bit of white visible just to the left of the summit of Guyot is probably the tip of Mt. Washington. Two large glacial cirques appear at the heads of the long prominent valleys descending from before Guyot and Bondcliff.

ABOVE: Kicking snowshoe steps up a steep slope.

Merle Whitcomb swimming out of a hole.

As we finally looked down once more on Galehead Hut from the summit of South Twin, heavy dark unattractive clouds were pouring in. Was this a bad omen for the second trip which we had hoped to make from Galehead? By the following day we had to admit that the one wonderful day which we had already enjoyed was all the good weather we were going to get. After quite a trip down into the valley of the Gale River through deep and fluffy powder snow we reached the logging camp and the jeep. Here we learned that "Those two rangers were just here, looking for you. They've been here every day." We telephoned as soon as we could.

Now that I think of it, how would the A.M.C. have felt about having a signal fire built on the roof of their Galehead Hut?

V. OWL'S HEAD

On several camping trips we joined forces with Bob Collin and his group of hardy winter climbers and campers. For our contribution we often made a trip or two ahead of time, to get a little trail breaking done; theirs was a lot more trail breaking. As for sociability, it was occasionally on the order of "Here comes Bob Collin—wasn't it?" They hadn't much spare time. On the Owl's Head trip they left Boston Saturday morning and camped that night near the foot of the big slide on the west face. A long day.

We, on the other hand, with our advanced years, could enjoy a more leisurely way of life. Robert and I, on the previous Thursday, pulled our toboggan from the dam above Lincoln, the head of jeep navigation at that time when the Kancamagus Highway was not plowed or paved, to a beautiful brand-new shelter which I believe is now known as Camp 9 Shelter, and left some supplies there. The snow was wet and sticky after a storm on Wednesday. By Saturday Merle had arrived and we three went in again to the shelter, arriving in plenty of time for lunch.

We spent the night in our open shelter. Inside my large down sleeping–bag I wore a down jacket, down undershirt, and down underpants besides, of course, regular climbing clothes and fur hat. I felt just wonderful. I never mind hardship as long as I am perfectly comfortable. Robert offered to lend me his air mattress, since I had not brought any, but with all that resilient down underneath I didn't need one and so was not put to the inconvenience of sliding off slippery nylon. Boots are the only things that I take off at night and, since I prefer to keep my boots outside my sleeping–bag, by morning they are frozen rigid and it is impossible to get socks and feet inside. But I have licked this contingency. I put the boots on with just one thin pair of socks. With feet inside they soon thaw out enough to accept the regular outfit, one medium thick pair and one very thick. From Merle's diary I can add the information that it took me from 6 to 7 P.M. that night to help Robert get into his sleeping–bag. The diary says that when I urged him to try to inch down a little farther he replied that he could not move a millimeter.

Sunday morning we left the shelter at 7:10 in nippy air of 0° and were soon removing extra clothing as it became too hot. Each piece shed was hung on some trailside tree, to the entertainment of Bob Collin's party when they returned that afternoon. I have a picture of Robert changing clothes, sitting on top of the National Forest signs which direct walkers to the Franconia Brook Trail and the Lincoln Brook Trail. The signs projected above the snow just enough to make a very comfortable seat.

To find the summit of Owl's Head in the Pemigewassett, the real highest point, is a puzzling job. When we first walked over this long, level, thickly wooded ridge one summer day our two sons, Bob and Brian, were with us. One of them would climb a tall tree now and then and peer in both directions. It was most difficult to make out whether another elevation ahead or behind was a few feet higher. We ended up by walking this pathless ridge along its full length, being careful to stay on the high points—and was that a chore, shoving our way through the frightful blowdowns and tangles. We then deduced that we must, at some moment, have been on the top. Finally, Al Robertson's Four-thousand-footer Club found and marked a tree which, by decree, was appointed the official summit.

I told Bob Collin about this tree. I said there was no difficulty in finding it, since we had again been up there the summer before and tied on some guiding red rags. The standard method of marking a route through wilderness has long been a quick chop with the axe, "blazing" or "spotting." But to mark a tough bushwhack we like red rags, one of our better innovations! Blazes are objectionably permanent and advertise every mistake you make, and I, for one, am not certain of finding the best route the first time. Unlike a blaze, a red rag can be taken off and put somewhere else. A quick gesture ties them, and a pull on one end unties. You can use them over again—unless, that is, birds have taken possession. We have seen many places where birds have bitten them off, but never once have I seen a nest with red streamers. Perhaps it is because red rags are tied on in summer and it is only in the following spring that the nests are built, when the rags, after spending a New Hampshire winter outdoors, are wan and bedraggled and would not stand out in any bird's nest.

We tied the rags as far up as we could reach, often pulling down a branch with an ice-axe. Even so, high in the mountains the snow is so deep that, come winter, there may be no rags in sight. I remember a trip to Cabot in 1959 when the area around the cliffs was more open than it is today. No rags were to be seen. Finally somebody discovered one underneath the snow. Sure enough, that's where they all were. Our party spread out, and with ice-axes and canes beating the snow we uncovered enough of the row to guide us.

On Owl's Head the slide was a crampon job, with snowshoes dangling behind the pack. When we were part way up we met the others coming back down, sinking in well above their knees, with their snowshoes over their arms. (Nobody likes to keep shifting back and forth, snowshoes to crampons and vice versa.) We congratulated them warmly on having done this outstanding climb, the first "sporting" winter ascent of Owl's Head. We put in "sporting," for who knows whether some logger of the old days hadn't gone up there timber cruising? (If he'd gone for fun, he'd been making a mistake.) They replied that we, too, were members of the party who had made this ascent and entitled to the same congratulations. Not so, we insisted. Even disregarding the fact that we had not been there yet, we still would not have been in the "first" party. But they were determined, as well as courteous, gentlemen, and would have it no other way.

We followed their tracks to the marked tree, and then, not having to be at the office desk the following morning, we spent a delectable hour and a half wandering here and there along the ridge, particularly fascinated by the wide views. For in the summer, according to the A.M.C. guide book, "The views are restricted." I should amend that to say that the views are restricted right down to the point of not being there at all. No views. But in winter the leaves are off the deciduous trees and the snow is so high that we could look over many of the others. At one moment, to our surprise, we found ourselves walking uphill and a little father along, somewhat off to the side, walking uphill again. We got together and examined every step carefully. There was no doubt about it, we had found a point perhaps six feet higher. This was startling. And it was also the time when we began to feel that perhaps after all we did belong to the group who had made the first winter ascent!

We decided not to tell. The difference was so slight, it really did not matter. So many people in summer had trustingly patted the marked tree and added Owl's Head to their list of Four-thousand-footers. And finally, it was I who had told Bob Collin that the marked tree was the summit, and perhaps prevented him from looking around for himself. All my fault!

We spent a second night in our cosy little shelter and this night the temperature was $-10°$. Lying in bed after supper, at about six o'clock, Merle told us that she had brought a great many things for which she had found no possible use: extra socks (dry), change of underwear, change of shirt, comb, washcloth, soap, towel, toothbrush, and so on. What she didn't mention then, but did eight years later, was that in her trousers pocket she had been carrying several hard-boiled eggs which had frozen, thawed and then crumbled.

Later, down in Boston, those who had been on the winter climbs, got together to look at each other's slides. When some of mine, taken on Owl's Head, came on they met a chorus of exclamations. "How did you get those pictures? We saw nothing like that," and, straight out from the shoulder, "Did you find a higher place?" Not being a quick thinker, I hesitated for just a second and did not need to say anything. They knew.

I believe that the Four-thousand-footer Club gives credit for Owl's Head to those who reached the marked tree before the higher point was discovered, which is certainly fair enough. But the Collin group went back another year and repeated the climb.

VI. HANCOCK

The Hancocks took a little longer. Starting in the afternoon from the dam above Lincoln, Merle, Robert and I had not progressed more than a few miles up the Kancamagus Highway, with snow gently falling, before it began to get dark, which is when the wise winter party stops. And this is how it then proceeds: quick, while you are still glowing from exercise, put on all the clothes you have, every one. Then get ready for the tents. Stamp around with your snowshoes to make a reasonably firm floor. Cover it with large evergreen branches, for an air space between tent floor and snow does much to keep you warm. Set up tents. Add more branches around tent doors to keep from tramping snow into tents. Get water from brook. Set up stove, fill it, get it running. Unpack food. Set out food for tonight. Cook. Put rucksacks in tents. Pick up everything while you can still see it (it's snowing hard now) and put that in tents, too.

(About this time Robert drew himself up and announced, "And this is my seventy-first birthday.")

Though this schedule may sound laborious, with three experienced people moving at once it all rolls off quickly and efficiently. In winter we never really cooked, but just heated water into which we tossed one thing or another. Hot water, milk powder, sugar and shredded wheat make a fine breakfast. Hot water, powdered soups, canned chicken or already-cooked meat from home make a good dinner. Hot water, apricots . . . Apricots! Once, when a group of us were on a red-rag-tying trip the apricots were served a brilliant, glowing red. With them someone had boiled the end of a red candle.

The following day we continued pulling our toboggans—two this trip, on the theory that two light are easier to handle than one heavy—up to a campsite on the Hancock Notch Trail, just short of a deep brook crossing. We had no desire to pull toboggans across chasms, since many of the brooks were open. The snow walls on each side were often six feet high above the water, and one time it was a good eight feet. Sometimes we slid down to the brook and then struggled up the farther side by breaking down a lot of snow. Once Robert decided that he would simply jump, snowshoes and all. To our surprise he did arrive on the farther bank—arms, head and shoulders at least. The snowshoes were waving in the air. Although he asked for help, Merle and I took the pictures first.

In summer you cross a brook by just leaping from rock to rock. In leaping from rock to rock in winter, you won't slip if the rock is above the water or entirely below it. But if the rock is near water-level, and being occasionally sprinkled, leap somewhere else. That rock is iced and slippery.

We decided to camp and walk a little farther the next day, rather than get the toboggans over those brook crossings. Our orange tent looked nice in the bright sunshine. Many winter climbers, including us, were building their own tents. Chris Goetze and the Collins built a great many, gleefully dashing up above timberline when they felt a hurricane might be on the way, to see if the tent would stand up. The fact that they went several times indicates the answer to that question. Ours is a splendid tent, lightweight (five pounds including fiberglass wands to hold out the sides), a two-man (Robert and Miriam) double-layer tent, nylon outside, light cotton inside, with a three-inch air space between. The floor of waterproof horcolite (plastic-coated nylon), is sewn to the inner layer, and extends about eight inches up the inner sidewalls. Touch it, pile things against it all you like, it won't leak.

The following winter the local Senior Citizens Club organized an exhibition of the handwork of us old codgers. What handwork could I enter? The tent, of course; just the thing. But Robert said nothing doing, it was his tent, I had given it to him for Christmas, it was too valuable to go to an exhibition. I put in some flower pictures instead.

We were to meet the Collin group on Sunday morning at the fifth brook crossing on the Cedar Brook Trail, and had allowed one extra day with a view to going farther along, perhaps, and doing more breaking. But as things turned out all we did on that extra day was get our cache, which we had left near this crossing in October. (We keep out of the woods in November on account of hunting season.) Up towards the cache the snow was deep, above Robert's knees even on snowshoes. Our cache consisted of a strong wooden box, built by Robert and painted green to make it less visible to hunters and bears. This he nailed, standing on his toes, onto the trunk of a spruce tree as high as he could reach, fairly well concealed by branches. After packing the box, he screwed on the front. Attached to the box at one end and to the tree at the other was a long, strong string, also green. If the bear succeeded in ripping the box off the tree we could follow the string and perhaps retrieve at least the aluminum bottle of gasoline. We put up no markers of any sort to indicate where the box was, not wishing to arouse the curiosity of hunters. Actually we were the ones inconvenienced. But after a long hunt we saw a small green corner projecting from the snow underneath our feet. No bear, no hunter, had disturbed it. We promptly got out and consumed a canned cake which we would not have much cared for at home, but here it tasted wonderful. We had in the box, also, some canned ham. Robert, realizing that when found, it would undoubtedly be frozen hard, had included a small saw blade. And to keep the saw from getting rusty he had smeared it with vaseline, a new sauce for ham.

To transport our summer loads, our son Brian had rigged up a bicycle wheel with a saddle-bag on each side, and handles projecting behind to push it along. A second, shorter set of handles in front enabled a second man to help lift it over obstacles.

On the way over from the main Hancock summit to the South Peak Robert stepped beside one of those treacherous little evergreens and plunged down into loose, fluffy snow above his head. With every motion he made he just sank in deeper. But he did manage to reach my ice-axe, which I was holding out to him. At the same time I threw my other arm around an old dead tree beside me. As Robert tried to pull himself up and more weight came on me and, worse, on my dead tree, my feet sank deeper and deeper down towards Robert's hole, until one of them was entirely without support. Was Merle helping us? No, but she had her camera in operation.

After climbing the two Hancocks and traversing the ridge between them, on our way down we stopped in for tea with the others, who had finished before we did. They were in shirt-sleeves, stifling hot in Bob Collin's new tent, an enormous navy blue model.

VII. JEFFERSON

You'd think that Jefferson, practically in our own front yard, would have been one of the earliest climbed instead of the very last. We did make gestures toward it. Between December 30, 1959, and March 21, 1960, accompanied sometimes by Merle, by Iris and Bill Baird, or by Klaus and Erika Goetze, we four times got well above timberline, only to become enveloped in

ABOVE: Camp on the Hancock Notch Trail, and BELOW: Robert landing after a jump over a brook. OVERLEAF: Approaching the summit of Mt. Monroe.

On the trail with our gear packed on toboggans.

Lunch at Edmands Col Shelter on the way to Mt. Jefferson.

clouds or battered by wind. I am not counting a couple of times when we merely spent the night at the Log Cabin (with little ermines dashing around in the dark), ready, in vain, to storm up the peak the next morning. The worst defeat was one when Robert and I, alone, got to Edmands Col, whereupon clouds came in. Too small a party, we thought, to go higher when we couldn't see. And suppose one of us had broken a leg? All this time we kept our crampons at timberline, hidden between two rocks in a gray, rock-colored bag which we had great trouble finding again ourselves. We were a little surprised and chagrined to reach the end of winter in March, 1960, with every peak over 4,000 feet climbed except Jefferson.

But winter rolled around again the following December and in the meantime Bill Baird had made some plans for us. The Log Cabin, said Bill, was too low. Crag Camp, although farther away from our goal, was higher and should be our base, to take quick advantage of any spot of good weather. We ought to live there. They would see that Crag was kept stocked with provisions and gasoline for the whole winter if necessary. And they would come up to bring us fresh food every weekend! Although I am not sure that the entire program would have been carried out as sketched, we at least started in on schedule. In October we cached a large stock of supplies, carried up mostly by the Bairds and John Nadeau, between two large boulders near certain trees on the trail just below Crag Camp.

December 22 was the starting day. Our son, Bob, was going to leave college a day early in order to be present at this historic event: the Fall of the Last Winter Four-thousander. In Harvard Square he ran into Chris Goetze, who came along, too. George Hamilton also joined the party, with instructions from Brud Warren of the Berlin *Reporter* not to come home without pictures. These were powerful reinforcements.

We all went up to Crag on December 22. Along the trail where we thought we had left our cache there were no boulders at all in sight or anywhere within reach. Nobody could recognize the trees. I lay on my stomach on the snow and plunged my mittens in here and there. Finally I brought up a branch which had been cut. Although I couldn't remember having cut any, it proved that human beings had been there, and gave me new strength and longer arms to burrow farther. Finally we found everything.

We left Crag Camp the next morning with a gorgeous red sunrise over Gorham. It was lovely, but "Red in the morning, sailors take warning." Sure enough, as we approached Edmands Col wisps of cloud started blowing rapidly by. What did we care? We sat for a minute or two, for a bite to eat, in the lee of the emergency shelter on the col. George had been having trouble that winter with the coffee in his canteen freezing. He didn't like that. This time he was going to outsmart the elements; he would leave the coffee at home and put in something which would stay liquid—namely, sherry. On opening the canteen at Edmands Col he found a solid block of ice in the middle and, sloshing around outside of it, pure alcohol. "Who would think a thing like that would happen?" inquired someone, to which a more knowledgeful friend replied that it was one of the recognized methods of obtaining pure alcohol.

We did not stay long. The official weather records for that day on the summit of Mt. Washington, and Jefferson is close enough to use the same, were: high, $-7°$; low, $-18°$; wind, 72 miles per hour. When somebody wanted a string tied I removed a mitten for not more than a couple of seconds and felt a little crackling in two fingertips. Frostbite. I was interested to learn that it would take place so quickly. We left our snowshoes at the Col and traveled up the cone on crampons. Chris, who had recently been up Jefferson, recommended that we avoid the summer route, now pretty icy. (Firm snow, which gives the crampon points something to bite into, provides easier going.) Chris led by a good route: a snow slope, traverse left, then straight up hard snow again. In an hour or less we were all on top, now in thick clouds. And such wind! Nobody stayed any longer than was necessary to climb, or just touch, the summit cairn. Chris stood by nonchalantly swinging his own thermometer. This read $-8°$ on Jefferson, $-11°$ on Adams, whither Chris and Merle took a little side-trip because she had not done it in winter, and $-1°$ inside Crag Camp when we got back there. These temperatures, with a wind of 72 m.p.h., make for cold weather.

We have repeated several of these climbs, chiefly to accompany Merle, who finished one year later. Since then, several others have also reached all the summits of the four-thousand-footers in winter.

Index

Italic figures refer to photographs adjacent to that page.